D1595908

The Extraordinary Life of Jane Wood Reno

UNIVERSITY PRESS OF FLORIDA

Florida A&M University, Tallahassee
Florida Atlantic University, Boca Raton
Florida Gulf Coast University, Ft. Myers
Florida International University, Miami
Florida State University, Tallahassee
New College of Florida, Sarasota
University of Central Florida, Orlando
University of Florida, Gainesville
University of North Florida, Jacksonville
University of South Florida, Tampa
University of West Florida, Pensacola

UNIVERSITY PRESS OF FLORIDA

Gainesville

Tallahassee

Tampa

Boca Raton

Pensacola

Orlando

Miami

Jacksonville

Ft. Myers

Sarasota

# THE EXTRAORDINARY LIFE OF
# Jane Wood Reno

## Miami's Trailblazing Journalist

George Hurchalla

25  24  23  22  21  20    6  5  4  3  2  1

Library of Congress Control Number: 2019954692
ISBN 978-0-8130-6645-5

The University Press of Florida is the scholarly
publishing agency for the State University System
of Florida, comprising Florida A&M University,
Florida Atlantic University, Florida Gulf Coast
University, Florida International University, Florida
State University, New College of Florida, University
of Central Florida, University of Florida, University
of North Florida, University of South Florida, and
University of West Florida.

University Press of Florida
2046 NE Waldo Road
Suite 2100
Gainesville, FL 32609
http://upress.ufl.edu

# Contents

# Introduction

## Genius

While serving as US attorney general for eight years under President Bill Clinton, Janet Reno told a lot of stories about her late mother, Jane Wood Reno. Usually they involved the unlikely story of her mother building the family home largely by herself from the ground up—hacking a foundation out of the limestone that underpinned the Dade County pine scrub and constructing a sprawling rustic house that Janet lived in her whole life. Sometimes she mentioned her mother wrestling alligators, or the 104-mile beach walk her mother undertook alone over a six-day period. The stories were usually intended to reinforce Janet's steely determination that a woman could do anything she wanted to if she put her mind to it. The general portrait the public got of Jane Wood Reno was of a mildly irascible, eccentric pioneer woman raising her children on the edge of the Everglades, with a strong adventurous streak.

Her daughter Janet usually avoided the stories about her mother that had been more embarrassing to her personally, like when her drunk mother called a state trooper a "baby-faced pipsqueak," poured beer on the heads of company who offended her, or trapped skunks that she later released outside the local police station. Nor did Janet Reno talk about the formidable depth of her mother's intellect, and her exceptional career as a prize-winning reporter for the *Miami News*. As much as Jane Wood Reno's children proved to be intellectual heavyweights in their respective fields, her daughter Maggy reflected that none of them was an intellectual match for their mother. Lost in the annals of Florida journalism history was the recognition that Jane Wood Reno was, in her prime, a titan of an investigative reporter, winner of two national and many local awards, and one of the rare woman journalists doing substantial hard-news reporting for a big-city paper in the 1950s.

Jane Reno was equally at home among tugboat captains and the greatest minds of the twentieth century. One of her favorite stories was of the night she spent drinking with playwright Tennessee Williams in Key West. Toward the end of the evening, Williams announced, "Jane, you're a bitch." He paused, adding with a big smile, "And I love bitches!" She fell asleep in the swimming pool that night, and Williams later paid tribute to her by including a bit character in one of his lesser-known plays that drunkenly falls asleep in a pool. In the complex personality of Jane Reno, the intellectual side was capable of impressing any company she chose to keep. Neither those who enjoyed her gregarious company nor those who incurred her displeasure soon forgot it.

In the 1950s she worked on a memoir with Dr. Sarah Sidis, who along with her husband, Boris, produced one of the greatest child geniuses ever known, William James Sidis. By the age of eleven, William was lecturing at Harvard and pointing out flaws to Einstein on the theory of relativity. As a child genius herself, Reno was able to relate. Fellow adventurers also captured her imagination, and she interviewed Amelia Earhart as a cub reporter at the *Miami Herald* in 1937 during Earhart's final, fateful attempted voyage around the world. The Miccosukee Indians' close bond to nature and the Everglades fascinated her. She became one of their most trusted friends from the outside world of white people and learned to wrestle alligators from them. They concocted an honorary title for her of Indian princess and named her Apoongo Stahnegee, the "messenger," for her accurate reporting on their affairs and her championing of their land claims as the last undefeated tribe of nonreservation Native Americans in the United States.

Her life was marked by an unlimited freedom of the spirit, which travel helped stoke. At the age of seventeen she caught a glimpse of fascist Italy en route to spending two years immersing herself in Greek life at the beginning of the Depression, with eye-opening adventures in the rapidly modernizing Turkey of Kemal Ataturk as well. She took her children on endless adventures all through the wilderness of Florida and the mountains of the Carolinas. She shared Greece, Turkey, Iran, Australia, New Zealand, and the Galapagos Islands with her grandchildren.

New technologies fascinated her. She walked away unscathed from a small plane crash as a student at the University of Miami in 1929, eventually got a degree in physics in 1937, and was in on the ground floor—or reef, as it were—of the pioneering of scuba diving in south Florida in the early 1950s. To help promote a new scuba regulator that was one of the first competitors to Jacques Cousteau's Aqua Lung, she did what was likely the first underwater scuba interview in history. Her young children became her guinea pigs with whom she shared the wonders of the ocean, and her daughter Maggy became a proficient diver by age twelve.

Reno's groundbreaking career as a woman journalist was inspired by writers like Marjory Stoneman Douglas, whom a fifteen-year-old Reno interviewed while still in high school. After getting her Depression-era training in the women's section of the *Miami Daily News* and in the home and design columns for the *Miami Herald*, Reno took a break from journalism to raise her children and then returned to it with a vengeance. Her first freelance article for the *Miami Herald* in 1949 after a twelve-year hiatus won her a national *Big Story* award, the first of two such awards. No other woman journalist in the country during the 1950s could claim such an accomplishment.

Her intellectual curiosity was limitless, both inside and outside her professional lives. She excelled as a reporter and initially got around the sexism that forbid women from doing certain kinds of reporting by writing prolifically under a number of male aliases. The chauvinist publisher of the *Miami Daily News* could not bring himself to have her on staff the first few years, which suited her as it allowed her much more freedom to pursue topics considered "quirky" by the staff news writers. Do-it-yourself articles and home and design were her bread and butter at first, but she quickly expanded her repertoire to include stories on timber men, lighthouse keepers, tugboat captains, watchmakers, scuba divers, and a wide range of other topics. When her worth to the paper became indisputable, they brought her on staff and gave her a hard-news investigative reporting feature that allowed her more latitude than most of her male colleagues had. She wrote immodestly of her success and the slings and arrows that came with it in a letter to her sister: "I am certainly the best known and best newspaper woman in Florida, having become twice blasted in the current session of the Legislature. . . . I get a good deal of hammering in return on some of these things, and am subject to plenty of acid criticism within and outside of my office—things that begin with, 'You and your goddamn vain hyperthyroid, look what you did now.'"

Always with a flair for the dramatic, she thrilled in going undercover on behalf of the Kefauver Commission, a Senate investigative panel, to expose the black-market baby racket in Miami. Wearing a fake diamond ring and driving a Cadillac, she pretended to be a wealthy New Jersey socialite in search of a baby to adopt. For her second *Big Story* award, "Scoop," she raced north to a Florida state prison with a Miami detective to hear a prisoner's confession implicating accomplices on the Miami police force. She constantly received laudatory letters to the editor about her tackling of topics that rarely got detailed attention otherwise.

Her grounding as a social worker during the Depression gave her keen insight into systemic failures, which came to a head after the most savage storm of the twentieth century decimated the Florida Keys in 1935. The various failures of government that resulted in the deaths, during that hurricane, of World War I "Bonus Army" marchers who were working on federal relief programs in the Keys drove her out of social work and back into finishing her education. Social work also left her with a great deal of empathy, which served her well as a journalist in championing the downtrodden and underdogs.

She exposed the conditions in which migrant farmworkers lived, forming the basis for a colleague to write a Pulitzer-winning series on the plight of migrant workers the following year. When a psychologist testified to the US Senate about beatings at an unnamed reform school, Reno followed the story to Marianna, Florida, and revealed the alarming abuse of boys taking place there. The governor expressed concern but failed to act; fifty years later, while the school was still open, unmarked graves with fifty-two bodies were discovered in the burial ground at the school.

Although sharp-witted intellectual women were not an anomaly in the early twentieth century, ones as fearlessly practical as Reno were less usual. After her small sailboat flipped in Biscayne Bay in 1935 with a friend on board, she left her friend sitting on the hull of the boat and swam a mile and a half to shore to get help. During World War II, she raised hens and did stints for Civil Defense watching for Nazi planes. She could shoot a rifle with uncanny accuracy, once dispatched a bear ransacking their cabin in the Smoky Mountains, and was happy as could be camping rough in the wilderness. In her sixties, she comfortably wielded a chainsaw while removing all the invasive species on her property to convert it to the subtropical oasis that it is today.

Her final career as a public-relations woman allowed her dramatic side and lightheartedness to flourish. She brought Buckminster Fuller to the Miami Seaquarium to speak about the power of dolphins, got humorist Art Buchwald to escort a dolphin to its new home as a mate for a lone seaquarium dolphin in Italy, and nearly lost a finger handling an alligator that National Airlines was sending to a zoo in Baltimore, among many other imaginative PR stunts. When the *Miami Herald* eulogized her by saying, "she did it all," it wasn't hyperbole. For the better part of the twentieth century, she experienced life beyond boundaries, interacted with extraordinary people, and excelled at her professions to a degree to which few other people ever come close.

Jane Wallace Wood came into the world on May 28, 1913, in Macon, Georgia, when Daisy Hunter Wood gave birth to her first child. The third child in a family of nine, Daisy had seen tuberculosis take her two elder sisters, and a brother died at seven months. When her father remarried after his first wife died of tuberculosis, Daisy Hunter was sent to Macon to live with her uncle, Will Sloan, while her younger siblings ended up scattered. Their mean and shrewish stepmother had no interest in having them around. Her brothers Bat and Parks were placed with other relatives, and her youngest sister, Peg, was farmed out to a school for children who had nowhere else to go. After marrying George Wood II in Macon, Daisy brought the family back together. Peg had been living an especially miserable existence, and the relatives the brothers had been with did not particularly want them. The Hunters were an old Scottish family from Mecklenburg County, North Carolina, part of a proud heritage that went back to Henry Hunter signing the Mecklenburg Declaration.[1]

George Wood II had grown up on a small farm in Sunnyside, Georgia. The Woods had deep roots in this part of Georgia, never straying more than forty miles from Macon throughout the entire nineteenth century. Five brothers emigrated from Leicester, England, in the 1740s to Great Falls, Virginia, and the lineage that George Wood II came from moved to Georgia soon after the American Revolution.

In the 1880s, George's father came up the railway line from Americus until he found a town that didn't have a general store. Aside from running the general store and post office and serving as stationmaster, George Washington Wood made the rounds of the countryside as a Baptist preacher, following in the footsteps of his preacher father. He had tanned features from the time he spent outdoors, and once an attendee at one of his sermons marveled afterward, "That high yellow negro sure can preach."

Although he was all fire and brimstone on the Baptist circuit, he was essentially a lazy man around the house. His granddaughter Winifred, the youngest sister of Jane Wood, recalled that her grandmother worked every day from 6:00 a.m. to 10:00 p.m., only taking time to say her prayers each night before going to bed. Lillian was the second wife of the preacher and the sister of his first wife, Winifred, who died fairly young. It was Lillian whom the grandchildren knew as Grandmother Lil.

"Grandmother made marvelous large rolls for Sunday morning breakfast which we had with syrup and fresh milk," Winifred remembered. "She did the cooking for all those people all those summers plus working in the garden, hoeing, killing chickens by wringing their necks, milking the cow, churning, and I couldn't begin to guess what else. Some lady!"

Hard work had been Lillian Wood's life. The intelligence, temperament, and independence that Jane and the other young Wood girls inherited seemed to be a direct product of their father's mother, Winifred. Though they loved Lil deeply, they also knew that they were never going to live a life like hers. In 1937, Jane Wood wrote:

"Lil's home was broken up when she was very young, and she was brought up by her aunt, who worked her all the time. She never had much formal education and was always working. Grandmother Winifred was brought up somewhere else. She was supposed to be the brilliant one, the talker, the thinker—a woman of very forceful personality and much charm.

"Uncle Roy has told me that she was the driving force for Grandfather. He was rather drifting, I have gathered. She made him pay his bills, instilled in him what ambition he had, and was immensely ambitious for her children and saw as far as she could that they go to school for as long as they could. She made them want to. But the only thing Daddy has ever said about them was that 'Aunt Lil was nearer a real mother to me. My own mother was always giving me lickings.'

"Lil finished out somebody else's life, you might say. It would have looked a thankless job to anyone. But I think she did it better than her sister might have, the finishing. There is something almost archaic about such a life. The chances of it happening to someone young now are not very high. It wouldn't be one you would cut out for yourself. But all I saw of it was finely done, and most of all because Grandmother never felt noble."

The house in Sunnyside became a gathering place for generations of family

Wood family, 1913. *Front row, left to right:* Jane's father, George Wood II; Jane's two-year-old cousin George Cain; grandmother Lilly Hardison Wood; four-year-old cousin James Cain; George Wood II's sister May Wood Cain. *Back row, left to right:* Lilly's sister Nancy Missouri Hardison; Jane's grandfather George Wood, holding newborn Jane; Jane's mother, Daisy Hunter Wood; James Cain Sr. (married to May).

members during Jane Wood's lifetime, and the lives of her grandmothers provided her with an early lesson that it was southern ladies who kept the South running. While the men went off to war, preached, or sat around doing nothing, the women did most of the work. Jane's father was determined to escape the mold, and despite his poor, rural upbringing, George Wood II graduated from Mercer University at the age of eighteen. He was a very academic man who earned one of the best records in the history of the university. Education planted the seed in him to aspire beyond the limitations of Georgia farm life, as his mother had desired. His Aunt Lil was fond of saying, "George is plowing in the west field, with his mind on Milton and his eyes on Greece and Rome." He went on to Mercer Law School and afterward opened a practice in Macon. When his father died, the Baptist church didn't have a burying ground in Sunnyside, so they buried him at the Methodist church. His tombstone simply read: "For twenty-seven years pastor of country churches in middle Georgia. He preached Jesus."

Married in 1910, George and Daisy had five children in eight years—Jane, Dorothy, Daisy, Winifred, and George. By the time Jane was six years old, she knew she wanted to write. When she was a fourth-grader at Winship Elementary in Macon, her teachers recommended that she skip a grade. At first, her parents thought it might be a bad idea to push her too hard, but field consultants from the ominously named National Committee for Mental Hygiene came to Macon to establish a child guidance clinic. Upon the advice of their family physician, the Woods sent their daughter to the clinic for testing. A battery of tests revealed an IQ of 167, indicating that Jane, who was a month short of turning eleven, was mentally more than nineteen years old. The *Macon Daily Telegraph* wrote: "Miss Falk says that she has examined literally thousands of children and that Jane is one of the most brilliant, if not the most brilliant, she had ever passed on. Dr. Robinson made practically the same remark, and his 157 examinations have been made all over the United States."

Jane's early notoriety as a genius and the troubles it caused became the subject of one of her favorite stories: "There was a story in the *Macon Daily Telegraph* with a headline I remember: 'Jane Wood Declared Genius.' It said I had the highest IQ in Georgia. I found out something. I found out there was nothing like being declared a genius to make people hate you. I had to go out and fight all of the boys on the block to prove I was still me." She completed the work of the seventh grade in two months and began high school at the age of eleven, the youngest student ever enrolled at the Lanier High School for Girls. Her passion for athletics and the outdoors proved as great as her intellectual curiosity. An article in the *Macon Daily Telegraph* of December 14, 1924, followed up on her progress:

"Dickens, Scott, Kipling, history, all are old friends of Jane's. She likes boys'

Jane Wood in Girl Scout uniform, Macon, Georgia, 1923.

stories and stories of adventure and animal stories. She loves nature and studies it. On a recent trip through Florida, one of her teachers who was a member
of the party says Jane failed to name only two of the birds they saw, and, not
only knew the names of all of the others, but their habits as well.

"Jane's dramatic instinct is highly developed. She 'acts out' everything.
Cherokee Heights, her home community, is to her a veritable Sherwood Forest where Robin Hood and his men make merry. Sometimes she is Robinson

Crusoe, and sometimes his Man Friday, or any other character to whom her reading has introduced her."

In 1925, Jane's father, attracted by the booming growth of Florida, boldly did what few Woods had done in the past century. He left Georgia, moving his family from Macon to Miami. In his eldest daughter's worldly intellect, he saw many of his aspirations, and he thought the new environment and financial opportunity would allow the family greater freedom. As Jane Wood became a teenager, she became something of a separate entity from the rest of her siblings and was initially excited by the move from a static social environment to a dynamic one.

"When we left north Georgia in 1925 and came to Miami to live," Jane Wood wrote, "my family was leaving a land with an economy blighted by the boll weevil for a bayside city enjoying a fantastic boom. The traffic to Miami on the old Dixie Highway was worse than anything in rush hour today.

"Downtown Miami was exciting, I discovered. The city had really become itself—jubilant, high of heart, wild. Binder boys, dressed in knickerbockers, thronged Flagler Street, selling their 'binders'—options to buy land—to people who hoped to double their money in a few weeks. The port of Miami was crowded with ships, including five-masted sailing ships and freighters of all sizes. They were helping the railroad bring building materials to Miami."

The landscape was transforming before her eyes as hotels sprouted everywhere, and existing ones stayed open during the summer months for the first time. In the winter of early 1925, Miami was a hotbed of entertainment. Stars like Madame Galli-Curci, Flo Ziegfeld, and Ignacy Jan Paderewski performed at the Royal Palm Hotel, while Paul Whiteman played at the Coral Gables Country Club, and the legendary Russian opera singer Feodor Chaliapin sang at the Biltmore Hotel. The newly constructed Venetian Pool of the Biltmore was the most luxurious spot to swim in the city, and statesman William Jennings Bryan was paid a yearly salary of fifty thousand dollars to give daily speeches from the island in the middle of the pool.[1]

The boom was outrageous in magnitude, more dramatic than what any other American city had experienced in such a short time. What the gold rush had been to the West, the real estate rush was to Miami. The city had been a tiny provincial outpost scarcely a decade before, with Key West considered a much more important trade center in Florida. But now, amounts of money were being thrown around Miami that would still seem like substantial sums more than fifty years later. Titles to swampland were printed as fast as possible and sold to any unsuspecting northerner who wanted in on the boom.

Along with everything else, illegal gambling was going on all over town in the 1920s. Slot machines took dimes in grocery stores. There was an elegant casino on a pier on south Miami Beach, complete with roulette wheels, faro, dice tables, blackjack, and striptease artists. Jane Wood's father was a gambler by nature, and it was all he could do to resist getting caught up in it.

Prohibition added more spice to life in Miami during the 1920s, when it was dangerous to be on Biscayne Bay in a small boat at night. Rumrunners raced up the bay loaded with the booze, chased by hijackers who were shooting at them, chased by Coast Guard boats who were shooting at both.

Hard liquor was run in from the Bahamas and Cuba, and stills on remote Everglades islands turned out moonshine. The illegal liquor was shipped north from Miami in cars with reinforced springs so that the body of the car wouldn't sag with the weight. During Prohibition, Miami was the principal source of most of the bootleg liquor sold in the eastern United States. Years after Prohibition was repealed, a gray-haired captain on a tugboat told Jane Wood:

"I came to Miami in 1923 from up around Cedar Key. I got me a fast little boat with a thirty-horse motor. It wouldn't hold more than about twenty, thirty cases of whiskey, but it would outrun anything the Coast Guard had. A bunch of us had boats like that and we were running whiskey in from Bimini to Miami. We came through Bear Cut, and the Coast Guard knew what we were doing, and we knew that they knew, but they couldn't catch us.

"So, one nice afternoon there were maybe twenty of us over in Bimini, and we knew the Coast Guard was waiting. But we decided to run for it. They could only catch one, if any.

"We hit Bear Cut about dusk, and there was the Coast Guard cutter, and we tore past. Well, they had stretched a cable across the Cut, a foot or so under water. We hit it and you should have seen the scrambled boats! Wrecked, sunk! Nobody killed, and it was a wonder. But for some reason, I don't know why, I hit that cable and it swung so that it lifted me up and over, and I was on through! No damage at all. I got out of that business then. You don't have to have something that lucky happen twice."

As the city of Miami had scarcely existed before 1910, hardly anyone living in the heady boomtown knew what a hurricane was when one of the tropical furies bore down on south Florida in 1926. Still feeling somewhat ambivalent about her new home, Wood was one of those whose life would be changed by the storm.

"On the whole Miami was dumb, dull, and flat," she remembered. "I had loved the pines and oaks of north Georgia, and those I saw around Miami were shrimps. I had loved going barefoot in the summer in the soft red clay dust of my homeland's hills, but the grass along the beaches down here had sandspurs. I was twelve years old.

"My contempt for Miami was blown away on September 18, 1926. Actually, my love affair with south Florida began the evening before. We were living in a rented house on Collins Avenue and Fourteenth Street on Miami Beach, a block from the ocean. Mother and I walked down to the beach in the late afternoon to admire the most beautiful sunset we had ever seen. High-flying cirrus clouds and widespread cumulus floated across the sky from east to west. Everything was gold and pink and blue and calm. It was a classic hurricane sunset, well known to meteorologists.

"It was the morning after that sunset that I fell in love. At 7 a.m. my mother shook me and said, 'Wake up, Jane! There has been a terrible hurricane!' I sat up in bed and said, 'Why didn't you wake me up?' She said, 'It's over now!' I ran to the window and looked out. The sky was a clear and beautiful blue. There was not enough wind to blow out a candle. Miami Beach was covered by more than thirty inches of water. Cars were wrapped around fire plugs. Was I thrilled!"

Her father and one of her uncles, Parks Hunter, had nailed the French doors shut, but the storm refused to be denied entry.

"Daddy was asleep on a sofa," Jane recalled, "and the younger kids were asleep on the dirty clothes in the dirty clothes closet. Those were the only dry places in the house. The windows had been blown out on two sides of the house. Mother and Uncle Roy and I put on our bathing suits and waded four blocks to a friend's apartment, Blanch Kell, to see how she fared. A big, tired snapper was swimming slowly down Michigan Avenue, four blocks from the ocean. We took him home to dinner.

"So many newcomers to Miami did not know that this was the lull in the eye of the hurricane. Then it hit again! The winds blew away the wind gauges after registering 138 miles an hour. Gusts were later registered at up to 200 miles an hour. Mother decided to stay at Blanch's apartment. My uncle and I walked home together, holding hands, leaning against the wind, grinning at each other. Nothing blew off and hit us. I loved it so! There is something in the heart of a thirteen-year-old that loves vandalism."

During the eye of the storm, her sisters and their uncle Parks explored in a different direction and found a sobering reality of the hurricane's power—a dead sailor on the beach. It was the first dead man Winifred Wood had ever seen, washed up onto a porch like a piece of flotsam. Other random things the Wood girls found on the beach included a side of bacon and a trunk with doll clothes inside it.

Many of the storm's causalities in the Miami area—one hundred dead and eight hundred seriously injured—resulted from people traveling from the beach to the mainland while the eye passed over. The second half of the storm caught them unawares on the causeway, flinging their cars like toys into the water and drowning them. As surprised as people had been by the ferocity of the first onslaught, they were even more shocked to be hit again with roaring winds from the opposite direction.

"I remember us driving across the causeway after it was all over," recalled Winifred Wood, "and seeing cars floating around all over the place from people who had been caught out in the eye."

In the aftermath, there was no city water, and only one man could be found who had a working well. Faced with long lines queued up for his precious resource, he became one of the earliest Floridians to get the idea of making money from a natural disaster. Suddenly he told everyone the water was no longer free. This enterprising notion was quashed almost as quickly as it was thought up, though, when Jane Wood's six-foot-four giant of a father walked up to the man and said, "I don't think that would be a good idea."

Jane's future husband, Henry Reno, had started work at the *Miami Herald* two years before as a crime reporter. No one at the paper had any experience of hurricanes. As the storm approached, the paper reported in a small story that gale-force winds from a hurricane were lashing the coast, but no serious damage was expected. An advisory from Washington was included at the end of the article, noting that it was a severe storm expected to track through Nassau and hit Florida. Still, the optimistic new residents of Miami had no frame of reference for such a warning.

By three o'clock in the morning, hurricane winds were blasting the city, and soon the power went out at the *Herald*. The news editor turned to the young Reno and said, "Henry, run over to the Weather Bureau and find out what the hell's going on."

Had the editor known what he was sending Reno out into, he may as well have laid a revolver before him and asked him to play Russian roulette. Reno took a flashlight, walked outside into the hurricane, and began his fruitless journey.

"I made my way east on SE Second Ave to the Gralynn Hotel without too much trouble," he recalled forty years later. "But when I turned that corner—boy!"

He found himself facing into northeast winds of well over a hundred miles per hour, with electric lines sparking, signs and debris flying by him, and the rain pelting him like flying needles.

"Somehow I made my way to the corner of East Flagler St and First Ave. The wind was getting stronger. Things were beginning to happen that scared me. I aimed my flashlight up at the old First National Bank building, and watched the wind fold a huge sign like it was a toy.

"I have never heard anything like the roar of the wind. For a few moments it had me pinned against a wall, but I had to get across Flagler St. I couldn't stay on the exposed southwest corner."[2]

He did make it across Flagler Street, but only as far as a group of shops on the other side. When he reached the corner, he met howling gusts that knocked him to his knees every time he tried to move forward. Windows began exploding around him, and he wisely retreated to the safety of the Seybold Arcade on the north side of the street. He was trapped there until the eye of the storm passed over just after six o'clock in the morning.

In Miami alone, the property damage was over $100 million. It was somewhat astonishing that the loss of life wasn't greater, considering the lack of preparedness and the fact that the hurricane destroyed nearly five thousand homes between Fort Lauderdale and Miami. The storm took its worst toll on human life to the north when it collapsed the small dike on the south shore of Lake Okeechobee, sending a fifteen-foot-high wall of water through Moore Haven. Half of the nine hundred residents were drowned. Tragically, this was but a stage rehearsal for the horror that was to befall the southern lake communities two years later, described in mesmerizing detail in the Zora Neale Hurston novel *Their Eyes Were Watching God*. The new, larger dike crumbled and drowned more than two thousand people.

The 1926 hurricane marked the beginning of Miami's collapse. While the economic failure of the country was still a few years away, Miami got a head start. So much was destroyed by the hurricane that many developers walked away, cutting their losses. The wild and heady optimism was smashed. Newcomers fled, both because the promise of the city had dwindled and because none of them wanted to go through a storm like that one again. All but one of the banks failed. Four acres of land and a home in South Miami that sold for forty thousand dollars in 1924 sold for nine hundred dollars on a tax deed in 1929. The Wood family, however, stayed on. There was nothing that would tear Jane away from the city.

She continued her fast track through school, inadvertently skipping another grade when she told Miami High administrators that she was a sophomore. Two years after the hurricane, she was associate editor at the Miami High School *Stingaree,* and she wrote about high school sports for the *Miami News.* In 1928 she read a story about the 1926 hurricane by Marjory Stoneman Douglas called "Beautiful and Beloved" in the *Saturday Evening Post*, and the intrepid fifteen-year-old journalist did her first interview with the woman who was to become known as the "queen of the Everglades." Wood was so nervous that her pencil broke while doing the interview.

Finishing high school at fourteen, Wood enrolled at the University of Miami at the age of fifteen. She began as an English major, but she didn't always concentrate on her classes. There were many other diversions for the university's youngest student. On January 30, 1929, the *Palm Beach Post* ran the headline: "Four Miami U. Co-Eds Elope; Police Looking for Runaways."[3]

"We were sitting in a car, four of us with nothing to do," Wood recalled. "The other three were flunking college and they decided to run away. Heck, it was just a lark, something to do. I said, 'I'm going too.' I wasn't flunking, but I was damned if I was going to be left out."

The four—Jane Wood, Jane Bostwick, Agnes McCully, and the last unidentified—hitchhiked north on a Monday morning, easily getting rides up the Dixie Highway to Palm Beach. They continued on to Orlando, spending the night in a hotel. Tuesday morning, they reached Ocala before deciding they should come up with a story so as to not worry their parents, who assumed they had been kidnapped. Jane Wood wired home that all four of them had simultaneously gotten married and eloped. This only brought forth more questions than answers. Agnes McCully's aunt said the families had compared notes about who the possible husbands could have been, and no men from their social circle were missing. Wood also telegraphed that she was staying in Ocala while the rest of the girls made their way to New Orleans. Police were alerted to be on the lookout for them as far north as Atlanta. By later in the day, though, enthusiasm waned for the adventure and deception, and the girls turned themselves in to a police station in Ocala and asked to be brought home.

Daisy Wood boarded a train to retrieve them. When Jane got home her father asked only, "Are you okay, honey?"

An article in the January 31 edition of the *Palm Beach Post* began: "Four restive young college girls with a longing for whoopee and a talent for fibbing were safe under their respective rooftrees tonight, while all Florida wondered."[4]

The lack of censoriousness in the coverage of the episode reflected the spirit of Miami toward the end of the Roaring Twenties, which would change considerably in the next decade. Between an increase in high-profile kidnappings and the hardships of the Depression, such behavior would be little tolerated in the future. Any infamy Wood might have achieved after this ill-fated incident did not dampen her adventurous spirit. Her proudest accomplishment in her early college years was learning to hold down five home brews before lunch. While the amount and timing of her consumption may have been unusual, home brew was a staple during Prohibition.

"Nice Coral Gables ladies made home brew for their husbands, even if neither they nor their husbands liked the taste of the stuff," she recalled. "It was the thing to do, like being a member of the D.A.R."

Her mother was a member of the Daughters of the American Revolution (DAR), a mark of gentility that Jane not-so-gently ridiculed during her teenage years. Still, she dutifully played the part of hostess as her mother required, periodically appearing in the social columns of the *Miami Daily News* serving at her mother's DAR luncheons. Her real interests lay in less ladylike pursuits, however. Among twenty girls chosen to appear in a page of *The Ibis* yearbook for their exceptional characteristics at the end of Wood's first year at the university, she got the dubious honor of being chose "rattiest." Whether the meaning at the time was the American "unkempt" or the British "irritable," neither was flattering. Once in the late 1920s she was asked if she wanted to smoke some marijuana, and she asked what it was like.

"If you're feeling good, it makes you feel better," she was told. "If you're feeling bad, it makes you feel worse."

"Let's go get a fifth of booze," was her reply.

At the same time that the whip-tongued Dorothy Parker was holding court at the round table in New York's Algonquin Hotel, Jane Wood was developing outrageous behavior similar to the poet's. She smoked, drank, gave her opinions bluntly, and was well aware that she was smarter than almost everyone she knew. In the Roaring Twenties in New York, Parker's behavior was controversial but not altogether unexpected in the intellectual circles in which she operated. For a fifteen-year-old in a relatively provincial outpost like Miami—and one who came from a long southern heritage—Wood's behavior was rather startling.

Jane Wood at her family home in Coral Gables, November 18, 1930.

Jane Wood with her mother, Daisy Wood, Coral Gables, November 18, 1930.

Eventually diversions began to crowd out scholarly pursuits. Home brews and restlessness caused Wood to fail both journalism and physical education, which should have been her best subjects. Her expectations for college weren't great when she started as a fifteen-year-old; in fact, she had asked, "What's college?" when her father first asked her if she wanted to go. The university had only opened in 1926 and was not developed enough to challenge her.

The University of Miami (UM) was sometimes called the Cardboard College because it was housed in a half-finished hotel with walls of cardboard until after World War II. The university paid professors in scrip for months after first opening and gave working scholarships to many students. Parents were allowed to sign notes, payable over a lengthy period, for tuition. Though many Miamians who could not have attended any other college got a good education there during the Great Depression, Wood was somewhat disgusted with the shambling institution after her first two years.

Toward the end of her second year, she was willing to do anything for a thrill. A fellow UM student, Vincent Jablon, asked in April 1930 if she wanted to come flying with him and another student, and she agreed. They took off from Coral Gables field and only got two hundred feet in the air before developing engine trouble. Flying too low to return to the field, Jablon picked out the nearest orange grove and crash-landed them into it. The plane was damaged, but miraculously all of them walked away unhurt.[5]

Remembering his own visions of Greece and Rome at her age, Jane Wood's father agreed that the best opportunity for her might be to spend some time overseas. Her mind wasn't being stimulated nearly as much as she craved, and her rebellion against boredom was placing some strain on the family. With the Depression already in effect in Miami, Jane's behavior was seen as increasingly selfish as times grew worse. Her aunt Peg and uncle Bal were living in Greece, and they welcomed the idea of Jane coming to live with them. Aunt Peg was her mother's younger sister, Margaret Hunter Balfour, and Uncle Bal was Dr. Marshall Balfour, a pioneer in world public health who was in Greece working on malaria control for the Rockefeller Foundation. The family scraped together the money to get her a first-class ticket on a ship out of New York, and she put her college education on hold.

The trip was a sacrifice during difficult times that the rest of the family was going to have to bear for the next few years. George Wood could not endure seeing his daughter's mind and spirit held back on account of lack of money, though, and his wife, Daisy, was already at a loss at how to handle her wildly independent daughter. Whatever had been said five years before about her did not reflect Jane Wood at seventeen. An unassuming child she was not.

After arriving in Greece at the age of seventeen, Wood continued maturing at an astonishing pace. She spent a lot of time reflecting in her letters on what she had discovered about herself, and the foibles and quirks of humanity in general. Unlike many, her ruthless self-awareness prevented her from ever being satisfied with "just enough" knowledge. She knew that her two years at the University of Miami, however recklessly spent, had imbued her with enough learning that she had an intelligent appreciation of most things.

"Yet every day I get shown how darn little I know *definitely* about anything at all," she wrote. "Most people 'talk loosely and expect to be taken seriously.' They have such a hazy idea about facts. I'm learning to keep my mouth shut about things concerning which I know nothing by watching other people make fools of themselves. I don't give a damn if people haven't got great mental prowess. But to pretend to have! Intellectual pretension can be just as disgusting as social climbing."

As letters from home began to arrive, Jane responded with her characteristic exasperation toward her mother. Daisy Wood could only wonder at how her long, proud southern lineage had given rise to a teenager who so blithely addressed her—"Darling Mum, still worrying about my wardrobe! You precious jackass, it's alright. You are such a dear idiot."

Though the Acropolis was the most obvious attraction to see in Athens, Wood resisted it for a while simply because of that fact. She had no desire to rush her sightseeing and had mixed feelings about ruins. She dallied with it from a distance, stealing lover's glances, unsure it wouldn't be a disappointment close up. After a visit to town, she wrote:

"From the street of blood—where the butchers carry knives in huge scabbards, wear red aprons, and hang meat on hooks in front of their shops—I got a lovely view of the Erectheum. From there looking up it seemed in perfect condition, and the line of the columns and the proportion was absolutely right. Perhaps I wouldn't like to see it closer. It seems like a great many folks affect an interest in things just because they are the Temple of this or that and are double-marked with stars in Baedeker. But the Erectheum from where I saw it would have been famous if it had been built in 1925."

The perfect Doric columns proved too tempting, though, and she finally went up there on a clear, cold day, with a biting wind blowing. The Parthenon didn't let her down. After descending, she waited for her uncle Bal on the side of Lycabettus and sipped a *cafethike* at a little place on the side of the mountain. Sitting at a little round table and eating chestnuts while having her shoes shined, watching the Monday market below, she admired the ruins again from a distance.

"I love the priests of Greece," she wrote. "They all have fine noses and great beards. But the nicest thing is that they have such a jolly twinkle about their eyes. They look like they laugh and enjoy life immensely. I suppose their religion is a bit pagan. Because the idea of a priest enjoying himself is so foreign to our religion. The idea I was trying to frame while having my *cafethike* is that the people and the country here haven't a great deal of our hypocrisy. There is so much bunkum built up around age—like around religion—and a sort of reverential, hypocritical awe. These English tourists miss the fact that those columns that still stand would be beautiful if they were built just yesterday. What I'm trying to get at is that there's a kinship between the priests' eyes and the line of columns where you can see the sky at the other end in the shape of a cock-tail shaker. And if it's not reverent for me to think of a cock-tail shaker in connection with the Parthenon—to hell with reverence."

Wood had left the strictures of Prohibition behind in America, along with the home brew, and she was discovering new drinks to take the place of beer. Most common was the ubiquitous *ouzo*. Her first introduction to the resinous wine, which foreigners tended to find a very acquired taste, was on a family outing to the Temple at Delphi. The narrow, unpaved road through the mountains at night, with hairpin curves dropping sheerly off to blackness three feet from the edge, was scary enough that Aunt Peg joked that Jane's mother would require two *ouzos* every hour to make the trip. When they stopped in Thebes for lunch, Jane got her first taste.

"You drink this right down, Jane," said Uncle Bal, throwing back his own nonchalantly.

She followed suit. "It took my tonsils with it," she observed, and left her pleasantly quiet for the next hour.

Jane Wood, Aunt Peg, and cousins Nina and Tink at the Temple of Poseidon, Sounion, Greece, December 1930. Jane wrote of this trip: "I can say that the bay was blue and the mountains were purple, but I've said that about other water and mountains. I can say that the columns of the Temple of Poseidon were white against a sky that was really as blue as the water, but—hell! The trouble is, I started with superlatives, and when I come to the 'est' of scenes, I've said 'glorious,' and 'loveliest' so much I'm faintly sick at my stomach of my own writing. We went to Suniam today. It is the very tip of the Attican peninsula. Right on the last end of land, with a drop of two hundred feet to the water directly in front of it, looking out on all the islands in the Aegean Sea, are the marble columns of the Temple."

Her first shock of Depression reality from home was a blow, both in how sorry she felt for her family and how bad it made her feel for enjoying Greece so much. The next-eldest sister, Dolly, delivered the doom-and-gloom news with some relish. In light of her parents' proud and somewhat muddled views on money, Dolly was forced to be the practical voice of reason and make the family accept that they couldn't put pretty faces on the situation anymore. Jane was getting an opportunity that Dolly was unlikely to ever get for herself, and she wasn't shy in making her older sister aware of it.

Despite Dolly's stark portrayal of bank failures and the impact on their father's law practice—if it wasn't his bank, then it was one in which his clients had their money—Jane's detachment from the financial situation at home became obvious as the months went on. She blithely dispensed advice on how they could tighten their belts and run a better household, not knowing that her father was matching quarters on the courthouse steps and playing bridge for money to keep the family housed and fed. When they moved into new houses, they portrayed it as a change of pace. It sounded better than the reality that they were no longer able to afford rent and had been kicked out. Determined not to worry her child too much, Daisy Wood related bad news with a laughing sarcasm: "Oh, a bank failure is just the thing to have at Christmas. And isn't it wonderful not to have any money to lose in it!"

After beating herself up a bit for being a faraway burden, Jane would usually resign herself to the idea that it was better being happy than miserable, and return to her normal ways. She added Parnes to the inscriptions on her new walking stick. The 4,635-foot peak that loomed over Kephissia was an eight-mile hike up and down, and she hiked it in the company of a taciturn acquaintance and his dog.

"Honestly," she complained of her hiking companion, "after you've been with him all day, you can't remember one interesting thing he's said. But you can't talk and climb. Even I can't. And it's rather nice to be with people who don't think at all now and then. I mean that abstract thinking and generalizations are the curse of mankind. They have no more bearing on the business of living than cross word puzzles. I can stand anything in a person except their being a talkative ass."

The intellectual pretension that flourished in society circles continued to irritate her. Though much of her learning had been achieved by seeking knowledge outside the classroom, she looked upon intellect as something that needed to be carefully cultivated over a long time.

"Have you ever noticed that the first generation with 'intellect' is as bad as the first generation with money?" Wood wrote. "The *nouveau riche* overestimate the importance of money. People who have discovered when they start high school that they have brains, who have no background of the mind or of mental culture, are just as bad. They take thinking and literature and communism so damn seriously. Even when they study ancient Greece they miss the old ideal of a balanced man."

The innocence of the peaceful era between the wars was reflected by one of her festive ruminations. She found herself more in sympathy with Germans than the French or English, solely based on the idea that you can judge a nation fairly well by its drinks.

"America, cocktails, which I can't develop an immense liking for. England, whisky and soda. A straight-forward drink, but brutal. Quite masculine. France, wine. It is sparkling. It's a good thing to have with people, with a dinner. It is a sort of social drink. Germany, beer. That is my favorite. It is a sociable beverage. You need to drink it with one other person. It doesn't increase wit and clever-ness, but it furthers conversation. It goes with big meals, and big laughter, and warm thinking. Of course it makes you fat in time, but it seems like that's my doom anyway."

For the next dance she attended, Wood had to be chaperoned by Mrs. Pappa, the wife of the minister of health, to satisfy local convention. During one of their many long talks, Wood and Aunt Peg argued the merits of chaperones. To Wood's surprise, her aunt was all for the idea. She felt that it kept parents in close touch with their children and helped prevent the children from making mistakes they would regret. Wood was aghast. The entire foundation of her teenage life was based on her parents giving her enough rope and trusting she would never hang herself. Generations of her family to come succeeded with the liberal approach, amused at the dire warnings American society issued de-cade after decade about the necessity to monitor their children's every move.

"Parents can be sympathetic and keep in touch with their kids without tag-ging around wherever they go," she wrote to her family. "The more I think about it, the more I am convinced that I am very lucky in my parents. Thank heavens you trust me. Even though I have often made a fool of myself, thinking that helps a lot. Yes, though you are often jackasses—worrying about my clothes, Mum, and shouting at the top of your voice, Pud, you suit me. *Don't* you feel flattered now?"

Another disagreement she had with Aunt Peg was about smoking. Her aunt claimed that Wood was too young to be smoking so much and that eventually it would take her two packs a day to be satisfied. While that was all well and good, Wood thought, it wasn't the real reason Peg or her mother objected. What they dared not say to her was that smoking wasn't ladylike. Even more than that, she decided, it was because she enjoyed it so much. "No real lady ought to like to smoke as much as a man," Wood wryly observed. "That's the last reason a lady ought to want to smoke, because she enjoys it."

While Wood had been warned before coming to Greece that she would love it except for the climate and the people, she found that she doted on the climate. Further, she found the people preferable to her fellow countrymen, complaining that "half the Americans here are such damn fools. If I ever really live abroad, I'm not going to know a single American. It's rather disgusting how most of the people here don't know anybody but their own country people."

After two months in the country, Wood felt like it was a new home. She observed that it was not a country that gave itself away to mere acquaintance: "As you get more friendly with it you find a deep, warm affection is taking the place of your first polite admiration for it." On a more particular level, she realized one day while driving in to Athens that she had never really *seen* Mount Hymettus before. She had noted the beauty of the sunsets before on it but thought that "many things never penetrate any further than the outer layer of your consciousness. You can look at a thing, appreciate it, admire it, but never really see it."

On her ramble back to Kephissia that afternoon, she marveled at how deeply she had fallen in love with the landscape in such a short time: "The wind blowing the short leaves of winter wheat, the shepherds' eyes, the pine trees; the sunlight lying in pale pools in low places; donkeys; a biting wind blowing your hair back as you come over the crest of a low hill; the smell of thyme as you rest and smoke and think of nothing at all; a hot bath and tea when you get home. Truly, it is the little things that count."

She felt like she was getting a sense of proportion in life that the ancient Greeks possessed. Noting that the work they left wasn't ornate, she observed that the keynote of it was simplicity, a perfect rhythm. No clutter. To her mind, they couldn't have lived in much of a hurry. Since she felt there was no possible way she could experience all of life in some seventy years, and didn't even want to try, the idea of reincarnation appealed to her. Curiously, she wanted to return as a buzzard.

"After all," she wrote, "eating carrion is merely a matter of taste, and it must be rather wonderful to float as smoothly and effortlessly as buzzards do."

In mid-February, she went to Athens College to see another play by Charles Koon, a local playwright who taught at the college. Ever since seeing one of his plays, she had been enchanted with him without having any idea what he looked like. She realized that she was more in love with him than ever, "but my passion seems doomed to flower unseen and unheeded." If she had just been attracted to him physically, or to his charm, or any number of other reasons, she could have approached him. But being attracted to a mind was a more difficult proposition. Rather than press the issue, she thought it best to keep living her life and see if an opportunity presented itself.

"I never believed in love at first sight for people or for things," she wrote. "Love takes time, and is gentle in its coming. I've decided that people, especially today, expect too much. They prepare for the big times of life and don't enjoy the commonplaces. Life may be as a race, certainly, to some, but I'd rather mine to be as one of my walks. I don't go anywhere, but I enjoy the going immensely. I have a rather bad quality of not particularly enjoying races, keen competition. I like fighting, but more because of the fighting itself than because I care much about winning."

Despite her relentless walking up and down mountains and along every goat trail around Athens, Wood had been gaining weight ever since her arrival in Greece. Three months after debarking at Piraeus, she had put on eighteen pounds and weighed 149 pounds. Part of this was due to the erratic winter weather keeping her from being outside as much as she wanted. She was just short of five foot nine, towering over other women at social gatherings and often taller than men she met. The extra weight made her the most voluptuous she had ever been—and ever would be—but in predictable teenage dissatisfaction she declared herself "fat-headed."

After reading *The Romany Stain* by Christopher Morley, Wood developed a curiosity about gypsies. One afternoon, she encountered a pair at the palace gardens in Athens. Wood was sitting in the sun reading *Tristram Shandy*, when an old woman and a young one came by. The young one was attractive, with braids down her back and big brown eyes.

"I think most of these 'liquid brown eyes' look cow-like," Wood wrote, "but hers certainly didn't. Even while she was offering to tell my fortune, they looked like they were laughing at me. They were both quite straight and thin-nish, and brown, and the old one was puffing a cigarette. They were certainly not defiant or arrogant toward society, they just didn't give a damn about it. I think it would be great to be born a gypsy and have eyes like theirs, aware and independent."

Poking around the dusty back shelves of bookshops was one of Wood's fa-vorite pastimes. She discovered a copy of *The Prussian Officer* by D. H. Law-rence, whose writing she was familiar with and liked, though she warned her mother that "you might not approve of him in spots." Lawrence had just died the previous March, in France, after a tumultuous career that had constantly pitted him against the sort of moralists for whom Wood had such disdain.

Another of Wood's favorite authors was Joseph Conrad, and she found a copy of his *Victory* in an Athens bookstore. She had read it before but was entranced by the rhythm of Conrad's writing. "Perhaps Conrad handled the English language so beautifully because it was an effort for him to learn it," she speculated, "because he was always aware of each word."

Two days before an unseasonable heavy snow in late March, playwright George Bernard Shaw and William Inge, dean of Saint Paul's Cathedral in Lon-don and an *Evening Standard* columnist, visited Athens. They were shepherded through the museums and monuments for a morning, and Wood was "rather peeved that I didn't get a glimpse of them, touch the hem of their gowns, or something."

The day finally came in the first week of April for her departure on an out-ing to Constantinople, which she had been dreaming of for the past month. Whereas Greece was cloaked in classical history, Turkey was cloaked in the mystery and intrigue of the East. The decaying Ottoman Empire had only re-cently passed into history. "Young Turks," led by the charismatic nationalist Mustafa Kemal Pasha, were in the process of changing Turkish society into a secular state along Western lines. All traditional dress of the East had either been outlawed or shunned, including the banning of the fez in 1925. Even the style of names was changed to reflect the new ways, and thus Mustafa Kemal transformed into Kemal Ataturk. It was Colonel Mustafa Kemal who had led the Turkish forces at Gallipoli, where his brash—if also costly to his own side— leadership so bloodied the Allied forces that he immediately became a national hero and was catapulted to the rank of general.

Relations between Greece and Turkey were just beginning to approach cordiality again at the time of Wood's visit. The Turks, perhaps as punishment for Gallipoli and other bruises they had inflicted on the Allied ego, were treated abominably after the peace settlements were signed in 1918. The Allied powers gave little heed to the letter of the treaties, and the Turks were subjected to continued humiliations. One of the worst cases was when the Greek fleet moved in to occupy Smyrna in 1919, with the Allied fleet looking on. The Greek army massacred Turks on a large scale, without a finger lifted in protest by the British, French, or Americans observing. The Turks elicited little sympathy from the Allies, having been a wartime enemy and also having committed genocide against their own Armenian population during the war.

For the Turks, the war was not over. They had to fight a campaign of guerrilla warfare for four more years, led by General Mustafa Kemal, to finally secure their republic in 1922. In 1923, after seven centuries of control, the house of Osman was dismantled and the caliph eliminated. No longer would sultans rule Turkey.

To some of Wood's shipmates, an unchaperoned young American woman taking on Constantinople in 1931 seemed absurdly rash, but Turkey was more enlightened than many parts of the world at that time. In the sweeping legislative reforms to build the new society, one of the early results was that women were given the vote. A year before Wood arrived, women were voting and standing for office in municipal elections. In the new Turkey, with its liberated women and Western style of dress, a bold American woman was considered no more amiss than in some Western countries.

The ship left Piraeus at noon on the April 8. To be sailing on a Turkish vessel under the star-and-crescent flag thrilled Wood, as did rule seven of the regulations in her cabin: "Not to touch piano unless play well."

While Wood was fascinated by the new cultures and people she encountered, her Achilles heel was the prejudice against blacks she had learned as a southern child. Though she might have been given to thoughtless generalizations about the English, French, Greeks, or anyone else, she never let the attitudes affect her judgment of an individual. Toward blacks, though, she had not even a charitable ignorance. Although she mocked her mother's dedication to being a southern lady, she had not yet cleansed herself of the stain of racism:

"I had a slight shock when I walked into the dining room," she wrote, "and saw a Negro with his five year old kid in one corner. Of course there's no prejudice at all against them in Europe. Nobody minded him at all. But I was born in Georgia, so I sat at another table."

Over the next decade Wood began to outgrow her prejudice, with Miami being too new a place to constantly reinforce racism as Georgia did. Certainly, Miami was still segregated. But parts of Coconut Grove were founded by blacks who came from the Bahamas in the 1890s and were increasingly populated by blacks from southern states throughout the 1920s. Many blacks had escaped to freedom in Florida during slavery, harbored by Seminole Indians. The perverse southern notion that blacks were an inherited part of the landscape, an inferior servant class that could never be anything more, gave way as blacks built their own communities throughout Florida. The transformation did not occur overnight, by any means, but somewhat enlightened views imported from the North to booming south Florida prevented brutal acts like the 1923 massacre of blacks by a white mob in the central Florida community of Rosewood.

In the morning, Wood woke up and leapt out of bed excitedly to get her first glimpse of Asia through a porthole. A brown sandstone fort and minarets greeted her gaze, and she scrambled up to the deck to get a better view. By that time, they were passing the last of the Dardanelles and the Hellespont. Her first impression of Constantinople was that it was the most beautiful natural site of a city she'd ever seen, but as a man-made thing it left something to be desired. The ship arrived on a Thursday evening, and they had just enough time to go up to Pera—the business section where all the hotels and embassies were located—and have dinner. She dined with the Browns, the parents of two brothers in Athens she liked very much. Walking back to the ship afterward, they strolled along narrow and winding cobblestone streets, with the second floors of houses hanging out over the streets.

"As you go down the hill," she wrote, "everything seems to close down on you, the street-lights become rarer and finally give up entirely, cats hop out of alleys and garbage pails, you get brief glimpses through dirty windows of unshaven men smoking *chibooks*—the water pipes—and playing backgammon, and about that time you realize with a pang of fear and delight that you are in Constantinople."

Though she enjoyed all the sights of the guided first day, it was not the way Wood liked to see a place. The things that interested her were the irrelevant little facts that proved not only that you were in an unfamiliar country but that you were in a foreign one—"like respectable ladies as old as Grandmother smoking in ferries, and storks that stand on chimneys, and the way the muezzins wind their turbans." She preferred to see half as much and enjoy it rather than trying to do everything. In light of that, she set out the next day on her own and found it much more fun to ride streetcars, buy her own ferry tickets, and communicate with gestures. An American woman on the ship was shocked that Wood should do so with no idea of any other language than English, and said in despair that she was more than a "modern" girl.

Wood hopped a ferry up to Eyoub, at the head of the Golden Horn, and sat on the deck munching crackers and watching life flow by.

"One of the reasons I love Constantinople is because you feel not only that a great deal of life has flowed through it," she wrote, "but that it is still flowing. You get this idea watching the shipping more than in any other way. Everything is so busy, without being hurried."

At Eyoub, an old Turkish cemetery was set on a hill by the side of the water. Grand old cypress trees, tombs with Arabic writing, and a drizzling rain combined to make her feel shut off from the rest of the city. Since Eyoub was the last stop on the ferry, she hired a rowboat to go up the Sweet Waters of Europe, at the very head of the Golden Horn. Midway up, the boatman calmly doubled his price. Women had made some strides in Turkey, but a foreign woman was still assumed to be an easy mark. This time, though, the boatman had chosen the wrong person.

"We had a heated argument with gestures which ended in our turning around and coming back," she wrote, beginning what would become something of a tradition of hers of cursing Turkish transport. "He would have liked to make me get out and walk, but I was twice as big as him."

In the afternoon she went to the Grand Bazaar, the bargainer's paradise, which she loved as much as anything in Constantinople. Covering about six blocks, the bazaar drew an odd comparison by her to one of Georgia's most famous attractions. "It is sort of like Stone Mountain would be if arched tunnels were hollowed out, and booths and little shops strung along them."

From her experience in Flea Market and Shoe Lane in Athens, Wood was an old hand by now at market etiquette. She described the process as if she were an inveterate horse trader.

"There are a lot of ballyhooers that have as their chief object just herding you into their shops. They've a great line.

"'Right in here, Madam, not to buy, just to look. Look cost no money.'

"The actual business of buying is very complicated. You go in and sit down and have a half-cup of coffee and a cigaret, and exchange remarks about the weather. After about five minutes you look things over with a bored air as if you'd seen worse, but couldn't remember where. You show a vague interest in one or two things you've no intention of buying.

"After a preliminary discussion of prices you ask casually, 'By the way, how much is that?' That, you are informed, is two pounds—one dollar. You laugh like you were much amused and look at other things.

"Later you say, 'Well, I might give you twenty-five piastres.'

"'But Madam, it is impossible,' in a deeply offended tone.

"The next move is his. If you go higher then, you are lost.

"'Because you are tres sympathetique, madam, I make you a special price of one pound fifty.'

"You say 'Nevermind, I don't believe I want it anyway.' This goes on interminably, until you compromise on fifty piastres. At that, the buyer is always cheated."

In the afternoon she took a ferry across the Bosphorus strait to Asia and wandered through a graveyard in Scutari, admiring the cypress trees. It had been overcast or raining ever since her arrival, but it cleared in time for her to watch the sunset over Stamboul. Right then she truly fell in love with Constantinople. She was inclined to agree with what Mrs. Brown had said the day before, that the ancients were quite right to worship the sun. Returning to Europe in the dark that night, she got lost along the waterfront walking down from Pera back to the ship.

"It was then that I decided maybe this wicked, mysterious East stuff has some truth in it," she wrote. "I was distinctly scared, but not panicky."

Sunday morning Wood went on a ferry up the Bosphorus. She got out at the last stop and walked up the cliffs, where she sat on a ledge and dangled her legs over the Black Sea. Bread, cheese, and figs from a little fishing village made for lunch. The Bosphorus wound along between high cliffs, with old towers and walls punctuating the heights. Along the shore, the path was narrow and lonesome, with the waves all breaking together in a great roar. Every village had an enormous drying rack, where sardines and other small fish hung out in the sun. The smell reminded her of Tahiti Beach, a popular Coconut Grove beach on the shores of Biscayne Bay, where a low tide could bring forth all manner of smells from the exposed muck and sea grass.

When she was talking with Mrs. Davis back in Athens a month later about where she had been, Mrs. Davis said that the area had been extremely dangerous when they had lived in Constantinople in 1923.

"We had to take three men with guns and paper-cutters when we were walking along the Bosphorus," she told Wood, assuring her that it was probably much safer in 1931.

"I know that even if brigands hid behind every rock," Wood joked, "all they would do to me would be to ask, in motions, to have their pictures taken."

Just before dusk, she walked out to the old Roman walls and heard a squealing at the foot of one of the towers.

"There were tiny kittens with their eyes not open yet," she wrote. "They were just about four days old, and so soft and squirmy that I put them in my hat and took them to the boat. These people abandon their kittens instead of drowning them, which I think is a dirty trick. They slept under my chin, and just meowed a little. Madame Alexiou gurgles in her sleep, so I was glad to get even.

"I tried to feed them with an eye-dropper, and every other way. All Monday morning I spent chasing around the Bazaar trying to find a mother cat. Explaining in detail to everybody that spoke English and tried to sell me something—just what I wanted—was kind of funny. That's one thing the Bazaar doesn't supply. The kittens seemed doomed to starvation, so the kindest thing I suppose was to drown them quickly. The cabin steward shuddered at the idea, so I did it. I'm not much good in that role, though." Though she was as enamored of pets as any other person, she had the farm child's practicality about putting doomed animals out of their misery.

The sun finally came out in full force on Monday, and Wood went to see the *serai*, the sultan's palace. She felt that the splendor of an eastern monarch had not been overrated but that the scale of wealth was so absurd it was difficult to appreciate.

"If there had been one emerald as big as a walnut it might have aroused me," she lamented, "but when you see three that big in a dagger hilt they don't mean much. Somehow a throne with three hundred odd pearls in it leaves me cold. There was a chess set with rubies in the top of half the men, and emeralds in the other half. In anybody but a sultan it would have been vulgar ostentation. If you just saw one of each thing, and that was the most perfect, you'd be able to grasp the beauty better. It must have been lovely in the palace in summer, because there are wide terraces, and rose gardens right above the water looking over to Asia."

The night before, she began talking to a young man she had seen sitting in the second-class dining salon whenever she went in. Wood discovered to her surprise that he was a stowaway, an ex-Communist, and homesick. She didn't think that he looked like any of the three, but more like a harmless, blond fellow of twenty-one. The lonely man had had his own company for two or three days, she found, "so he was quite ready to tell his life's history, or discuss Mills." She wrote:

"It seems his parents were Russians, but he was born in the United States, in California. Six years ago his folks decided to come back to Russia, because they thought it was a free country then. Well, they got in and couldn't get out.

"'Geez,' he said, 'I wish all these Communists in America could try it out in Russia.'

"Then he cussed Russia awhile.

"'There, why you can't even get what's called black bread in America. The bread's so lousy they wouldn't sell it there. In Russia if you do anything against the government, they just come and take you away, and nobody knows what happened to you. They've got women's rights there—my sister, she's eighteen—she's a bricklayer. Why, you ought to be ashamed sitting here talking to a dirty Russian.'

"I asked him why more people didn't try to get out. 'They don't know any better. The Googlys—that's what we call the government agents—stick up notices everywhere about school children fainting from hunger in the U.S. and that sort of bunk.'

"I asked him about the drive against churches. He said, 'Well they don't tear down the churches, but if they want a new school building, they make them into that. They put up posters, "Religion is a trick of capitalists to make the workman satisfied with his lot. God didn't make man, man made God!" They used to be a religious people, but religion doesn't fill your stomach, so nobody cares much now.'

"He got fed up, but it's as hard as the deuce to get out. At every port he says, you have to go through a huge wall, guarded heavily, before you get to a ship, and you have to pass a guard getting on the ship. 'You have to have a pass, and they look you up and down for half an hour before they let you by.'

"He was acting as interpreter for some Americans, and he bluffed the guard into letting him go on to 'help them.' He had a friend on the ship and they found a canvas covered box that he crawled into.

"'I had a heavy shackle under my belly, and my ear was all crumpled up in a heap of rope and I couldn't breathe, and I got hot. Geez, I said I was going to get out or get shot. I thought I was a man, and I didn't care much about people. But I got so home-sick I almost bawled. Geez, I thought I might never see my folks again, and they wouldn't be there to take care of me. I would have gone back, only my friend said, "You're here now, you might as well stay." But I wouldn't want to be in that box again.'

"After the ship left port he crawled out and got down in the American's cabin. He crawled under the bunk, and the steward found him in the morning. He couldn't speak French, so he had the deuce of a time, but he managed to bribe the steward and the maid and they brought him food. They got him ashore at Constantinople as a sailor. He didn't have any passport or visa, but the American consul fixed him up with the first. They sent him on our ship because he didn't have a Turkish visa. He had to stay there until an American boat came in and the consul got him a job to work his way across. He left this morning. I think that's a grand story, but you can't imagine anybody less fitted for the role. The things he said about Communism and stowing away made me decide never to try either one."

On Monday night when Wood came into the dining salon, there was a funny-looking little fellow with big ears with the escaping American. They drank some beers together, and she learned that this person was a naturalized American citizen who was trying to escape from Turkey. According to an agreement between Turkey, Albania, and the United States, Turkey claimed him as a subject. He asked where Wood was from, and when she told him, he started laughing and said: "Know where Joe's Restaurant is on Miami Beach? South Beach? I was a waiter there."

She couldn't believe how small the world could be, to find a stranger on a boat in Turkey who had worked at Joe's, famous for its stone crabs and a venerable Miami institution that still exists today. He had left Miami a year before, and she caught him up with all the news on the bank failures. He found it nearly impossible to believe.

When the boat left on Tuesday morning, Wood sang to the seagulls until Constantinople dropped out of sight. Watching the coastline reminded her of some lines in Conrad's *Youth*, which she quoted to the seagulls: "And this is how I see the East. I have seen its secret places and have looked into its very soul. But now I see it always from a small boat, a high outline of mountains, blue and afar in the morning, like faint mist at noon, a jagged wall of purple at sunset."

With the weather warming, Wood felt a mental laziness set in that began to concern her to some degree. It was all well and good being a Romantic and living for sights, sounds, and smells, but she felt twinges of guilt about not aspiring toward anything substantial. Still, convention held little attraction. People who led unusual lives did.

Her motivation to explore increased yet more when her friend Mrs. Davis loaned her a bicycle for the duration of her stay. All the bicycle needed was some air in the tires, but Wood managed to break a bolt when tightening up the front hub. Because she couldn't get a replacement bolt, she had to buy a whole new hub, and then found herself faced with the nightmarish task of replacing all the spokes. Though she lived her life with the idea that she could do anything if she put her mind to it, there were some things that it paid to have others do for you.

"I ruined my nails, a kitchen fork, the color of my arms, and my temper," she fumed, "and then the darned thing was off center. The bicycle shop man did it for twenty cents."

Uncle Bal wasn't at home much, as travel to the out stations along with trips to other parts of Europe consumed most of his days. Greece, and much of the Mediterranean, had devastating problems with malaria at the time, and hundreds of thousands of lives depended on bringing the disease under control. He lived the life, as their friend Mrs. Keays described, of an "animated pendulum" between the field stations of Drama and Maurla. One was almost in Bulgaria, and the other in the Peloponnesus.

"Traveling on trains that go about thirty miles an hour on the average," sympathized Wood, "and sleeping in bed-bug ridden hotels isn't exactly fun when you do it at least three days out of every week."

Relations with Wood's parents had come back to an even keel, with the agreement that it might be best for her to come home at the end of the summer. She was beginning to second-guess her attempt to be a noble martyr, though, having half-expected her parents to tell her not to be silly and to stay put. With her appetite whetted for world travel, she didn't want to leave Greece just yet.

What appealed to the teenage Wood about her parents, and about family for the rest of her life, was that she could fight with them. Her love of fighting encompassed her whole life, often to the exasperation of family members forced into bare-knuckle verbal matches with her, but she assumed that family had the strength to take it and still love her at the end of the day. She expressed to her parents her appreciation that they did not treat her as any older or younger than she was: "Parents so often patronize their kids—and kids their parents. With all our fighting we have steered between those two rocks. I think when I am old and grey and telling my thirty-six grandchildren about my parents I will say conclusively, 'My blessed father, I could fight with him.'"

While she liked fighting on an individual level, she had very strong antiwar feelings as a result of World War I. The stench of useless death from the modern world's most horrible conflict still offended her. She reconciled her pacifism with her personal love of fighting by explaining:

"The thing about war that is most horrible, I've decided, isn't that men kill each other, it is that they don't do it spontaneously. They are led, and driven, and worked up by propaganda. Street brawls appeal to me more than international ones. The worst thing the war did was to use the things people believed in—no matter how foolishly—things like honor, and bravery, and glory, and then let them see that they were nothing but words and catch-phrases all along."

The more time passed, however, the more reluctant Wood became to follow through on her promise of coming home. She went through the motions of finding steamers and arranging a schedule, but it hurt her to do so.

"Miami is a nice place to be home," she wrote to her parents, "but it can be that for years and years, and once I get back there I won't be able to return to Athens in a week. It doesn't seem that while I'm here I'm so much more expensive than I would be at home. In the six months I've been here you've sent me sixty dollars. I owe Aunt Peg thirty-five dollars for my trip to Constantinople. A hundred dollars in a half year, $16.50 a month, doesn't seem so awful."

Thus began her campaign to prolong her stay, suggesting that October seemed a better time to return. She knew that with enough manipulation she could tug at the heartstrings of her father, and she was still not aware of how desperately he was trying to make ends meet for his family in Coral Gables. Though she had downgraded to student third class to save money, she wanted to travel through Naples, Rome, Florence, Venice, Milan, Lyons, Paris, and Cherbourg en route to New York. In fact, the only thing that tempted her to travel earlier than October was that she was desperate to see more of Italy. Her letters home, mixing sympathy for her family's hardships with firm declarations about what was best for her, no doubt made her parents wonder why she was seeking their approval. It was clear that Wood was going to do whatever she wanted in the end, anyway.

She turned eighteen on May 28 and celebrated with a trip the following week to the islands of Mykonos and Delos.

The boat left from Piraeus at two o'clock in the morning under a nearly full moon, with everyone in high spirits. While the cabins could hold a hundred people, there were four hundred on board. Wood sat up on the top deck with Sam Ives, whom she had met at the Gennadius Library in Athens. He was assistant librarian at what Wood had discovered was one of the finest collections of Greek history and literature in the country, and she had recently been spending some time there and immersing herself further in Greek history. Reading Thucydides made her lament:

"Five and a half years of Latin, and I can't read anything, which is my fault, and I wouldn't enjoy it if I could, which isn't my fault. To think of reading Caesar when there's Thucydides! It is depressing to think that 2300 years ago men were quite as civilized, quite as full-grown in every way as they are today. For it is the stature of the Greeks that I am humble before."

Though Wood was as happy as anyone to launch into her first *ouzo* or beer at nine in the morning, she did not consider herself much of a drinker. Visiting a young man who knew a friend from home, she noted that both he and his sister "seem to be in the whirl of young English and American hard drinkers. That may be all right, but Athens isn't the place for it. You should see the Kit-Kat, the raciest nightclub. Christian Endeavour [a youth ministry founded in 1881 that had more than four million members in America at the time] is wilder and more hilarious."

In the dog days of summer, Athens grew scorchingly hot. It was the hottest summer since 1916, and just before noon one day Wood almost collapsed of heat exhaustion trying to ride her bike up the hill outside Kephissia. The family spent more and more time in the backyard pool, which Wood viewed as something of an overgrown bathtub. They stretched out on steamer chairs in the evening, with two candles burning and the shadows of the pines in the water, and Peg and Jane engaged in long rambling talks. The Balfour family had taken to calling her "Ginger," a nickname that paid tribute to her spicy personality. Uncle Bal was still away much of the time, and on one of his trips to his study areas he took Wood with her. She described her newfound sport of mosquito catching with great enthusiasm:

"They have several study sections for malaria in Greece. They are spots where malaria conditions are rather bad or unusual, from ten to thirty square miles in area. In these sections, they study the malaria among the people, the breeding of the mosquitoes, and do a good deal of preventive work. At Marathon, about twenty miles from Athens, they study the breeding particularly. They have nine catching stations in three different little villages, merely the houses and stables of accommodating peasants. There are several marshes around Marathon. There they catch wiggle-tails and tumblers, larvae and pupae. I went hunting with Uncle Bal yesterday. For three hours we tramped through the marsh collecting wiggle-tails. We sank in mud and water halfway to our knees.

"The marsh grass came to our shoulders, and reminded me of the 'glades and Tahiti Beach both. The thing that added the spice of excitement was having to continually inspect for leeches around your shins. They wouldn't hurt you, leave a little wound if they stayed on a couple of hours, but I hardly fancy the idea of these flat little worms fastened on to me and sucking my blood. I knocked three or four silly. When I came out of the marsh my old white skirt was brown for six inches around the bottom, and my legs looked faintly like I'd been out on the jetties, and my blouse was sticking to my back. I was having a grand time.

"Then we went catching in a couple of little villages. You catch with a long rubber tube and a thin glass vial. One end of the vial is funnel-shaped. You suck the mosquitoes in but they can't get out. You should see Uncle Bal, looking as bedraggled in huge boots as I did, with the tube in one hand and a flash-light in the other under a low bed, with the lady of the house, three or four brats, and Jane squatting in an entranced circle around him. The people of these villages are all nice to you, very curious, but hospitable, and sort of naturally gracious in the way they receive you. Eighty percent of them have malaria, and it seems to me they're brighter than the normal poor white trash of Georgia. They have a flashing curiosity, the old Athenian desire for 'new things,' and a receptivity. They have an aliveness that is nothing like the dullness, the plodding, that is bred in the bone of the same class in northern countries. They aren't provincial minded. They don't have a distrust of people and things not like themselves.

"I liked the peasants much better than I did the malaria students. Nine of them came out after we'd finished with swamps, to learn something about field work. They belonged to the newly respectable, 'dry-feeted,' as Uncle Bal calls them. Couldn't get their feet wet or roll up their sleeves. After an hour of stables they were ready to knock off and sit in the shade. There was one dumb cluck that tried to impress Uncle Bal and went up to the village of Marathon with us. I rather admired her for having ambition enough. She opened her parasol and trotted along in the dust dabbing her brow and talking French steadily. I can discuss malaria and play bridge in French now, though I can't carry on an ordinary conversation."

Just as Wood had begun to think that she had steamrolled her parents into seeing things her way, she received another reality check from home. Her mother had been suffering from kidney stones, and the ever-nagging fears about Daisy Wood's frail health leapt back to the fore. In addition, her mother criticized her for her ignorance concerning her father and the family financial situation. Predictably, Jane went on the offensive once again to berate her family for not making the situation obvious enough to her. Given her carefree and idyllic life in Greece, the pain of the Depression was an ugly reality that she didn't want to face. Although her sister had continually painted the situation starkly, Jane had let herself be reassured by her parents' acquiescence to her staying on in Greece. Both her parents had experienced poor childhoods, and their ascension to the middle class as adults made them into the kind of people who desperately, for their children's sake, did not want to lose their station. That kind of class pride disgusted her, and she lashed back at her mother:

"Don't you suppose I feel ever so much better for knowing more how things stand? Do you think Aunt Peg minds? She's not mealy-mouthed about money. I guess she knows what it means not to have much.

"I know you do, too, Mum, but you will never admit to yourself and the kids exactly how things are. Of course I'm not blind. I've known often that we were frightfully pinched at times. But if everybody else sort of looked around and over that fact, it was rather easy for me to do so. Too easy. I think the trouble is, you and Dad have always taken all the responsibility. You have thought, 'We'll save them worrying anyway. If they look, they can see the trouble we're carrying. They'll help by and by.' Don't you think kids would be much better off if they were *given* part of the load themselves? If it was said, 'Just this is expected of you.' Because you know kids ignore facts which might hinder their pleasure unless they're stuck right under their noses. Do you think it makes them any happier to discover what you've been carrying all the time they were going blithely along bluffing themselves and being bluffed? Do you think I don't feel disgusted and sick over *my* blind selfishness?"

Jane talked over the situation with Aunt Peg, and they agreed that the Woods' financial straits were nothing to be ashamed of. Given Peg's extremely difficult childhood, poverty was a fairly ordinary fact of life to her, and courses of action were simply adjusted to reflect it. The first decision Jane made was that she wouldn't be returning to college for some time. If she did return, she only wanted to attend Columbia University, because there was no "college life" there. The hours spent contemplating Greek history in the Gennadius Library had made her regret not taking her education seriously enough.

Next she decided to rule out returning through France, which was an indulgence she had no trouble giving up. "My dreams are true in themselves, and sufficient excuse for their own being," she wrote. "The mere fact of going or not going to Paris means very little as far as my anticipation of it goes. Anybody can go there." Finally, she decided it was time for her to buckle down, get a job, and pay her own way in Greece. This was also an easy decision, for she was having enough trouble already justifying her aimlessness to herself. "We are going down to the Consulate tomorrow and find out what an ambitious and willing young lady can do, even though she's a Puddin' head."

The trip to the consulate gave her some leads on getting teaching work. Two American women with six-year-olds were impressed by Peg teaching her children at home through the Calvert system, and they wished the same for

Jane Wood with Peg Balfour's daughters, Nina and Tink, Greece,
1931. She captioned it at the time: "This looks too darn much like
me to be any good. Don't you like the scarves, though. The dress
is Aunt Peg's creation and partly my execution."

their children.[1] They did not have the time to undertake the homeschooling, so
they were seeking someone to take the boys from nine in the morning through
noon, five days a week.

"The main requirements for the teacher are patience, thoroughness, and a
fairly even disposition," Wood wrote to her father. "Laugh if you like at the idea
of me being a paragon of patience and all the rest."

While waiting to find out whether she would be accepted to teach the boys, Wood continued to inhabit the Gennadius Library. Her librarian friend Sam Ives gave her a copy of *Ajax* by Sophocles to read, and it opened up a whole new world for her. She struggled to read it in Greek, and while she felt she was probably missing much of the beauty, she thought at the same time that she was comprehending it without being distracted by the beauty. Of Sophocles, she waxed: "Here is sophistication, maturity, civilization. This man doesn't hand you taken-for-granted truths, which you forget because they are so true. To me he gave something greater than a truth; he gave a question."

Ives and Wood found themselves in a heated argument about their perspectives on *Ajax*, breaking the silence of the normally peaceful library. The librarian saw Ajax as a man doomed by the fates and thought that was how Sophocles saw him, whereas Wood thought that Ajax was doomed by his own weakness and that Sophocles shared her view. The argument brought to bear the fundamental outlook that Wood would have on people throughout her life. She recognized weakness in men and scorned it, feeling that too many men blamed "fates" and "the world" for problems that were due to their own lack of strength. And she was no more sympathetic toward women. If they blamed "men" for stifling their progress, she saw weakness.

After finishing *Ajax*, Wood turned her mind back to Conrad and read *Lord Jim*. She was astonished at how alike the two characters seemed, noting that "Jim makes you wonder and be afraid of your own weakness." Though her father was fond of Thomas Hardy, she preferred Conrad and considered his viewpoint to be in line with hers, quoting: "I suspect that the aim of creation cannot be ethical at all. I would fondly believe that its object is purely spectacular—a spectacle for awe, love, adoration, or hate, if you like, but in this view—never for despair."

On the other hand, she was fond of Hardy's poetry, and he was the only writer who had ever made her weep over an entirely abstract matter, through making the abstract personal. The poem, "We Are Getting to the End," was one she quoted for the rest of her life:

We are getting to the end of visioning
The impossible within the universe,
Such as that better whiles may follow worse,
And that our race may mend by reasoning.

We know that even as larks in cages sing
Unthoughtful of deliverance from the curse
That holds them lifelong in a latticed hearse,
We ply spasmodically our pleasuring.

And that when nations set them to lay waste
Their neighbours' heritage by foot and horse,
And hack their pleasant plains in festering seams,
They may again—not warily or from taste,
But tickled mad by some demonic force—
Yes. We are getting to the end of dreams!

The finality of the poem had made Wood weep in the small hours of the night, and the terrible casualness upset her. She wondered to her father if he had known just what he was recommending to her in Hardy.

"The danger of this attitude is that it leads to resignation," Wood told him. "Shaw somewhere speaks of people who, when the actuality of the world shatters their picture of it, blame the world."

In the first week of September, Wood received a cable from home. Her family was losing their patience with her making the decisions on her future, and her father notified her that he preferred that she return as soon as possible. She stalled for time, trying to read anything out of the cable but the glaringly obvious, and replied: "Is your 'prefer' as strong as Coolidge's 'choose,' or is it merely 'we'd like'? I have a sad feeling it's the former. When you get excited enough to start cabling you mean to say definitely 'Come on home.'"

Although she once again restated her position that it seemed to make more sense to stay on, she did agree that she would sail in October if they made a firm agreement. The terms Wood set were that she would take over all her mother's duties and that her mother would rest. Having seen that her father was no longer susceptible to manipulation, this ploy was aimed at her mother's weak spot. Wood knew that her mother would refuse to be treated like an invalid. She made one final appeal to her father in a letter of September 8, putting forth a view of family love as eloquently as any teenager could:

"Don't think I'm being hard-boiled when I say that the fact that you think a year and a half is a long time to be some seven moons away from home is no reason at all. I think it's silliest of all to let distance and separation make any difference between parents and kids. It seems to be the only sort of love you don't outgrow or grow away from. That's simply because always, where-ever I go, I know you're there, that I can go back to you, that you're my Dad and my mother and that if I wore a lorgnette and rolled my r's you'd always love me. And parents feel sure of their kids. My being yours doesn't depend on whether I'm in Athens or China or Ojus. The one thing that makes me think parental love is so grand is because it is so free. When I say parental I mean love for parents as well as from. There is no jealousy in it, and it doesn't depend on what you do. Do you think I'd care much if you robbed banks or chewed tobacco and let it dribble down your chin? I don't honour you, I love you."

As usual, she was too much for her parents. While there is little record of Wood's life in Greece over the next year, she did take on teaching the two American boys and remained until the following August. Her unrequited passion for Charles Koon remained so, and she wrote in 1932:

"One day last summer, when I was up at Mrs. Davis,' he came in. I was listening to them talk, or rather, watching him. I don't know what it was—nothing he said—a giggle, or his freckles, or something. My heart or some organ did a quick flip and after that I was in love with him. I suppose that was the reason I used to ride down to Mrs. Davis' that summer, sort of hoping I'd meet him on the hill. Occasionally, I did see him, you know. I never admitted to myself that was the reason, and I really did want to borrow books. But you know a person might be in love there for fifty years, and matters would stand on the same plane as they were at the beginning. There was nothing I could do about it, and I don't trust myself to be able to walk on eggshells. If there had been anything I could have done, I'm not sure I would have.

"Seeing his outlook opened new windows for me. As for being in love with him, which was something apart from that, I believe the warm joy that I got from occasionally dancing with him, from hearing him giggle, was about as much as I could expect under any circumstances. I may be being dumb about this. Maybe if you don't snatch things from the little gods they aren't going to break their backs stretching out to drop things in your lap. Maybe I was right when I said I was too lazy and it was too hot to be in love. I didn't trust my clumsiness."[2]

# 4 | The Depression

When Wood returned from Greece in 1932, the Depression had spread across America. She rolled into Sunnyside in early August, thrilled to see her family again. Climbing off the bus, she fell into the arms of her sister Win and her brother George and was astonished to see how much they had grown in the two years she had been gone. Even Winifred was already over five foot seven. Her mother was healthier than Wood expected and resigned not to worry as much anymore now that her eldest was home. The middle-class snobbery about "keeping up appearances" had mostly fallen by the wayside after long enough of not knowing where money for the next meal was coming from. Still, her mother had been making the young George go to the butcher when they had twenty-five cents to buy meat to save the girls from the embarrassment of only being able to afford such a small sum. To be eating any meat at all was a luxury.

The phone had been disconnected the previous winter, and the car had sat idle most of the year until they were able to acquire a license at half price. With the harder times, though, the family had banded together. Jane marveled at how well her sisters got along with each other and how smoothly the family functioned. Noting that her hell-raising at the age of fifteen had been a strain, she wrote to Aunt Peg:

"I think when I left I was one of the irritating elements. I come back not one so it's swell. Mother and I have talked. I have said everything to her I have wanted to, and she has said her say. I think I can see now how she could have brought you and I up the way she did, or rather leave it to us to do alone, in spots. While we were talking a lot tumbled out that I hadn't meant to let go. I painted the dangers of growing up in rather lurid colors. She was really frightened, which maybe wasn't fair."

Still given to characterizing her mother as "dumb," Jane clarified it by saying that she was "sort of glowingly optimistic." It was the same characterization Henry Miller made of himself and Americans in general, writing of the same time period in Paris in *Tropic of Cancer*: "Incurably optimistic! Still have one foot in the nineteenth century. I'm a bit retarded, like most Americans."

In her sister Dolly, Jane saw much of her own practicality and no-nonsense approach, but Dolly was also blessed with a keener wit—"she is off-hand in her relationships and funny enough to keep us all giggling violently." In contrast, she described Daisy as "soft, giggly, clinging, and in an awful lot of danger during the next few years because of her amiability." With a mild combination of envy and disgust, Jane lamented: "The reason people think she is so beautiful is because she is pretty, and she has a downy, just-hatched air about her that gets men. Her appeal has nothing definite about it, nothing hard."

From the beginning, she had formed her strongest bond with her youngest sister, Winifred, now thirteen years old, and it only grew upon her return. "It is a very lucky thing," she wrote, "to find that one of your sisters is such a rarely lovely person that you would have been captivated by her when you first met her and loved her ever afterward. In a pair of old blue overalls she is so lovely that I would have to follow her around if she didn't follow me."

Like their Grandmother Winifred, the girls were thinkers and talkers who never discussed any topic at less than a dull roar. Little George sat back and watched his sisters with great amusement, making his contributions in tones half the volume of theirs. "He has an adaptability," Jane mused, "a sort of good-humoured tolerance of people that no one else in the family has."

Wood had taken for granted the anachronism that Sunnyside represented, but it still surprised her how little the place had changed in the time she had been away. The girls helped Grandmother Lil churn, draw water from the well, wash clothes, and press them with irons heated before the fire: "I got again the idea that events here move very deliberately along a line almost at right angles with the path the rest of the world follows."

She sadly realized the old people were wholly responsible for the archaic nature of the place and that when they died the atmosphere would disappear: "Grandmother is Sunnyside to me. Without her it would be a dull place, full of rather stupid people. My country life, the rather precious isolation Sunnyside has always meant to me will go, and life here will be the same thing that is lived in towns, almost. There will be girls with chalk white complexions and over-painted lips and boys with purple shirts."

While her grandmother lived on, though, Wood enjoyed the same simple pursuits that made her love the summers there so much: eating green apples, shucking corn, going fishing, making popguns, churning butter, and eating watermelon. For as much as she loved Miami, she still felt stronger ties to the red clay roads she grew up on and the "sloppy talking" than she did yet to anywhere in Florida.

"I have never been a 'true Southern lady,'" she conceded, "but I am a rather good Georgia cracker."

A cousin, James Cain, drove down from Atlanta every so often, and Wood found herself now old enough that he enjoyed her company. He was an ensign in the Naval Reserve and planning to attend medical school at Emory the following year. To her surprise, he told her that he expected a war with Japan by Christmas. At first she dismissed the notion as macho "war talk," but she learned he had no interest in going to war and was especially fearful of getting submarine duty. Since January, Cain had been under orders to prepare to report for duty within seventy-two hours. The entire Japanese fleet had appeared off the coast of California in July, he told her. Wood realized that rumors were just as rife in the military as anywhere else, so she didn't give too much credence to the dire prediction. Her transition into adulthood was giving her less interest in great upheavals. She wrote: "Knowing that there could be one—and it would be so easy—gives me a pretty weary feeling. I have also lost much of my zest for hurricanes. I can't forget that they make such a damn mess, and take so much cleaning up afterward."

The event would be delayed for nine years, but the war with Japan by Christmas eventually became a reality. Cain's early fears proved justified, and he served as a captain in World War II before eventually becoming an admiral. Whether or not the original probing had been just a rumor, it was not unreasonable to think that Japan contemplated an opportunity in 1932 to strike against a militarily weak, avowedly isolationist nation already crippled by the Depression.

Wood's father was back in Miami, struggling to keep his law business going. Although he had a steady stream of clients, collecting from them was a painfully slow process. When he could, he played bridge for money to keep the family afloat, though he kept this secret from them. He played socially with his wife to keep sharp. A few weeks after Jane arrived in Sunnyside, the family traveled back to Miami to rejoin her father.

The drive took them twenty-four hours, even with Jane and Dolly convincing their mother to let them drive all night. As the car overheated when they pushed it over forty-five miles per hour, they didn't find the enterprise to be too risky. Once back in Miami, Wood realized that she loved it just as much as anywhere. If her mother's conventions exasperated Jane at times, her father's indifference to conventions endeared him to her even more. The sheer size of George Wood projected a solidness Jane found reassuring, as well as his wordless affection.

"It was the sudden picture of him walking down Miami Avenue," she remembered of her time in Greece, "with his hair uncombed and his shirt sleeves rolled up and his trousers too short—and he looking rather god-like—that would make me feel gulpy at nights."

Wood was impressed by so many of the absurdities in her father that she knew better than to make any attempts to reform him. One of his small enthusiasms during the Depression was waffle cooking. The family had them for supper every Sunday night, and various friends and extended family members would drop in. Against the furious protests of his wife, George Wood insisted on cooking the waffles while shoeless. The children, who loved this, threatened to go about bragging, "Our father can cook waffles with his feet."

Jane and Dolly settled on a routine to divide up the housework in the morning, allowing Dolly to practice music much of the day, and Jane to go in and look after her father's office from eleven to five. Dolly was an elegant piano player, and Winifred loved sitting and listening to her older sister play. With no money available for Dolly to attend college, Dolly felt to some degree as if her aspirations had been "fobbed off." She had no interest in attending the Cardboard College—"that messy place!"—but there were no other options available for higher education that the family could afford. Feeling some small degree of guilt over her sister's situation, Jane happily took on the office work. At five o'clock she would dash home to help fix the family supper.

Communities became closer during the Depression, and Wood found her ideal second family in Charlie and Angeline Graves. They lived nearby in a house with their parents. Wood wrote:

"You wander in the garden and a monkey drops down and grabs your cigarette. A macaw two feet from beak to tail flies up from the hibiscus bush and perches on the telephone wire. You find a note on the door saying: 'Back in

Jane Wood writing in 1933 while working as a cub reporter for the women's section of the *Miami Daily News*.

five minutes. Come in and make yourself at home. Beer in the ice-box. Ange.' You go in and drag a huge greyhound off the sofa and sleep until they return. And they make you at home. They tell you to get your own ham and mustard. Angeline said sadly when I first met her: 'Every now and then we try being polite to people. But we always break down finally and then they are shocked and surprised. It's better to let them know what they are in for right away.'"

Miami was one of the better places in the country to be poor, Wood came to realize, but it was also harder to find decent work there. In taking care of her father's office, Wood soon discovered how many bargain eateries there were around Miami. For fifteen cents, she could get a meal of "baked beans, one slice of ham, a fair scoop of potato salad, as much bread and butter as you can eat, and coffee or tea." Still, she was aware these luxuries were open only to those who had fifteen cents. The dollar had doubled in value but was twice as scarce. One night, unable to sleep, she got up at one o'clock in the morning and took a two-mile walk through Coral Gables. She marveled at being able to do so, safely, along clean streets: "Coral Gables is by no means typically American, nor is Miami, principally because of the cleanness and a sort of vague, hazy optimism that comes from the climate or too many Coca-Colas. It isn't an optimism—people don't hope—it is a refusal to be depressed by rather depressing facts."

The Biltmore Hotel—and its $10 million price tag that made it the pride of Coral Gables—was a popular summer gathering place because of its swimming pool. Winifred Wood recalls: "There was a flagpole hanging above the pool, off a balcony on the second floor. Two people used to climb out on the flagpole, and hang upside down, locking our feet around it. The game was to see who knocked the other person off first. I landed flat once and you don't forget that. There was a loud groan from everyone." The Venetian Pool was the other hot spot to cool off. One of the centerpieces of the Mediterranean vision that developer George Merrick had of Coral Gables, the Venetian Pool was an old quarry pit that was sculpted into a series of fountains, porticos, loggias, towers, waterfalls, and high-dive platforms. Artesian wells fed the pool, which was initially called the Venetian Casino. Made even more famous when segments of *Tarzan* movies were filmed there, it remains one of the most remarkable examples of pool architecture in the country. Despite her self-deprecating remarks about her femininity, when Jane Wood strode out on the high dive most of the guys would stop and watch, with their whistles acknowledging her figure and form.

George Merrick, the founder of Coral Gables, had been driven to poverty and drink after the land bust in Miami, but his legacy lived on. At its peak, $150 million had gone into the creation of the small city of Mediterranean houses and lush green lawns. Less than a decade later, people couldn't give away their homes. One of Merrick's sons, Dick, was a young artist who was doing beautiful engravings of the Florida Keys for one dollar apiece, and Wood was eager to save enough spare money to afford one. Though some neighbors were going hungry, she had a limited amount of sympathy for the difficulties of the middle class. She wrote to Peg Balfour: "I could see that our class of people call what they have 'cutting things to the bone,' where a Greek refugee family of eight could scrape enough off that bone to live for a month. There are plenty who haven't, but don't be misled by the yelping of people situated as we are. Some of them yelp a good deal."

The correspondence from Greece kept Wood reminded of a simpler way of life, kept her "from drifting wholly under the influence of this Coca-Cola civilization." "It is so insidious," she wrote. "Here you seem to be in a briskly moving current. It doesn't whirl you, but you can never climb out and sit on the banks. In Kephissia either the current moved so gently that I was never aware of it, or else I was asleep on the banks most of the time. Anyway, I was out of time, it never really mattered. And I am back in it, but it doesn't actually matter."

Continuing her education was still out of the question, so in 1933 she got a job at the *Miami Daily News*, where she covered obituaries, food, and fashions. Her boss on the "women's section," Mrs. Hall, kept her in a state of perpetual jitters. "Even the fact you are a budding author," Wood wrote during the summer, "doesn't overweigh the fact that you know you are going to be called stupid, no matter what you do."

The small income that she made helped the family's financial situation, and a move into one of the most spacious houses that they had ever lived in also made things seem brighter. The constant downward adjustments of most middle-class families kept a transitional flow going through many of the homes in Coral Gables. George Wood was receiving five hundred dollars in payments from the government for work as a special master on judicial cases, though Jane knew the upswing was only temporary: "The nice thing is I know the brightness won't last so long that it will become monotonous."

Electricity use for the house was reduced to the bare minimum needed for lights and the refrigerator, as they had a solar water heater and an oil stove oven that she procured at the Woman's Civic Club swapping post. Describing the women as "a bunch of hard-boiled traders from way back," Wood was fascinated by the pure barter of the system: "They prefer not to handle money. You take your article down, set a tentative price for it, and say what you want to get for it. They get ten percent of each trade, and really do produce the goods. Cows are swapped for dentistry, roofing work for meal tickets—the list is endless. The club gives itself its ten percent in credit in the stuff that passes through the post. It shows that the system is still badly broken somewhere, but it also makes me feel like pioneer days."

An item that caught Wood's attention at work one day was the news that Eleanor Roosevelt was going to have a letter page in the *Woman's Home Companion*. Her husband had not been in office for more than six months, and though Wood professed to have no great admiration for Mrs. Roosevelt, she was inspired by the involvement it suggested:

"I like the fact that she can do it and still keep her prestige. In the second place, she invited everybody who wants to to write to her, and I believe from the account of the thing that she will actually give personal attention to what comes in, all of it, and dictate the answers herself. Best of all, she is doing it both as the president's wife and as a person in her own right. She presumes in her announcement of the Page that people will be interested because she is the president's wife; and yet she intends to keep them interested because of her own personality. And I believe that she does it because she is really voraciously interested in people, not generally, but as individuals.

"If you think, you will realize what this means, because you can't conceive of any other president's wife doing a thing like that. Of course, the others were not the sort of woman Mrs. Roosevelt is, but the office as other presidents held it would not allow them to do anything of the sort. There has always been more than a hint of the pompous, more than a hint of the withdrawn-from-the-world-in-clouds about the U.S. presidents who have gone before. And when we have shaken our heads about the way we killed them off, and about the heavy responsibilities on the shoulders of one man, we have meant not the actual work, but the clouds of our own weaving of greatness and the clouds of the presidents' weaving that we have surrounded them with.

"Most presidents—certainly Hoover, for instance—fell for the hooey about the immensity of the office, and allowed themselves to be weighed down. I don't mean it is conceit that ruins them. They just fall for the idea of the vast *intangible* responsibility that is supposed to be theirs, and it awes and crushes them. Roosevelt has rid himself of that weight simply by shrugging his shoulders, simply by not seeing it, and he goes at the job as though it were a big job. He's capable, able, but doesn't have any idea that he's infallible. I think it is a sign of the growing up of the nation, that he can do it, abandon the pedestal. We have stopped asking for nobility, goodness, greatness, and we ask for capability."

Roosevelt was lucky to assume the presidency at all, and may never have done so if it wasn't for the courage of a woman named Lillian Cross. On February 15, 1933, just weeks before his inauguration, President-elect Roosevelt had been speaking in Bayfront Park auditorium in Miami. A little Italian bricklayer named Giuseppe Zangara suddenly lunged forward and fired a .32 caliber revolver bought at a pawn shop. At that moment, Roosevelt bent down to examine a six-foot-long telegram that supporters had sent to congratulate him, and the bullet missed. Next to Zangara, Lillian Cross screamed and clutched at his arm. The man kept firing, but his aim was ruined by Cross. Bullets sprayed through the crowd. Mayor Anton Cermak of Chicago was on the podium, and a bullet struck him. A retired policeman and the wife of the president of Florida Power and Light were also hit, and two more were grazed.

After Zangara was wrestled into submission, he was tied to the luggage rack of a car and raced away from the scene to keep the crowd from lynching him. On February 20, he was sentenced to eighty years in prison, but Cermak died on March 6, which resulted in Zangara getting the electric chair. He was an Italian immigrant who had been a military marksman in Italy, and he blamed the chronic stomach pains he lived with on capitalism. The pains grew worse, he claimed, when he was around the rich and the powerful. In record time the execution was carried out, taking place on March 20.[1]

The Wood family managed to scrape the money together in the autumn of 1933 to send Dolly to Florida State University, in the days that it was still a women's college. Though Jane distrusted Dolly's motivations—the resentment that Jane had gotten all the advantages and that she wanted something Jane had gotten whether she was truly interested in it or not—Jane also conceded that Dolly deserved it. Although George Wood had no idea how he was going to continue to afford it, he felt a duty to send all his children to college and was not going to let financial realities deter him from fulfilling this obligation.

A great opportunity appeared at the beginning of the winter that looked as if it could set the Wood finances through the next year. The landlord consented to let them sublet the huge house they were living in, through which they could fetch one thousand dollars for the three months from January through March. In turn they planned to cram into a fifty-dollar-per-month duplex for the interim. The plan was another of those fleeting bits of wild hope, though, that disappeared almost as soon as it surfaced. Another plan for the winter that Jane had hoped might provide a lucrative side income for herself was holding fashion sales at the Biltmore, but resistance from the shops at the Biltmore soon scotched the idea. The newspaper raised her to a six-dollar-per-week salary, and she made do on that, helped along by the fact that clothing and material possessions had little importance to her. When Peg Balfour expressed concern from Greece about the Depression in America, Wood responded: "Don't feel like you have to worry about America and hard times here. We aren't so bad off, meaning both the family and America. The times of stress come occasionally, but they are not continuous, and when they are with us it gives you a good tense feeling, like you were in for a good fight. You draw in your stomach muscles, actually and figuratively speaking. It is not so hard a world, and there are as many moments of beauty as there are of pain."

A transfer to the city desk and covering the hotels on Miami Beach led to Jane's salary soaring to fourteen dollars per week in 1934, though increasing prices and the need to pitch in to the family's survival meant that finding a nickel to mail a letter to her sister Dolly was still a challenge. The good fortunes that the Wood family had enjoyed in 1933 seemed to dwindle the following year, and the spring semester at FSU would prove to be Dolly's last one there.

The little boat Jane was sailing that summer, the *Tinker Bell*, seemed doomed for misfortune. Later in the summer the rigging, mast, and rudder were stolen, and she spent the next year working on and off to get it back in the water. Dolly was already committed to her future husband, Bill Denslow, though it had been Jane whom Denslow had been first to notice. He had seen her jump topless off a bridge into a Coral Gables waterway, the sort of act that rarely fails to make an impression on a teenage boy. He soon became good friends with the whole family. Jane wrote to Dolly in Tallahassee:

"Bill is a cute thing. He and Kenneth took the sailboat out Sunday afternoon and rammed the side of a yacht—a yacht, any yacht—and busted the bowsprit. They were very sad and crestfallen when they came round to tell me about it, and had it fixed by the Incredible Risley, the younger, the next day.

"Mother said, 'I'll bet Bill said unprintable things when he rammed the side of the yacht, Kenneth. Was it worse than 'damn'?'

"Bill said, 'Gleeps,' Kenneth answers.

"Which is very fine and shows Bill is a true artist, because then is the best time to say 'Gleeps,' when you are ramming the side of a yacht and seeing the bowsprit slowly break. But most people are not so instinctively true artists of conduct. I, under similar circumstances, would be cursing anyone else in the boat, oh, just anyone.

"But to show that at least I am an artist in action, if not in word, I went out Wednesday, after they finished the new bowsprit, and broke it by getting the peak of the mainsail caught in a cable. I think that was a beautiful and considerate thing to do, and it made Bill and Kenneth feel fine. They came around last Sunday and offered to fix it for me, and incidentally to go sailing. I had already got the wood, but was working on it very slowly. They did a neat job. I should varnish the spar now. I am thinking of running the thing down to Risley's this afternoon and beaching it and concentrating on a little serious work on it.

"Dolly, over the obituaries I began thinking philosophically with more than a mere trace of melancholy this morning, as one will over the obituaries. I was writing the obit of Diefenderfer, Horace, 78. Do you realize all the implications contained in that sentence? Do you see how happy I would be if I had a sister one day whom I could introduce as Mrs. Diefenderfer? Can't you feel how happy I would be? For me there is no hope for being a Mrs. Diefenderfer, for I have sworn to marry a man with only one syllable in his name so no one can tell whether I am drunk by making me say my name. You can see that I can not be a Mrs. Diefenderfer. But it would make me so happy to have a relation named that. Now I am working up to the crux of the matter and treading on delicate ground. But you are willing to make me happy. Daisy will never be Mrs. Diefenderfer, the name would scare her off before she got anywhere, she is so conventional. And Win is young—ah, young.

"I do not wish you to become that, even for the pleasure it would give me, for I know your troth is plighted. But oh Dolly, Diefenderfer Denslow would fill me with an overwhelming, super-joy, a double delight, a delicious delirium. Dorothy, that is all I shall ever ask you in repayment for the short story which I am going to produce after lying fallow between two and three this afternoon.

It is not so much, after all, and you know the idea appeals to you, in itself, on its own merits and ex officio, as it were.

"I will send you some more money when I get some more money. Laconic, but not cryptic, that remark."

*Miami Daily News* sports columnist Jack Bell—who seemed to alternate between the *News* and the *Miami Herald* in the early 1930s before settling on the *Herald*—observed her sailing efforts in 1934 from the *News* building across from Bayfront Park. The Danish schooner the *Prins Valdemar*, which had sunk in the Miami shipping channel in 1926, had been righted and moved against shore to serve as an aquarium in Bayfront Park. The aquarium housed manatees, and one of the manatees later born in it in 1946, Snooty, lived until 2017. Jane Wood had tied her sailboat up against the aquarium. Though Bell's telling of events no doubt has to be taken with a grain of salt—the eighteen-foot boat was not as tiny as he made out—Wood did seem determined to repeatedly do in the bowsprit of the beleaguered *Tinker Bell*:

"Yesterday we watched her leave the building, dart across the street and into the aquarium. Soon she emerged on deck of the old Prins Valdemar and clambered down the side, using portholes and deck piles for footing. She dropped into a little boat about 10 or 15 feet long. Another girl was there (at least I guess it was a girl—wore a cap like the commodores of the yacht club, and white trousers), and they hoisted a couple of little sails, each about as big as a good-sized handkerchief.

"Soon they were ready to set sail. The 'sailing craft,' as Jane in all her unsophisticated naivety calls it, immediately tried to ram a hole in the side of the aquarium. Jane backed it off with practiced hand and tried again. Once more the aquarium shuddered as the impact woke even the sea cows."

With the help of some young black boys paddling a dinghy, who threw Jane a line, she got reoriented in the right direction. Bell concluded: "Captain Wood, in her mighty sailing craft, soon cast loose from her tug, and majestically sailed away. The last time we saw her she had just missed ramming a great white yacht and was heading resolutely in the general direction of the land of the midnight sun."[2]

# 5 | The Best We Could

At the age of twenty-one, Wood decided she wanted to go to Key West as a social worker. The southernmost city in the United States, a once-proud haven of fiercely independent people, was economically devastated. Residents who called themselves Conchs, descendants of pirates and wreckers—people who salvaged wrecked boats—were suffering 80 percent unemployment. The staple jobs of Key West, cigar making and sponge diving, had migrated to the Tampa Bay area and Tarpon Springs. The city was incapable of functioning on any level, and in desperation Key West gave up its charter on the Fourth of July and threw itself at the mercy of the federal government.

In stepped Julius Stone, appointed as the Southeast director of the Federal Emergency Relief Administration (FERA). FERA was the brainchild of Harry Hopkins, a former Red Cross social worker who had showed President Roosevelt how effective social work could be in New York State. Stone was a young, bright, and arrogant Harvard graduate who immediately became a lightning rod for criticism. He turned things around quickly, organizing an unpaid army of four thousand men to clean the mountains of rotting garbage off the street. (The garbage was all dumped in the ocean.) Guest houses and restaurants were renovated, WPA artists were brought in to do watercolors and paintings, and the Key West Aquarium was built on Mallory Square. Though it was hard to argue with Stone's results, many were incensed at his attitude and methods. He was a law unto himself and paid no attention to any sort of regulations or guidelines. Newspapers labeled him the "Kingfish." Later he admitted that he had only been able to get away with his actions because Harry Hopkins had been on an extended vacation and because Key West was so far from anywhere that no one had any idea what he was up to.

Ernest Hemingway, who had taken up residence in Key West in 1931, was one of Stone's most vocal critics. Hemingway was one of the few residents who didn't have to worry about making a living, and he had no desire to see Key West changed radically overnight to reflect Stone's vision. Though Hemingway's legacy in Key West remains better known today, it was Stone who left the greater impact.

Hearing tales filter back up to Miami of the exciting and unconventional approach to overturning the Depression in Key West, Wood wanted to join up. She heard they were paying twenty-five dollars per week. She checked with her friend Ellen Knight, who was a social worker, and Knight told her there was a lot of work that she could do closer to home. While social services were being handled quite effectively on Miami Beach, in the City of Miami social services were a disaster. The head of the welfare department was a former truant officer who was said to resemble the Queen of Hearts in looks and temperament. Once FERA came to town, she refused to pay out a cent in city welfare money for food. On the other hand, she would readily pay transportation costs to ship non-natives back home again. Even if someone from Michigan had been living in Florida for ten years, she would persuade the person that Detroit was his home and that was where he was going back to.

Wood became a FERA caseworker in Miami for fifteen dollars per week. The idea of FERA was to provide individual compensation based on individual need, a rather novel idea for social work, and one that placed a huge amount of power in the hands of the social worker.

"Because there were so few qualified social workers in existence," she wrote years later, "it allowed people like me at twenty-one to call themselves social workers. And lots worse. We did the best we could, but a generation hates the name 'social work' largely because of us. Some were sadists, some were sentimentalists, some were bureaucrats—and these last were the worst. The emotions that activate sadists and sentimentalists ebb and flow. But the dead, total lack of emotion that infects a bureaucrat is with us always, and is one of the great threats of our lifetime.

"The philosophy behind FERA is still something that thrills me. The actual, fatuous day-by-day working of the thing was something that still gives me the triple vomits. I got the district on North Miami Avenue, from Fifth to Thirteenth Street. My clients were mostly unemployed Cuban cigar makers and aging prostitutes. Their problem was hunger.

"The Cubans had to face the fact that the cigar industry had migrated to Tampa. The prostitutes faced the fact that their youth had migrated—further than Tampa. While the Republicans beefed about lazy men raking leaves, my clients were showing me muck sores on their legs from digging ditches in the mangrove swamps around Matheson Hammock, the first Dade County mosquito control."

Her worldview shifted dramatically with her exposure to the worst victims of the Depression. Whereas she had escaped the most depressing aspects of it to date through being in Greece or the serenity of Coral Gables, living a money-poor but idyllic life, she was now faced with grinding poverty every day.

"The qualities you look for in people when you are writing for a newspaper," she wrote at the time, "have to do with their credulity, gullibility, aimless curiosity, and taste for exaggeration and sensation. Since you find what you look for, the world seems a very different place to someone who is drawing $14 from the *News*, and another who gets $15 from the government."

In a week when her clients didn't get a work card, they were sometimes able to get a grocery order of two dollars. Her allocation for direct relief for the eighty families in her district was often as low as two hundred dollars per month. As for medical help, she never forgot the county welfare head telling her, when she was trying to get a pregnant woman in labor into Kendall Hospital: "After all, Miss Wood, they's been born in a manger."

In October 1934, Wood wrote:

"Life is very complicated just now for it seems like a fourth of the women in my district—and there are 120 families—are going to have children, mostly within a month. I've gotten over getting so griped about their having children, but the county medical facilities of the section in which I work are practically non-existent, and half of the women don't get examinations or have any plans made for them at all. When I have a weary feeling some time that it would be wonderful if many of these people could die peacefully and painlessly to make way for a new crop, it is terrifying that a new crop is coming on to be underfed and undereducated.

"There is really something horrible about this whole business of local charity and federal relief. The efforts of the people who are in the work and in charge of it seem to be so much patch work. They are trying to plug holes in the dike when the whole dike is giving and about to go over. For instance: Dade County has one county hospital and one doctor only for home calls and clinics. A woman in my district is pregnant, expecting a child immediately. I dig up a layette for her from the Needle Work guild, blankets from the Red Cross, and by a balanced combination of wheedling, bullying, and slinging a lot of hooey get the county doctor to admit her to Kendall. Now that is horribly stupid. The woman has to go to the hospital—she's had two miscarriages and almost died at the birth of her fourth child. But she should go as a matter of routine. You shouldn't feel like you've won a great victory when you get her in there."

As a result of her battles, Wood took a keen interest in the ongoing fights within the medical profession for and against the socialization of medicine. Doctors within the American Medical Association were demanding that the government take over the costs of health care, causing the leadership of the staunchly conservative AMA to quash the dissenting views. It would be more than a half century before the AMA changed its position. Wood discovered a report from 1928–29 that noted that 62 percent of the population had no medical, dental, or eye care of any sort. The injustice of her clients' lives infuriated her:

"It's awful enough to fight against the loss of morale, and psychological twists, and all the things being without work and subsisting on too little does for people. But when they are sick, and there are not enough facilities to do anything at all for taking care of them, it is like coming up against a stone wall. The thing this world needs is not a five cent cigar. It is a thirty-six hour day.

"On most days I think that these people who are subsisting, living a sort of half life on less than what is necessary, are in their condition through no real fault of their own, and that when our rulers get this crazy economic machine patched up again they will be okay. But there are horrible days when it is obvious that thousands of people have been so beaten by four years of thin living that they are spiritually crippled, can not take their place as independent members of society again."

Her political views increasingly tended toward the need for socialist reforms. Though she did feel that things weren't getting any worse, she believed that it had finally soaked into everyone's minds that radical steps had to be taken to get the country back to people having any kind of security in their lives. She wrote:

"People are rather bleak, on the whole. I really feel that much of what Roosevelt's administration has done has been pills and palliatives. But if the country has not gotten much better under the dosage, people still know what might have happened without it, and have not forsworn their doctor by a long shot.

I believe there is not so much discontent with this present administration as a deeper discontent with this present economic structure.

"I have read of the effects of continual war on a country, of how it impoverishes, leaving the older generation broken and the younger one underfed, undereducated, with half of the vitality sapped. This has been a four years war, this struggle with insecurity. And while it may not breed revolution, because the lower levels of people have become too impoverished in body and spirit to fight, it will breed a great class that is half alive, forever handicapped and scarred.

"And it seems to me that centralized control of all production, and a gradual paring and final elimination of private profit is the only answer to this problem of insecurity. The trouble is, that sounds like communism, Red Russia, which it resembles to a certain extent. (Oh, if there hadn't been that idiotic wave of red-baiting along about 1924! Why can't we look at another country without prejudice and learn?) You would be surprised at the number of people in every walk of life who are beginning to feel that there is too sharp a division between the rewards of capital and labor. The idiotic thing about this whole collapse of the past four years is that America is almost the one country in the world that is almost perfectly equipped in its mechanical, natural and human resources to produce quite enough for all people to live on in decency and security. I believe that the average education, the mechanical and mental ability to do a good job, is unsurpassed by any race or rather nation. Combine this with the factories and the farms and you should have plenty.

"The trouble is, the visionaries, the intellectuals, the radicals, offer no practical way out of this wilderness. They yell 'There's a promised land, halleluiah, and you're in a desert!' But few follow them. When a man comes along with a map he'll have this country behind him. People want a way out."

Wood was probably more aware than most, from her conversation with the Communist stowaway in Constantinople, that Stalin was taking care of any chance of America looking favorably upon socialism. The greatest opportunity had been during the era of red-baiting that she lamented, when the Soviet Union was thriving culturally and experimenting with capitalism under Lenin's New Economic Policy. It was the most open society the Soviet Union ever achieved, before or after Stalin.

Because America was booming economically in the 1920s, capitalism was touted as an unquestionably superior model. The Soviet Union was far too weak to fear, so communism was portrayed as a domestic threat to all good and decent Americans. Nicola Sacco and Bartolomeo Vanzetti were represented as the face of radicalism: not only were they recent immigrants but anarchists and murderers as well.[1] It was only looking back a decade later that a great many Americans began to question many of the assumptions they had always lived with. Faith in capitalism as a system had been rudely shattered by the Depression. Wood went on to lay out her own program for rescuing America:

"The government is in so many executive and administrative fields, that its personnel must be made efficient, intelligent, and honest. This is an absolute necessity, for under this sort of system and attitude toward government work, where the failures in American business and the chiselers get the administrative jobs, you cannot do anything. It is on men and women that every system depends finally, and they should be the first consideration.

"Then—after you have intelligence and honesty in administrative positions—our august legislative bodies can begin to pass laws. These laws will regulate and control hours of work, amounts of production, and wages. And these laws will have teeth that bite. There won't be any of this drum beating 'come under the blue eagle because you love your country and otherwise you are not quite nice.'

"The reason I am for government control of business is because it will do away with labor unions, for one thing. One of the worst phases of the depression has been that it has set business and capital, represented by smug, frightened, foolish chambers of commerce, against labor, represented by unions grasping greedily for special privileges for only those who have paid their dues. There has been a real drawing of class lines. If you have labor controlling production, you would have what Russia is dreaming of, but not practically working toward. (For in Russia there is no dictatorship of the proletariat, as far as I can make out. There is a dictatorship of the top members of the Communist Party, of a few men.) If you have capital controlling business, you have this silly business cycle, alternating between depression and prosperity. The only alternative is government control, which means control by trained and intelligent men. That's why the civil service must come first.

"There are many incidentals: old age pensions, work insurance, socialized medicine, public ownership of utilities. But all these things are incidentals. The country must set its face toward steady intelligent socialization. People must know where they are going. There must be an announcement of the purpose by the government, by newspapers. The way things seem too often to be now is that the government and the press scrutinize closely the way the vast and sluggish stream of public opinion is going, and then mold their policies in the same direction. Men have made the machines, the system, the tradition, that keeps our lives going. They have made this system of economics. It seems so absurd, so a matter of begging the question, for economists to talk about business laws as though they are an unalterable part of the universe. They watch production, consumption, payrolls, freight loadings, as though they were barometric readings outside of human control. They sit dumbfounded before nakedness and overproduction of cotton."

For Wood, social work was both a chance to reevaluate her view on the economics of America, and reevaluate some of the stereotypes of race that she had been brought up with. The resistance of most Florida counties to having welfare on which a family could survive, she found, was that they were scared they would not be able to keep blacks in the fields any longer, paying them wages on which they could scarcely survive.

Because she needed a car for her job, Wood bought a 1929 Ford Model A roadster for one hundred dollars. Putting down a first installment of twenty dollars on it, she then proceeded to ruin her nails grinding the valves. Her parents were renting the garage to a pair of University of Miami students, and one of them was a good mechanic. Chester—"a naïve Bohemian slangster"—taught her the inner workings of the Model A engine, and soon she was proud of having done a job for $2.84 that would have cost her $12 if done by the cheapest gas station.

The two students were from somewhere near Chicago, and Wood's mother tried to make polite conversation with Joe the first night they moved in:

"And are you a Democrat or a Republican, Joe?"

Joe grinned and replied with a drawl: "I left Northwestern, Mrs. Wood, because I made myself pretty unpopular as a Socialist."

Blinking at the unexpected reply, Mrs. Wood turned to Chester to listen to an account of his life.

"I had a good job up until a year or so ago, then it stopped on me. I've been working in a Puroil station for the last year, outside of finishing high school. But since I couldn't get the good job back I decided maybe I'd better get some more education until something else opens up."

"What sort of job was it, Chester?" asked Mrs. Wood.

"Oh, I was driving a rum truck between Cicero and Chicago."

Jane enjoyed the consternation this caused her mother and was sure Daisy Wood didn't sleep well that night with the addition of the questionable young men to the household. The two worked out well as tenants. Most nights they played hearts with Mr. Wood and one of the girls and were entertaining company. Tapping into their respective fields of expertise, Jane learned auto mechanics from Chester and socialism from Joe. Another tenant and University of Miami student they had in the garage was David Douglas Duncan, who went on to become a legendary photographer after his graduation in 1938.

Duncan first achieved success while traveling the Caribbean on a schooner, photographing the hunting of sea turtles, which became the material for an article in *National Geographic*. He joined the Marines as a combat photographer during World War II, and his images appeared everywhere during the war. Between fighting with Fijian guerrillas behind Japanese lines on Bougainville, shooting photos from a Plexiglas belly of a P-38 over Okinawa, and witnessing the Japanese surrender aboard the USS *Missouri*, Duncan proved himself one of the most versatile combat photographers of the day.

With his success as a combat photographer, he became a staff member of *Life* magazine in 1946 and documented the conflict in Palestine before Israel became a state. The work was only the beginning of a long and storied career traveling the world, much of it captured in his 1966 autobiography *Yankee Nomad* and his subsequent 2002 autobiography *Photo Nomad*. He would cover two more wars, in Korea and Vietnam, and his social conscience came to the fore with his book of photos on the Tet Offensive in Khe Sanh, entitled *I Protest!*

Perhaps even more remarkable than his war photography was Duncan's deep personal study of Pablo Picasso, spending seventeen years on and off with the painter and taking more than ten thousand photos of the artist going about his daily life. The Wood family could hardly have dreamed that such a future lay in store for the handsome young student in their garage, though Jane regarded him as good company. Through their love of travel and adventure, they both developed an international view of the world that would make them rail against the shortsightedness and ignorance of American foreign policy in the decades to come.

While Dolly Wood had abandoned college after her first year to take a five-dollar-per-week job in the art department of the *Miami News*, young Daisy was

Jane Wood portrait, early 1930s.

just starting her first year at the University of Miami. She had a scholarship but had to work two hours a day in the school bookstore. Jane maintained her contempt for the institution:

"It is costing her those two hours," she wrote, "where it cost me nothing. I did not feel those bruises on the family pocket-book, and what 16 year old does? I'm hoping that she may discover some excuse for the existence of the damn place. I still nurse a bitterness against that place, and always will. It is so poor an excuse, so shoddy. It seems to me my family would at least see the advantage of using me as a trial horse in some things, whether they take my theoretical advice or not. Perhaps it's just as well. I turn out to be wrong more than half the time."

Though she wished better for her sister, Jane also thought Daisy's experience at the university would be different. She knew that she reacted in greater extremes to her immediate environment than Daisy did and that her sister was much more careful about proprieties, appearances, and conventions. Running away from home and consuming too many home brews were not on Daisy's agenda. On the other hand, she feared that Daisy's habits were too easily molded by her associates and environment, whereas Jane thought herself able to "bounce out of habits with the greatest of ease."

Winifred was a blossoming fifteen-year-old at Miami High School in whom Jane recognized the potential to be a real beauty "when we can lure her away from a shade too much rouge. I'm trying to sell her on the idea that lipstick is much more sophisticated, since it suits her freckles far better than rouge. She has compromised by using too much of both lately." While her older sisters all had varying impressive degrees of brains, practicality, and beauty, Winifred proved to be the most boldly stylish of the Wood girls, carrying a natural elegance and fashion sense that was well suited to her future as an aviator.

Even as a twenty-one-year-old, Jane still maintained an immense affection for her father. With the elder girls making an income, the lack of money that George Wood was bringing in was less of a problem. She thought him a rare person. Given to pure childishness at times, he was also capable of such unusual loyalty, gentleness, and devotion that she could scarcely believe it. He had taken to amusing himself by alternately criticizing the American Legion and the French nation and wrote "an idiotic story set in Oxford and a western mining camp in 1892." Recognizing that she couldn't think of two things he knew less about, Jane recalled what their family friend Colonel Seymour told her mother one day: "George is a great man, one of the finest young lawyers I've ever seen anywhere. The only trouble, Mrs. Wood, is that he has a screw loose."

Looking for a new way to amuse himself while waiting for paying clients, Mr. Wood let himself grow a red beard for ten days in the late autumn of 1934. Jane was proud of his effort, and he was delighted with the results himself. The rest of the girls were not so kind. Winifred refused to play rummy with him, and Dolly observed: "If you were a fastidious dresser you would look like a man growing a beard, but as it is, you look like you just don't care."

His wife grinned slyly, leaving him in doubt of what she thought. Combined with the disapproval of most of his daughters, the numerous comments of strangers on the street finally did him in. He was sad about it, and so was his eldest daughter.

"But all he said when I looked sad about him shaving," Jane wrote, "was 'People won't even let you grow a beard in peace. Could you use a pack of cigarettes?' He thought to buy off my sadness, but I was not consoled. It only goes to show that American society is becoming governed by women. It's bad."

As Wood continued the frantic scramble to get her clients what medical aid she could to keep them and their families alive, she became more and more sure that being a caseworker was not what she wanted to do with her life. The initial appeal had been the boldness of Julius Stone's vision, which, while working grandly in the small community of Key West, was proving to be an abject failure in Miami. The rules and regulations of FERA had to be followed in her job, and all she could do was provide pathetically small amounts of stopgap relief. Unlike in Key West, there was no plan to turn around the economy of Miami, to provide enough jobs to make the welfare caseload manageable. Aside from the miserable ditch digging on WPA projects—which able-bodied men were glad enough to take—there was only a smattering of temporary jobs for women, like sewing blue curtains for Julius Stone's yacht.

If there was one concept that was anathema to Wood, it was doing things by half measures. She wanted overwhelming reform. In order to be a reformer, though, she needed credentials. The all-important letters after one's name that opened doors for advancement in society were missing as a result of her refusal to finish school at the University of Miami. She was sadly disappointed to miss out on a scholarship to Tulane—four months tuition, rail fare there and back, books, and $12.90 per week to live on—because she did not have her bachelor's degree. The setback caused her to finally overcome her distaste for the Cardboard College, and she made plans to take night courses and summer work to work toward her degree. Ideally, she still wanted to graduate from Columbia University, but that was a far-off dream.

"It is really not at all bad that things have worked out about my education just as they have," she wrote. "Now I very definitely know what I want to go to college to get, and I will finally get it. I think my groundwork for studying psychology and sociology isn't bad. I run across numerous people in this FERA who have had technical training for sociology on too narrow a foundation of general intelligence, education, and experience. I have, of course, overcome my blatant antipathy to formal education, but I still think that it is most valuable if it comes after a wider and informal education, rather than before."

Giving her stability amid the eye-opening nature of social work was her love of sailing the *Tinker Bell*. She made the news yet again in July 1935, when a sudden gust of wind flipped the craft in the middle of Biscayne Bay. On board with her was a childhood friend, Catherine Smith, who was visiting from Macon, Georgia. Wood swam a mile and a half to shore, coming aground exhausted near the Coast Guard station at Dinner Key. She ran to the station and alerted them that her friend was sitting on the overturned boat in the middle of the bay. Wood pragmatically explained to the press: "Catherine was a visitor, and we can't ask visitors to swim home, can we?"[2]

Wood left her friend with a lunchbox under one arm and a raincoat under the other. A Coast Guard speedboat was rapidly dispatched to fetch Smith and found her that way. On the way in, Smith waved the raincoat at a passing plane until it blew away.

While Wood had never given too much sympathy to the troubles of the middle class, she was finding more and more in her work that white-collar men were becoming the most heartbreakingly crippled victims of the Depression. One of her clients was a man from Virginia who had been a real estate salesman. With the onset of the Depression, he went into bankruptcy and began drinking himself to death. His wife's wealthy family cut her off because she wouldn't leave him, and the man ended up in a sanitarium for a year. They came down to Florida together and subsisted on what she could earn as a relief worker, along with welfare. Three years of this had worn him down, and Wood saw that he winced when he came into her office. During the Christmas holidays, he got a temporary job with the post office. They raffled off a quart of scotch, which he won. It started him on a two-week violent and dangerous drinking binge, which ended when his wife had to call the police. He was sentenced to ninety days in jail.

"The whole matter enraged me," wrote Wood:

"The man is a sensitive, quiet weakling, and 90 days in jail will just about finish any shreds of self respect he had left, which were rather few. I have cursed many things over this matter, beginning with the economic system and ending with wives who had their husbands put in jail. But of course, the final answer is—what could his wife do when he became violent for days on end. And the further answer is—if he had been able to get a steady job he would never have had to drink himself oblivious. It is rather a tough proposition. It seems to me so unfair for a society which refuses a man work to finally put him in jail for cracking under the tension of being without work.

"It is frightful to see people, not degenerate, but crack up, before your eyes—through no real fault of their own—except that of being just a little bit weaker, having a little less push than the average. My district is semi-rural. Most of the people are carpenters, laborers, plumbers, truck farmers. A frightfully reduced income is hard on them physically, but they can get down to the bare essentials of living without being broken psychologically. The men of the much touted "white collared class" have usually worked at no real work; selling, promoting, front work, middlemen really. Their jobs have been created by a stupid system that in the late great Twenties paid men who dealt in paper more than those who dealt in the production of actual goods by actual work. These real estate salesmen, little businessmen, have all their lives been divorced from the reality of actual production, no matter how hard they may have worked at middlemen jobs. Because this middle class has been paid more than laborers, they have added a thousand necessities to their existence—silk stockings and clean collars, magazines and curtained windows. These are not necessities, and the man who works with his hands knows it, his family know it. When he is without them it does not break him. Now this white collar class, in spots, finds itself cut to the barest necessities, and they discover they do not know how to really attack the physical details of living. They are not jacks of all trades, cannot pick up a little work here and there, do not know how to live on the fringe of odd jobs. And how they suffer: They lived under a system where workers with words and figures and paper rated too high in proportion to their worth. They knew only this condition. It is passing. They are out in the cold."

As she settled in to the routine of social work in 1935, Wood passed through the summer with the same bleak caseload. Then came another hurricane that altered her life. Two days before the Labor Day Hurricane hit the Florida Keys, she had been down on Matecumbe Key doing casework, interviewing the World War I veterans who were working on the new highway to Key West. The veterans—known as the "Bonus Marchers"—had been agitating for years, marching on Washington and demanding better benefits for their service to their country. Many desperate, unemployed men had formulated the hope for a veterans' bonus for their wartime service that would allow them to put food on the table and survive. When their ragged and unorganized trickle reached the nation's capital and set up camps, Herbert Hoover sent General Douglas MacArthur out on a white horse to charge the veterans and run them off.

Harry Hopkins, head of the Federal Emergency Relief Administration (FERA), had a better idea. A linchpin of Julius Stone's revitalization of Key West was the construction of a highway through the Florida Keys all the way to the southern tip. The veterans were sent to start work on the northern end, near Islamorada, with some others shipped out to work on restoring Fort Jefferson in the Dry Tortugas. If Key West seemed like the end of the earth, the Dry Tortugas were even more so. Sixty miles west of Key West, the tiny island chain was about as removed from civilization as you could get. But the scheme wasn't just based on relocation. The veterans had to be treated well and made to feel useful. Three tent camps were built on Windley Key and Upper Matecumbe Key, and only the veterans who had agitated were allowed in on this project, where they were fed steak, lobster, and ice cream every day. They received thirty dollars per month in pay, slept on cots inside of tents, and were given plenty of time off for fishing. According to Wood, the word was, "Keep them happy and keep them out of Washington."

The destruction and loss of life from the 1926 and 1928 hurricanes had made these storms part of the national consciousness, and the first question most of the veterans had upon arriving in the Florida Keys was, "What happens in the case of a hurricane?"

They were assured that FERA had everything worked out to the last detail. (In the twenty-first century, a similarly named federal bureaucracy, FEMA, would make the same empty assurances about an oncoming monster hurricane called Katrina.) The Florida East Coast Railway was supposed to evacuate the men, and camps would be set up on the mainland as soon as hurricane warnings went up.[1]

Wood went down to the camps as part of a task force of social workers. The government had decided that two years of the project was enough for the men, and the social workers were interviewing the veterans so that the camps could be liquidated on a casework basis. Very little progress had been made on the road construction. The wide channel between Upper and Lower Matecumbe Keys, Indian Key Channel, had only seen two hundred feet of causeway constructed across it in the previous two years. It was hard to blame the veterans for the lack of progress because they hadn't really been sent there to seriously work. The project had been a temporary solution to the embarrassing problem of how the nation treated its veterans. If the road was to be finally constructed, though, Julius Stone wanted an army of men working there who would get the job done. The veterans were soon to be sent elsewhere. Two days after the interviews were wrapped up, the hurricane hit. Luckily, half of the veterans were in Miami for a baseball game, and others were in Key West. The rest weren't so lucky.

Wood's future husband, Henry Reno, was one of the first reporters on the scene for the *Miami Herald* and filed a story for the September 4 issue about the incredible destruction they had found on Upper Matecumbe Key, which wasn't even where the worst of the storm hit. The railway bridge to Lower Matecumbe Key and Islamorada had been washed out, and they still had no way of accessing the veteran camps there to assess damage or find out what had happened. Nor did they know yet what had happened to the train that had been sent to evacuate the veterans. The destruction of Camp 1 did not bode well, however, for the fate of the rest of the veterans and the Keys inhabitants to the south. Of sixty-four buildings in the camp, all had been leveled save one, where ten of the most badly injured of the surviving veterans huddled.

"I would rather face machine gun fire again than go through an experience like that once more," said George Senison, a thirty-nine-year-old veteran who lost the use of both of his legs in the storm.[2]

On Tavernier and Plantation Keys, children who were washed out of their homes desperately clung to the railroad tracks or bushes all night long until the water subsided.

The following day Henry Reno and fellow *Miami Herald* writer Henry Cavendish made it by boat to Lower Matecumbe and Islamorada, where Cavendish filed a much longer account of the destruction. It was worse than they ever imagined. Cavendish himself counted thirty-two bodies in their travels, and hundreds more were washed away or buried under rubble. The train that had been sent to evacuate the veterans was at Islamorada, destroyed. Conductor J. E. Gamble told Cavendish:

"We left Miami Monday about 4:25 p.m. We arrived at Homestead and turned the engine on the Y-table there, and coupled back up to the train. We went on south and reached the quarry at Windley island just across from the No. 1 Veteran's camp. There was a large cable stretched across the roadbed there which we ran into, and it pretty near derailed the train. After working about an hour in the wind and rain we succeeded in getting the cable loose from the train. We proceeded on to Islamorada, stopping at the station there about 8:15 pm Monday.

"We picked up a number of people at Islamorada, and attempted to proceed on to the water tank when suddenly the entire train blew away. The train consisted of six coaches, two baggage cars, and three box cars. The box cars were in the rear of the train, and were hurled by the wind and tidal wave about 400 feet from where they were resting when the train came to a stop. Every car in the train was turned on its side. There were quite a number of people in the coaches, and the water came up in the coaches. In some of the cars it nearly drowned the people there. All of the people succeeded in getting out, however. The water was about five to six foot deep in most of the coaches. The Florida East Coast depot and the commissary of the Florida Emergency Relief Administration all blew to pieces suddenly, and blew around over the engine and over the coaches."[3]

The wind howled until just after midnight, and when daylight came there were bodies lying all around and under the train. The locomotive was still standing upright on the track, and the engineer pointed out that the storm surge had gone up over the driving wheels of the locomotive and extinguished the fire in the firebox. *Herald* reporter Cavendish estimated that it would have taken a tidal wave of thirty to thirty-five feet to do that.

In the following weeks, a great deal of outrage was directed at the National Weather Service, whose headquarters was still in Jacksonville and whose Miami branch had proved next to useless in providing advance warnings of the location of the storm. Based on the most up-to-date bulletins from the weather service, the train was only called for in Miami four hours before the storm surge washed it off the tracks in Islamorada. Such a narrow window made it impossible to rescue the veterans in time. It was a near suicide mission for the train's crew.

Jane Wood herself was called away on Labor Day to do FERA interviews in Mount Dora, a small town in central Florida, saving her from the storm. She returned in the aftermath, though, to interview the survivors. Hundreds of the veterans died on Labor Day as a result of the "temporary solution" to their grievances, with no protection from the most powerful storm to hit Florida in the twentieth century. It annihilated the upper Florida Keys with a staggering fury. Having just had conversations with these men and learned about their lives, Wood was not able to stomach the idea that bureaucrats—social work bureaucrats—had ultimately been responsible for their deaths.

"The bureaucrats passed the buck and the veterans died," she wrote. "More would have died had it not been payday, Labor Day weekend, when so many were in Miami. Their rotting bodies were burned, and the stench drove me out of bureaucracy—because I knew that if I had been responsible, I might have been one of the ones who played it safe and passed the buck and caused it all."

The aftermath of the hurricane, where organized relief was a widespread failure, made her decide she was done with social work. Neighbors failed neighbors, the head of the Red Cross had a nervous breakdown, and only the city of Homestead did a gallant job of relief. The failures of the Red Cross due to its stultifying bureaucracy particularly irritated Wood. As shell-shocked survivors made their way to Red Cross aid stations, they were told that nothing could be done for them because Red Cross headquarters would approve no applications for aid without a "permanent plan for rehabilitation" first.

Wood promptly quit her job, enrolled full-time at the University of Miami, and accelerated her plan to get a degree. Her focus was different now, however. Rather than pursue psychology and sociology, she turned toward the hard sciences. The choice was somewhat accidental. Her readings in Greece had given her a strong interest in metaphysics, a field of study that came out of Aristotle's treatise on transcendental philosophy. She asked at the university what would be the closest thing to metaphysics that she could study. Either she had the misfortune of asking a scientist with no patience for philosophy, or more likely, she consulted someone who wasn't quite sure what metaphysics was, but the end result was that she was told that it was physics she wanted. The term "metaphysics" comes from *ta meta ta phusika*—"the things after physics," simply indicating that Aristotle had done his treatise on the subject after he had done his treatise on physics.

As easily as she could bounce in and out of habits, she could bounce in and out of academic subjects. She took to physics with enthusiasm and was glad she chose it.

A year and a half later, she wrote: "I am far enough along now to get a good view of the vast fields of my ignorance on the subject, and I want to know more. It is soothing, the most soothing and peaceful work I have ever tried. I may perhaps never reach the border line, where I am facing the new and unknown work to be done in this field. That thought pleases me, if it is true. I know that this work will not play out on me. It is as big a field as I could want."

For the next two years, she devoted herself to her studies, intent on making up for the "darned foolish" student she had been in 1928 and 1929. She did publicity for the school to pay tuition fees and receive five dollars per week, and got a part-time job with the *Miami Herald* in November 1936. Working at the *Herald* three hours in the afternoon each day, she wrote "chamber of commerce junk," did rewrites, and was occasionally sent out on interviews. For four hours in the morning, she attended classes on mechanics, calculus, graphics, and physics, and wrote university publicity in the afternoon before catching a bus downtown to her job at the *Herald*.

"The *Herald* staff is nice," she wrote, "and the paper has more money than the *News* and is able to pay better. It is much the best newspaper job I ever had. Some days it takes me more than two hours, some days less—but the average is two. They gave it to me because I pestered them for three months."

Her daily column that she called "chamber of commerce junk" was "With State Clubs at Civic Center," which detailed the dances and shows put on at the civic center by state clubs from throughout the country that had registered with the Miami Chamber of Commerce. After four months of doing the column, she started writing some home and design features.

The University of Miami was steadily transforming into a real school, and the bitterness toward it that Wood had harbored only a year or two before began to fade away. The Winter Institute of Literature was created, which brought poets Robert Frost and Padraic Colum to teach. Wood took a course in the modern novel from Colum's wife, Molly, who was a renowned literary critic for the *New Republic* and had one of the most beautiful speaking voices for poetry that Wood would ever hear. In addition, Wood remembered her as one of the few great English teachers she ever had. One day in class Wood was doing calculus homework and not paying any attention to what Colum said, until she asked, "And how many of you have ever memorized a poem?"

Wood's hand shot up.

"Say it."

"Music I heard with you was more than music, And bread that I broke with you was more than bread . . ."

"No! No!" said Colum with exasperation. "I should have known better than to call on you, Jane. Go ahead and say it all."

Wood continued with the Conrad Aiken poem "Music I Heard."

Now that I am without you, all is desolate
All that was once so beautiful is dead
Your hands once touched this table and this silver
And I have seen your fingers hold this glass
These things do not remember you, beloved
And yet your touch upon them will not pass
For it was in my heart you moved among them
And blessed them with your hands and with your eyes
And in my heart they will remember always
They knew you once, O beautiful and wise

The reason that Colum was disappointed that Wood had responded was because Colum was depending on one of her average students to prove a point.

The professor said with a slight severity in her voice: "What I had been saying, Jane, is the verse most people memorize is not poetry. But that is the most beautiful modern love poem in the English language."

Despite Wood's full schedule, she also managed to find time for two weeks in February to do the publicity for the President's Birthday Ball on Miami Beach. She made forty dollars for her efforts, a minor windfall and an early indicator that she had a successful future in public relations work. Unfazed by the assassination attempt that had occurred four years before during his appearance at Bayfront Park, Roosevelt continued to return to Miami for public appearances. He loved the city, sharing the sentiment that Adlai Stevenson expressed during a campaign stop at Bayfront Park in 1952. When Stevenson was a boy his grandfather brought him on his first visit to Miami, at a time when it was still a sleepy little town. The young Stevenson looked up Biscayne Boulevard, and his eyes and voice lifted with delight as he proclaimed, "You have built a splendid city, shining in the sun!"

Having started the Depression three years early with the land bust, Miami was starting to recover ahead of the rest of the nation. Unemployed bootleggers had reemerged as bookies and heads of gambling syndicates, and gambling was becoming one of the primary attractions for winter visitors. The bookie racket run by Frank Hyde and Red Slaton was a $30 million per year business. While law enforcement had tried to cripple the operation by taking away the telephones, a judge ordered Southern Bell to restore service to the bookies. Hyde's lawyer argued successfully that though his client admitted he was a bookmaker, the phone company was not a defender of the public morals.

Still, gambling wasn't doing much for the local economy. The winter season, Wood lamented, meant "more hard work for anyone who makes any money at all, and more and more cheap people." Since the syndicate bosses were cleaning out many visitors' wallets, and other visitors were notoriously cheap to start with, the "snowbirds" were viewed with a less than favorable eye. Wages were going up some, but the cost of living was going up even more quickly. A decent apartment anywhere in Greater Miami during the winter season was hard to find for under $150 a month.

In March 1937, Wood received the news that her Grandmother Lil had died in Sunnyside. Wood had not been to Sunnyside since returning from Greece in 1932, and the sense of an era passing saddened her deeply. She wrote:

"I knew then that a time, an era of my existence—and of a good many other people's was absolutely intact as long as she was at Sunnyside, and that it would be quite gone when she was not there. When I was little, and when I spent my summers at Sunnyside, it was the place I loved, oh, with very immense happiness. I took Grandmother for granted. It wasn't until I was there last that I really realized that she was the place.

"Somehow, I think that was one of the finest things about her. That is why all her children and her grandchildren will miss her with a grief not adulterated by any tiny thought of 'Perhaps it is the best thing after all.' She made her place in our hearts entirely sweet, she never made any of us feel a responsibility toward her. That was partly luck, surely, that she had her own home to the last of her life. But she never placed an emotional responsibility on us. She gave and gave, and did not demand, and never let any of us feel that she ever felt lonely, old, or out of life. I do not think she did. She had her place right up to the time of her death."

In late May a great opportunity occurred that Wood treasured for the rest of her life. By a stroke of luck, the first of many cases in her journalistic career of the fates smiling on her, Wood was the only reporter in the office on a Sunday afternoon in May when word came in that Amelia Earhart was flying into Miami in a few hours.

"I drove out wildly in an ancient *Herald* Ford," wrote Wood to her aunt Peg two weeks later, "and saw her land."

"Her husband, George Palmer Putnam, was with her, and her stepson, David Putnam, a charming lad, met her. I've always rather liked her, thought she did the business of being much in the public eye with grace and without ostentation. She was quite gracious. I was the only reporter there, and she answered questions for me for about half an hour. She has a charming voice, lots of poise, and seemed to me to have solved the problem of how to receive lots of publicity without having your privacy disturbed. She and her husband seem very fond of each other. Probably only one man in a thousand would do what he does. For he was up in the *Herald* office for about a week after she took off, using this as his headquarters for managing her business of cables, news stories, etc. He has made his million, is a publisher, and obviously cares nothing for all the publicity and excitement of his wife being Amelia Earhart."

The flight had begun in Los Angeles, and the day before Earhart, Putnam, and her navigator, Fred Noonan, had stopped in New Orleans for the day to see the city. Flying 450 miles from New Orleans to Miami, the first two hours of it over the Gulf of Mexico, the plane landed in Miami a little less than three hours later at Pan American Field on Thirty-Sixth Street. Almost immediately it lifted off again to ferry over to the adjacent municipal airport, where Wood met it. Both airports would eventually become part of the Greater Miami International Airport, but they were separate entities then. Wood wrote that the creak of metal could be heard all around the airport when the plane came down with a thud. Earhart's first comment upon emerging from the plane at the municipal airport was: "I certainly smacked it down hard that time. That's the hardest letdown I've given you, isn't it, Fred?"

Earhart then added: "We sure are hungry. My navigator wouldn't let me fly high and I can't make good time under 1000 feet altitude."

Putnam sarcastically commented about his wife's impatience with Noonan's flight planning: "Our navigator erred gravely. Captain Noonan said that we would sight land at 12:11 and we didn't until 12:12."

The first round-the-world attempt had been aborted in March after the same plane had sustained damage on takeoff in Honolulu, but Earhart wasn't worried. She told Wood: "When you have two tons more fuel than a ship is supposed to carry, you can't expect normal reactions. But I've been taking off overloaded planes for six years now, and that is the first trouble I've had with them."

Wood asked her, "Just what of scientific value do you expect to get out of your trip, Miss Earhart?"

"Do I expect this trip around the world to be of scientific value?," she replied. "No, not much. I am going for the trip. I am going for fun. Can you think of any better reason?"

Wood could never forget how her eyes twinkled when Earhart spoke the last line, for she reflected much of Wood's own spirit. The interview took place just a few days before Wood's twenty-fourth birthday, and in her young life Jane had never thought to question whether there were any limitations on what a woman could do. If a woman wanted to fly around the world just for fun, she couldn't have approved more. As far as her own aspirations, it didn't occur to her that any man would ever try to limit her, because the most influential man in her life, her father, had never done anything but support the idea that she could do anything she set her mind to. In George Putnam, Amelia Earhart had a man with enough financial and personal security to be more than happy to stay out of the limelight and do all the groundwork to support Earhart's flying.

Earhart also showed detailed interest in a wide range of aviation-related topics and commented about the Soviets recently establishing an airplane base at the North Pole: "We need more meteorology stations all over the world. There are whole areas that we know absolutely nothing about. When you have daily observations from a station at the north pole you can have better long-range weather forecasting. I don't know very much about the feasibility of an air route over the north pole any time soon, but that will be the way they finally fly, I have no doubt."[4]

She also had thoughts on the *Hindenburg* disaster in New Jersey, which had occurred only a little over two weeks before her arrival in Miami. At the same time, she was willing to recognize her limitations in playing expert on aircraft radically different from those with which she was familiar.

"I was lunching last week with an authority on dirigibles," Earhart told Wood, "and I was expressing my opinion as to the cause of the disaster in some detail. He said: 'It would be smart for someone who knows as little about lighter-than-air craft as you do, not to express an opinion about the cause of the Hindenburg crackup.' I think he was right."[5]

Another person meeting Earhart's plane at the airport was a woman named Helen Day. She had been friends with Fred Noonan in her college days, when he had lived and worked in Miami as a navigation instructor for Pan American during the early 1930s. Day was rumored to be having an affair with him, and she spent time with him and Earhart during their stay, one of the few outsiders granted access to their inner circle. By chance, Day and Wood became close friends in the coming years, when Day married and became Helen Day Bible.

The similarities between Wood and Earhart were not just limited to their carefree, independent natures. Earhart had also been a social worker, which was what she had been doing in Boston in 1928 when offered the chance to be the first woman to cross the Atlantic by air. Though she laughingly referred to being no more than a "sack of potatoes" on that trip and hardly thought it an accomplishment, the adventure had been responsible for her falling in love with flying. When Fred Noonan was querying Helen Day about her blind mother during their stay, Earhart showed a keen interest in whether there were enough services for the blind in Miami.[6]

A week after meeting Earhart, Wood finally got the college degree that the Depression and her disdain for the University of Miami had put out of reach for so long. Though she had secretly been hoping to graduate cum laude, her four-year average was 89.1, just short of the needed average of 89.8. The erratic grades of the first two years had been too much to make up for, and her grades had fallen in the past semester due to her taxing workload outside of school.

"It is odd how you go along laughing at letters after names," Wood wrote, "and saying 'Oh, but a diploma means so little, just as such.' And then when you finally get your B.S., you are so tremendously excited. I didn't expect to be so pleased, but I was in a fine glow."

The job at the *Miami Herald* continued, with her hours extended from 2:00 p.m. to 9:30 p.m. once she was out of school. As a sort of graduation present, the *Herald* gave her a raise from $15 to $17.50 a week, which, she said, "does not set me afire with admiration for myself" but still was pleasant for her since it was the first raise she had ever gotten that she hadn't asked for.

Along with her other duties she became the church editor, an assignment that was richly ironic. While she knew religion well enough from her family, she described herself at the time as a "Presbyterian atheist."

With the undergraduate degree under her belt, she further contemplated her dream of attending Columbia University in the fall to pursue a master's degree in physics. The cost was formidable. After consulting with Columbia and talking with people who had studied there, she concluded it would cost her $1,000 to obtain the degree. She thought she could save $200 to $250 from work, and if she could borrow $250 to $300 as a student loan, she would be able to afford the first term. During the time she was at Columbia, she would try to work and borrow toward the $500 for the second term. Scholarships were scarce, though, and she was advised that until she was at Columbia, there was little chance of getting a loan or scholarship from the school.

In addition, the admissions department told her that while she was eligible for admission to the graduate program, they did not recognize the University of Miami's bachelor's degree as qualifying her for regular graduate standing. She would have to make up an additional term of liberal arts courses. That didn't worry her, though. Being admitted at all was what had concerned her, considering the standing—or lack of it—of the University of Miami among American colleges.

Wood chose Columbia for a number of reasons. Though the University of Chicago had the best physics program in the country—and she wanted to get her doctorate there—Chicago was unknown to her as a city. Wood wasn't sure she would care for it. In New York she had friends, could easily get a part-time job, and the physics program was excellent. While she was aware that it was easy to get distracted from studying in New York, she thought living in a dormitory could help minimize that.

"What I will do with my master's degree when I get it," she wrote, "I don't know. I know what can be done with it, and what I shall do if nothing better appears. I shall teach in a college. I say it confidently, and think I can get such a job. Women who can teach physics are far fewer than men, and I know that a number of women's colleges would like to have them. I should enjoy that, though I believe I would enjoy more working in a laboratory. But I like college existence, and teaching physics is a good way of getting it set in your mind. I could do that several years and then work on my doctor's degree."

Her plans abruptly changed one fateful day in June. Another member of the *Miami Herald* staff mentioned that the season for spiny lobster was opening the next day. The man was Henry Olaf Reno, who had been a police reporter at the newspaper for the past thirteen years. His father, Robert, was a *Herald* photographer who ran the newspaper's photo studio, and Wood had known the elder Reno since joining the paper. Robert Reno was over seventy, with blue eyes that twinkled and made him appear fifteen years younger. He was the patriarch of a family of Danish immigrants who had come to America from the city of Odense. After arriving at Ellis Island, they spent three years living in Wisconsin with relatives, moved to Bartow, Florida, three years later, and then to Tennessee. Henry Reno attended the University of Tennessee for two years, majoring in agriculture, before the family returned to Florida in 1923 and finally settled down for good in Miami. After Robert Reno got a job with the *Miami Herald*—he had been a professional photographer in Denmark—he got his son a job there as well.

Henry Reno, who was eleven years older than Wood, told her that he was headed down to the Florida Keys the next day to dive for lobster on the open-

Henry Reno aboard the *Vagabond*, 1930s. The boat took Jane and Henry on their first date—lobster diving.

ing day of the season. Wood was more attractive than she would ever admit to herself, and it was no surprise that Reno, a rather solitary bachelor, took an interest in her. He was doing little more than trying to impress her or leading up to the offer of a lobster dinner when she surprised him by enthusiastically saying, "Take me, take me."

"You know how to catch a crawfish?"

"Sure."

Though Reno had met few women yet with an enthusiasm for skin diving, he took her at her word. She told him to pick her up in front of the Coral Gables Theater to save him time looking for her house and also to avoid explanations to her sisters about why a handsome man was picking her up at six o'clock in the morning. He never really expected her to show, but at dawn she was sitting on the curb by the theater.

Reno had a boat named the *Vagabond* that they launched out of Key Largo, and Cobb's Creek whiskey for warming up between dives.

"Here's to the Argentine Navy," he would shout, knocking back a slug and diving back in for more lobster. Wood tried to keep up with his drinking. The rolling waves and the whiskey finally caught up with her, though, and she got sick and passed out.

Reno was the height of chivalry in response. Because his parents were away, he took her to his house, carried her in, and put an ice pack on her head as he put her to bed. The sun had set when she awoke, and a table awaited her with steaming hot lobster and melted butter. The *Blue Danube* was on the stereo. Wood was embarrassed with herself and thought she had ruined any further chances of seeing him again. She knew that he was something special, the first man she had met since Charles Koon that had such an effect on her.

He did ask her out before long, though, and within a matter of weeks, he proposed to her. Or she thought he proposed to her. Some months later, she asked herself somewhat abashedly, "God, was that what he really said?"

Eventually, her curiosity got the better of her, and she asked him if she had indeed mistaken his words for a proposal. He hemmed a bit and admitted, "Aw, I guess I could have gotten out of it—if I'd wanted to."[7]

They were married on July 20, 1937, at St. Stephen's Episcopal Church, and Wood remembered of her wedding day:

"I came down with slight poison ivy under my right eye three days before, but that was all gone. I will remember waking up in the dark of the morning. I will always remember the smell of gardenias, the candles, and the deep good intonation of Father Cannon's voice. But the thing that will remain bright and clear in my heart forever was the surge of pure elation as we started down the aisle, and those hilarious opening chords of Mendelssohn's wedding march broke out. I could feel the cool, tender freshness of early morning; the few faces that I saw were wiped clean by that happy reverence that comes when people attend a ceremony that seems to have heart as well as beautiful form. And best of all I could feel in Henry's arms and his stride that we were as one in our elation. We were absolutely in tune, coming down that aisle, and what a tune."

They spent a week honeymooning on Key Largo because they both loved the Florida Keys deeply. "They are the best," she wrote, "the essence of this

Henry and Jane's wedding day, July 20, 1937. The note to Jane's aunt May reads: "We're happier now than we were then. He is something rather special as a husband. Much love, Jane."

country." They had a shared intimate knowledge of the Keys from her social work and his reporting around the Labor Day storm. He knew exactly what she meant when she told him the smell of rotting fish was the only thing that ever made her homesick when she was away from Florida.

The absorption of Henry Reno into the Wood family, and Jane Wood into the Reno family, was so smooth that it relieved Jane of any worries that she would ever have to face in-law problems. Somewhat to her surprise, it was Dolly among her sisters that Henry most immediately hit it off with. Henry had a well-developed and mischievous sense of humor, and they engaged in thrusts and parries with enthusiasm.

"Strange that my marriage has brought us much closer together," mused Jane five weeks after the wedding. "Dolly never approved much of my taste in people, and it came as a surprise to her that I picked a fine person to marry, I think. She was grand in helping us get ready for the wedding. When she and Bill came over to dinner I could feel her wonder, that contained no trace of envy or jealousy. 'This is just what I want, and have wanted for years. And Jane never seemed to be aiming at this, and here she has it, a home of her own.' She has more courage and devotion than the average person in this world, and it won't be wasted. While it is truly tragic that she and Bill haven't been able to get married, they are wise."

Bill Denslow had recently acquired his own gas station, so things were beginning to look more solid financially for him and Dolly. Five years had gone by with income so threadbare they had not been able to seriously contemplate marriage, and Dolly had grown increasingly restless with her job at the *Miami News*. For them, the Depression seemed never-ending. One of the reasons was Denslow's father, a man from Pittsburgh who had been one of the white-collar men destroyed by the Depression. After losing everything, he had never regained an even keel. He remained a mean and hopeless drunk for the next decade, a burden that his son could not forsake.

Jane's father, on the other hand, whose law income had been running in ebbs and flows, saw his business become steadily more consistent in 1937 to the point that he and Daisy were thinking of buying a house. He got along well with Henry, and upon learning that Henry had good relations with the police force, observed, "At least we've got one diplomat in the family."

Though George Wood had always been gentle with his family, he was not a man for suffering fools and could have a hard temper when provoked. Rarely did this happen, though, due to his imposing physical presence. But one day during a particularly contentious divorce trial in 1937 in which he was involved with his law partner, representing a Colonel Elliott Caziare, his temper got the better of him. The trial had already experienced fireworks the previous day when Caziare's wife assaulted a witness testifying for her husband, a widow and doughnut baker named Pearl Mills, knocking her out of her chair and spraining her wrist. On top of that, Mrs. Mills said her landlord and neighbor, Harry Boehm, who was testifying on behalf of Mrs. Caziare, threatened her life in the courtroom. Boehm was arrested. The charges against Boehm were dismissed the next day by the City Court due to "lack of jurisdiction," and Boehm appeared as a witness in a separate proceeding that Boehm himself brought to attempt to place Colonel Caziare under a sort of restraining order, or "peace bond." While George Wood was questioning him, Boehm apparently said something exceptionally "vile" to Wood, causing Wood to reach over the railing and begin beating him around the head and shoulders.

Wood was promptly charged with contempt of court and hauled off to jail for two hours. In the meantime, as Boehm continued calling Wood's law partner, O. B. White, a "liar," Wood took off his jacket and proceeded to try to fight Boehm himself. This was the only time in his entire law career that Wood exhibited this kind of behavior in a courtroom, so it's hard to imagine what Boehm said that angered him so.

The following night, Saturday, Wood had retired early in the evening and Daisy Wood was sitting out on the screened front porch of their Coral Gables home on Minorca Avenue. Two men came to the screen door asking for George Wood and announced that their mother was a client of his and was waiting in the car out front to discuss her case with him. Daisy asked the client's name. The men hesitated for thirty seconds and then gave her a name that turned out to be fictitious. She went inside to get George, who got dressed and came out to meet the men. He walked alongside them toward the street, whereupon one man lagged behind him and raised what appeared to be a small hammer or cosh to strike a blow to the back of his head. When Daisy saw this from the porch and screamed, George turned around just in time to be smashed on the temple. The men fled before doing further harm, spooked by Daisy's screams.[1]

In his interview with police, George Wood expressed certainty that the attack was retribution for the courtroom incident the previous day. While police initially said they had some leads, it doesn't appear the attackers were ever caught. Harry Boehm, alternately spelled Harry Boehme, seemed to be a curious character who owned some bungalows just outside the city limits on NW Seventy-Fifth Street, and a variety of other properties in the area. At the time his occupation was listed as "gardener," but over time he became known as a Miami developer. Two years later, Pearl Mills was still a tenant and neighbor of Boehm on NW Seventy-Fifth, living with her thirteen-year-old son, Billy, and her mother, when her house burned down in the middle of the night. They all got out alive. In 1943, Boehm was arrested on nine counts of rent violations and later convicted, one of the first Dade County landlords to be successfully prosecuted. More than likely Boehm paid for the attack on George Wood, but nothing was ever proven. Somewhat curiously, for a family that loved stories, the episode disappeared quietly into family history and was never retold. As crime reporter at the *Herald*, Henry Reno almost certainly had some insight into the attack on his father-in-law which he shared with his young wife, Jane, but she never mentioned it in any correspondence.

Although Henry meshed well with Jane's mother, and Daisy Wood was somewhat bowled over by the idea that her daughter had found peace and happiness, Henry was unsure at first how to treat Mrs. Wood. At the age of thirty-five, he didn't feel like a son to her. He was the sort of man she understood and liked immediately, though, and they settled on being friends. There were a number of similarities between Henry Reno and Jane's father, a solidness and security they projected "that contains no dough, no insensitivity." When Jane had talked in Greece about wanting a "finished" man, who had a hard, defined quality to him, she found one who fit the bill with Henry. "Yet he has the most delicate perception," she wrote, "and consideration, and tenderness."

After five weeks of marriage, Jane's life had been turned upside down. Her school plans were abandoned, her work was cut back, and she looked forward to her marriage to Henry as being "the last job I shall undertake in this life."

"That married life could be full of immense terrors," she bemusedly wrote, "heretofore nameless, I had foreseen. But I had visioned nothing to equal refrigerator salesmen. They call us at nine in the morning—which corresponds to 4 a.m. in a normal life—when I am taking my nap. They beg, like prodigal sons, for 'one more chance' (to cut prices). They jump up and down on oven doors. They say with immense dignity, 'I had rather be allowed to explain my product than make a sale.' Henry, who is really the world's most amiable husband, leans on the range and smokes his pipe I bought for him. He gets down on his knees and looks at the ovens' elements. He listens with a diplomacy of which I have not yet plumbed the depths. We phone here and run there, because wise friends have advised, 'Don't be a sucker, I know the way that you can get 15% off—or 33%, or 10%. And both of us, to whom this is strange and new, shake our heads in amazement at the perfidy of men and their prices. Never, oh, never, believe that 'national advertising' prevents all the bargaining of the Flea Market."

Jane embraced the sudden change to a domestic routine, having tired somewhat of moving in the overly fast current of American life. Now she had the time she sought to sit or sleep on the riverbank. Henry worked from late afternoon to one thirty in the morning. When he came home, they had sandwiches and split pea soup or turtle soup, and Ovaltine, or what was called a "Thomas Collins" before the name got shortened. They usually got to bed between three and four in the morning. Getting up any time between eleven in the morning and two in the afternoon, they dallied an hour or two over breakfast and sometimes went to the beach. He would come home for dinner around eight thirty in the evening, and she concentrated on most of her household chores after ten, when it was cool and quiet.

"I will have to boast and say that I have the makings of a really good cook," she wrote. "I've a tendency to get dough all over the kitchen and use every pot and pan—but I am consoled by our best man [Bill Denslow] who says that no true artist ever was orderly and neat as he worked."

The lines John Steinbeck wrote in the preface to Log from the Sea of Cortez reflected the Reno theory of housekeeping, and it was a system adopted by generations of the family to come: "We must remember three things. Number one and first in importance, we must have as much fun as we can with what we have. Number two, we must eat as well as we can, because if we don't, we won't have the health and strength to have as much fun as we might. Number three, and third and last in importance, we must keep the house reasonably in order, wash the dishes and such things. But we will not let the last interfere with the other two."

If it had not been for the typical immigrant desire to blend into America, Jane might have become a Rasmussen rather than a Reno. Henry's father had changed the family name while they were still in Denmark, though oddly the ship manifest of the boat they arrived on showed the boys entering the country as Reno and their parents as Rasmussen. While living in Odense, Robert Marius Rasmussen had taken a random stab at a map of the United States, hit on the city of Reno, and decided that it was as good a name as any for his family. He became a great friend to Jane, and she wrote of him: "I've seen pictures of him when he was Henry's age, and truly, if Henry were nearly that handsome I would be uneasy. He took me and bought a beer and a dress for me and gave me much advice, and *all* of it was good. He is gruff, and an artist. The walls of his home are hung with paintings—some originals and some reproductions, and all of them interesting."

Jane also enjoyed the company of Henry's mother, Laurine, or Lau, who was a gentle and thoughtful Christian Scientist with whom she was able to talk for hours. Only five years before, Jane had despaired at her friend Shinnie's adoption of the religion, which Jane had viewed as "the last refuge of the tender-minded." The deep love and knowledge of music—especially opera—that Henry shared with his new wife was inherited from his mother.

Though Jane was the first to admit she had a rash and impulsive nature, it had rarely been evident when it came to men. With her unrequited love for Charles Koon, she had felt some of the strongest romantic longings of her life but was unable to act on them. The abrupt discovery of a man with whom she wanted to spend the rest of her life left some friends and family pleasantly baffled. Many had assumed that men weren't important to her, while others who knew her well knew that she was extremely cautious about expressing her feelings toward men she really liked. In addition, she did not play the game of romance well. She met most men boldly, challenging them intellectually and matching them physically, leaving all but the most confident of them feeling awkward about how to romantically pursue her.

"From the immense vantage of five weeks," she wrote to her aunt Peg, "I can tell you better now why I married this man. I did it because it seemed preordained. I do not mean exactly, as the girls of comedy and melodrama say, 'Henry and I were made for each other.' No, not exactly. I felt in the grip of a big hand that showed me the only possible way. Henry, I might say, was the

Jane and Henry, with Henry's parents, Robert and Lau, Avocado Avenue, 1937.

opposite of the refrigerator salesmen in putting pressure on me, in spite of the speed in which all this took place. I do not think it was romance, because I have known that, and this was not the same thing at all. You will not misunderstand me when I say I was moved by an immense feeling of fatality."

In late September they moved into the new house that Henry was having built at 3561 Avocado Avenue in Coconut Grove, which cost about three and a half thousand dollars. It was a low, long, concrete block house with a green

Jane outside the bedroom of her house on Avocado Avenue in Coconut Grove in 1938 with her mother-in-law, Lau, baby Janet, and sister-in-law Doris Reno and Doris's daughter Lisa.

shingle roof. The ceiling in the living room was beamed wood, and the small dining room had walls of knotty cypress, with windows all along one side. Soft, gray-green tiles covered the bathroom floor, and the kitchen was white and peacock blue. The bedroom, one of the most important places in the house for the newlyweds, was the highlight. It had a southern, eastern, and northern exposure with three windows and a French door. They expected to be in debt for years to pay off the house, but the mortgage was cheaper than rents in Miami.

Being familiar with the struggles his younger brother Paul suffered during the Depression, Henry Reno wasn't worried. Paul had met his wife, Doris, at the *Miami Herald* in 1930. She had just returned from California, where she got a master's degree at Mills College and won a scholarship to write poetry for a year. After the scholarship ended, she thought it unlikely that she could live off poetry in hard times and returned to Miami to seek work. Her uncle, Frank Shutts, was the owner of the *Miami Herald* at that time, and he gave her a job.

On a rainy day when she was in Robert Reno's photo lab waiting for prints to dry for a story, Doris met Paul Reno. His father had also found him a job at the *Herald*, working as a photographer, and he was attracted to the dripping-wet girl in the black rubber raincoat and black beret. Robert Reno made sure to arrange for Paul to accompany Doris on assignments, and a romance blossomed. In fact, it blossomed too quickly for everyone's liking, because they announced in 1932 over great protests that they were getting married. No matter how in love a couple was, the idea of marriage during the Depression was thought to be rash. Most people could barely take care of themselves, much less someone else. They eloped to New York and made ends meet living in Greenwich Village.

Soon after Henry and Jane built their house, Paul and Doris moved themselves and their two-year-old daughter Lisa back to live in Coconut Grove. Doris was to become not only a dear friend to Jane Reno, but also one of Jane's favorite poets. In 1940 Doris went to work as the *Miami Herald* music critic and held the position for the next thirty-one years. Associate Editor John Pennekamp supposedly chose her for the job by telling her: "Doris, you're a good writer and know nothing about music. Marian Burdine knows about music but can't write. It's a lot easier to learn about music than to learn how to write, so I'm giving you the job."

Henry and Jane Reno holding baby Janet, 1938.

Jane with baby Bob, early 1940.

Exactly one year and a day after she married, Jane Reno gave birth to a baby girl they named Janet. The following year they had Robert Marius, named after his grandfather. The family moved farther away from the city to 111 South Eleventh Street in South Miami, where Henry could fulfill the aspirations toward farm life he had harbored ever since studying agriculture at the University of Tennessee. They bought goats, chickens, and a cow.

In early 1939, around the same time the Japanese had taken control of much of China, Dr. Marshall Balfour moved his family from Greece to the International Settlement in Shanghai. His new work kept him out of China much of the time, roaming from Java to the Philippines. At home with Nina and Tinker, Peg Balfour wondered if they might not have been better off moving back to the United States. She wrote to Jane in July 1939:

"Shanghai's climate is vile. For a month we've had typhoon weather. Our whole district as well as many others is under from 5–12 inches of filthy water. Things in the house are moldy and grow beards and everything smells awful. Today we went out to the country to the Shanghai Municipal Nursery Gardens. There are lovely shrubs and trees and many birds. It's very like heaven after Shanghai.

"We can drive about five miles out to the old blown up aerodrome. There a sign greets us: 'Prohibited Zone by Order of the Japanese Imperial Commission.' To reach the country we must have a cholera certificate and wiggle our car through barbed wire entanglements, pass French and British sentries, then numerous Jap ones on the rail road barriers.

"There are always little troubles with guerrillas and we can hear machine guns, which are definitely not blank cartridges, from our house nearly every day. Out in the country, little boys always bring four leaf clovers to sell us. If things ever get right, we are going to live in the country. They have curfew 9 p.m.–6 a.m., so if people who live out there have a party in town they sleep in or get a special permit from the Japanese to return."

As the situation grew more and more tense over the next year, the international community in Shanghai began to realize that Japan's brutal occupation of China was inevitably going to swallow them. The Japanese had been careful to appease the fears about their imperialist aims by treating the internationals respectfully—Peg Balfour noted that "they have always been pleasant to us"—whereas they tortured and slaughtered the Chinese wholesale. The mask began to drop in 1940, however. Dr. Balfour sent his wife and children to New

York, but he remained behind to continue his work. Before the Japanese oc-cupied the International Settlement in December 1941, in conjunction with the outbreak of war with the United States, he managed to get out himself.

Before America entered the war, the conflict seemed a long way from life in South Miami, though Reno's world awareness made her more prescient than most Floridians. In a fragment of a 1940 letter to Peg Balfour, she wrote:

"One reason I haven't completed a letter before is because I would start with the war, and be overcome with a quiet horror and not be able to go any further.

"I represent the average American fairly well in my emotions about this business, and they are what count in our conduct more than our thinking. We are implacably anti-German, and feel toward them not especially hate or rage, but something more enduring, a deep firm dislike. We feel a wild, bitter rage against the British for their stupidity, a contempt for their leaders and their upper classes."

In December 1940 Reno gave birth to Margaret Sloan, or Maggy, who for the first months of 1941 filled her mother's life with dread. The new baby con-stantly appeared on the verge of death. Refusing to eat, yellow, and shriveled, Maggy was the strongest test yet in Reno's young career as a mother. In spite of these trials, she got pregnant again. Two days before Christmas in 1941 she had her fourth and final child, Mark Wood. Later she told the folk singer Pete Seeger, "I had four children in three and a half years so I could get on with other things."

The attack on Pearl Harbor and the subsequent declarations of war against both Japan and Germany changed Reno's outlook on war. While she had always ridiculed breast-beating and jingoism, when the fate of her country was in the balance, she had no doubt that the nation had to rally behind the war effort. Her commitment began somewhat dubiously.

"In a burst of patriotism—believe it or not," she wrote, "I am raising some chicks. As soon as I got 50 New Hampshire red biddies, the June rains started. So what with a sick baby and grappling with half-damp clothes and drying wet chickens in the oven, life has been strenuous."

Henry was driving a truck for civilian defense during the days, and work-ing at night. Appalled at the nation's lack of readiness, he told his wife that the state of preparation of the casualty stations was "ghastly," especially con-

Jane Wood on a mule, late 1930s.

sidering that it was not impossible that they would end up using them. For five hours each Sunday afternoon, Jane went to read detective stories and nap by a telephone as a link in the air-raid warning system. She watched the skies for enemy aircraft from the top of the Biltmore Hotel, assisted by a military airplane identification booklet issued by the Army Air Corps. "These things, we suspect, are gestures but we hope vaguely in the right direction."

One of the poems of Louis MacNeice, written on New Year's Day of 1939, was close to her heart and remained so throughout her life. She loved the lines:

Sleep to the noise of running waters,
Tomorrow to be crossed, however deep.
This is no river of the dead or Lethe;
Tonight we sleep on the banks of Rubicon,
The die is cast.
There will be time to audit the accounts later,
And the equation will work out at last.

While tourism had been steadily growing every winter, the war caused an abrupt change in the busy marketing of sunshine. Beginning in February 1942, Germany sent submarines to the Gulf Stream to torpedo ships carrying crude rubber and oil up to East Coast ports. Houses of Refuge, old coastal stations that had originally been built in the nineteenth century to aid shipwrecked sailors, were used as lookout stations to spot submarines. Other nineteenth-century structures, like lighthouses and abandoned brick forts, also got a new lease on life as watching posts. Still, little could be done to stop the undersea prowlers.

The savage U-boat offensive, Operation Drumbeat, sank nearly four hundred ships and killed thousands of sailors. Dozens were torpedoed just off the Florida coast. Cruising the surface at night with impunity, German submarine captains lined up their targets by watching for silhouettes against the coastal lights. A blackout was ordered for Miami and Miami Beach.

"We could see smoke from burning tankers," wrote Reno, "from the tops of tall buildings along Biscayne Boulevard."

The beaches were covered in clumps of tar and assorted debris, and oil slicks were everywhere. Occasionally, dead bodies floated ashore. Most men were burned alive, unable to escape the flaming tankers. Worse yet were those who reached the water and thought they had a chance, only to die in the blaze of oil on the surface surrounding the ship. The US Navy sent a huge dirigible to south Florida to scout for German submarines. It was housed in a hangar at the Richmond base until it was shot down by a U-boat as it flew over the Gulf Stream.

Rubber soon became a restricted commodity, along with gasoline. Rationing quickly extended to food. Before he was drafted, Bill Denslow—who in 1938 had finally realized his dream of marrying Dolly Wood—was among the men who went out in small boats and salvaged bales of crude rubber to sell. As the military increased its presence in Miami, most of the whorehouses were shut down, including the final site of Gertie Walsh's legendary bordello. Wide-open whorehouses flourished throughout Miami during the 1920s and 1930s, generally accepted by law enforcement and the public as part and parcel of the tourist industry. The most esteemed of such establishments had been Gertie Walsh's first whorehouse in an old stone mansion built in 1903 on Flagler Street by the Brigham family.

The mansion was the childhood home of siblings Peg and Ed Brigham, and Jane Wood became friends with Peg in the 1930s. The Brigham parents built the estate when Peg was two years old, on forty acres of downtown real estate that stretched from Flagler Street to the Miami River, and Ed was born there. Miami was such a marginal development in the wilderness in those days that when Ed Brigham was a little boy, a panther stuck his head through the window of the living room and looked around. The young Brigham and his father sat very still, and the panther finally went away. While the Brigham family did well in real estate during the boom, they lost most of it in the bust of 1926. They rented it to Gertie Walsh for a few years for her high-end bordello but eventually moved back into the old family mansion when Gertie Walsh was forced to shut down in the early 1930s in a vice-squad crackdown and the Brighams were no longer receiving rent money. Until marrying Jane, Henry Reno enjoyed student rates at Gertie's different establishments throughout the 1930s.

"You have never seen anything so stunning as Gertie, all 250 pounds of her, and her sister Blanch, all 200 pounds of her, coming down the stairs of the old Brigham mansion, dressed in pink satin, with ostrich plume feathers," Henry Reno told his wife.

Jane Reno remembered Peg Brigham, who died young in the 1940s, as one of the treasures of that era. Reno wrote of her:

"Peg was one of the great, the wonderful, people of the world—kind, wise, generous, brilliant. She wrote fine prose, though she never finished anything or published any of her writing. When Peg no longer had money with which to help friends, her strength and kindness were still there. She could listen to a friend's problems and find a good solution. She returned you to yourself feeling your very best, polished like a silver spoon. Her eyes had the sparkle of true beauty. Married five times, she died a baroness.

"The second time I talked to Peg after I met her, I came to her house and asked her mother if she was at home.

"'She's upstairs in bed, not feeling well,' said Mrs. Brigham, indicating that I could go up.

"When I went into her bedroom, she was propped up in a bed like Sarah Bernhardt dying of consumption, and I said, 'What's the matter, Peg?'

"'I have been to Ludlow Fair.'

"'What does that mean?'

"She replied,

"'I have been to Ludlow Fair

"'And left my necktie God knows where

"'Carried halfway home, or near

"'Pints and quarts of Ludlow beer.

"'Down in lovely mud I've lain,

"'Happy 'til I walked again.

"'The world it was the old world yet,

"'I was I, my things were wet

"'And nothing now remains to do

"'But begin the game anew.'

"Then she said, 'I was drunk.' She had a problem of getting drunk and doing things like falling in the Roney Plaza pool and being arrested for simple drunkenness."

After vacating the Brigham mansion during the brief spasm of morals enforcement, Gertie Walsh rented a magnificent house on the Miami River, the Palais Royale, when business as usual resumed. This was the first bordello in the area with a yacht basin offering boat access for wealthy clients. Walsh largely depended on a rich clientele that had not been hit by the Depression, and she was reported to be the only American ever allowed to run a brothel in Havana. One night as Henry was leaving the house, Gertie said to him:

"Henry, I know you majored in agriculture and I want to ask you something. I sent a couple of the girls downtown to buy two flamingos, and they called back and said, 'Gertie, they want five hundred dollars each.'

"I told them to buy swans, and they called back and said, 'They want five hundred dollars each for the swans.' I told them to come home.

"Then Blanch and I read an ad in the paper saying, *Ducks, catch them yourself. $1.00.* So Blanch and I put on straw hats and borrowed a truck from some workmen who were working here and went out and caught ducks. And they have been here for months and none of them have laid any eggs."

She took him out beside the yacht basin and showed him the redheaded Muscovy ducks swimming around. He looked them over thoughtfully and said, "Gertie, you caught all males."

# 8 | World War II

Daisy Wood, who had just completed her training as a nurse at Emory, was the first woman in Miami to muster out with the Army Nurse Corps. Though Jane still doubted her sister's adventurousness and tenacity, she thought that joining up "because she thought she ought to" was a good enough reason. She was afraid for her sister, and not a little bit disgruntled that Daisy was proving to be as capable of being practical, hard-nosed, and fearless as the rest of the Wood sisters.

"It's a good thing, and all," she wrote, "but when it's someone you love crossing the ocean—any ocean—just now, everything seems to drop away but that it's dangerous. She's stimulated, and somewhat nervous, but not unduly so. Daisy's a good nurse and a darn smart gal, and the army can use her. She's almost as smart as I, and almost as well-poised as Win. (Yes, even if I am raising chickens for my country.)"

In 1942, while awaiting her marching orders, Daisy Wood met a charming young RAF first lieutenant who was training with an American squadron in Miami. William Parsons was a Cambridge-educated twenty-six-year-old from an upper-class family, and Daisy brought him by to visit with Jane and Henry on occasion. Despite the contempt that Jane had professed toward the British upper classes in regard to the war, the two got along very well during their short acquaintance. Parsons was so impressed by Reno, in fact, that he turned to her for advice and psychological reassurance during his first year of flying missions in North Africa and Europe. Because Parsons was the censor for his squadron, he was able to express thoughts and dissatisfactions in eloquent detail, unconcerned with prying eyes. His first letter, addressed to Jane and Henry and dated December 14 of the disastrous year 1942, summed up the bleak state the Allies were in. The losses to American shipping, the stalemate in North Africa, and the failure to make gains in the Pacific did not provide much cause for optimism. Production of combat aircraft and other technology that was later to reverse the ride of the war was still not up to speed, and propaganda was being offered in its place.

"Time passes so rapidly and one lives such a hectic life from day to day that it becomes almost impossible to find time for the more sane things of life, least of all letter writing, so you really must excuse the laxity on my part, for though I often mean to write and in fact have begun at least three letters to you in the past six months I have never felt really confident of my ability to put in words what I really think and want to say to you both.

"Times have changed since those easy days when I was with you all in Miami and I really must admit that they seem so far away as to be almost unbelievable and certainly unattainable in the future. Don't for God's sake assume that I'm writing this in a morbid frame of mind, far from it for as far as it is possible these days I'm as sane as ever and in the pink of health. I say this because I want to explain to you Jane first what I think of the future and Daisy in particular.

"No doubt by now you will have heard from Daisy of my views, badly expressed I'm afraid for I find it most difficult to consider things logically when I write to her, but I'll endeavour to clarify by getting down just how I feel, for after all you know us both well enough to judge things in a much saner light than either of us will do.

"Seriously Jane you must agree with me that it is absurd for either of us to contemplate a rosy future together, for the continual prolongation of this war eliminates almost every opportunity of our ever meeting, and so on these grounds alone it is only right that Daisy should reconcile herself to the fact that the past can be nothing but a dream, and not a prelude to a terrific future. Surely I am right in writing to her and telling her this, after all what's the use of building up and living on vain hopes when you know there can be little chance of their materializing.

"I do hope this doesn't strike you as a defeatist's way of looking at life, but if it does I must excuse myself on the grounds that I'm getting old and war weary, so much so that I can't even visualise the end of it all and have definitely ceased to contemplate the possibility of ever being able to settle down and get married. If such a statement surprises you I can only say that a year ago I too would have laughed at the very idea of such a point of view. By now, however, I have realized just what war really means and I'm afraid to say that I've seen so many of the world's finest men die such bloody awful deaths that I've ceased to hold any beliefs in Christianity. If this really is a crusade to free the enslaved people of the world then surely to God we ought to get a little more spiritual assistance.

"Flying, Jane, is a soul destroying business. At first once I'd got over my initial nervousness I really enjoyed bombing the bloody Germans because I felt I was getting my own back. The first few times I was exhilarated beyond words seeing my bombs burst, especially when they started big fires, because I could visualise the dirty bastards trying to run away and hide. After a while, though, the thrill dies away and one becomes more or less old and cynical and it then seems bloody absurd and grossly unfair that the few who have the guts to fly should waste away their youth and so frequently have to blindly sacrifice their lives when the vast majority are doing so little by comparison. Still that's another story really, I won't digress too much on industrial achievements, though I must say it would be a welcome change if we could only see a little of what they profess to have done instead of only reading of all these wonderful achievements.

"Bearing all this in mind I began to realise some months ago how grossly unfair it was to expect Daisy to wait on the off chance that I might be one of the lucky few who will come out of this war alive and sane so I wrote and told her so. It took me a hell of a long time to make up my mind, in fact I didn't write to her for a hell of a long time because I hoped against hope she would turn up in England before I left on my travels. Well, I guess fate thought differently. Maybe that was a good thing, for if we had met it would have been impossible to part.

"You know, Jane, I wish to God she'd never joined up, she'll see such god-damn awful sights. At one time I used to imagine we'd meet again in an operating theatre but even those illusions were shattered the other day, for when we were shot down and crashed there wasn't even a nurse to hold my hand as I went under, let alone Daisy. As usual we were lucky, or should I say it's about the first time that I've ever noticed any providential intervention on my part.

"So much for the future, for the present here's wishing you all a very merry Christmas. I shall be thinking of you all, and by then God willing will be imbibing a few bottles of Scotch. Must say that at least there's one good point about this campaign in North Africa, at least we have liquor, this plus the fact that there are plenty of chickens and eggs to supplement our rations enables us to live a reasonable existence on the ground. Talking of food has reminded me that it's about time I tucked in to a good meal so will end this epistle, though before doing so I must thank you for your letter which I really appreciated, particularly so since I was glad to hear that you couldn't volunteer, Henry. That would have been a mug's game however patriotic you felt, for you've far too many family ties to start playing the fool."

Daisy Wood went to North Africa with General Patton's army, though she never met up with Parsons there. Although discouraged by his initial pessimism, she did stay in touch up through the summer of 1943. In the early part of that year, she met Phil Winslow at an army hospital in Louisiana where he was a doctor, and she a nurse. Despite a testy first exchange over her not having the patient's temperature for him, Winslow was warmed by Wood's refusal to be intimidated. The soft attitude that Jane Reno had always equated with her sister's soft beauty was absent when it came to nursing. While Daisy maintained social characteristics throughout her life that annoyed Jane—girlish flirtatiousness and the effortless ability to charm men—everyone who met her in a professional capacity came away impressed at how businesslike and efficient she was.

Though Winslow was on his second marriage at the time, he wrote to a friend, "I found my honey." The following letter from William Parsons to "My dear Jane" showed that he was second-guessing the decision to push Daisy away, but it was too late. She fell further in love with Winslow, and they got married after the war when he finalized his divorce. On July 24, 1943, Parsons wrote:

"During the last few days I have been penciling you a letter. Now however I am rewriting it whilest I'm sitting in my tent on a very hot afternoon.

"The flies and the heat have been exceedingly troublesome of late, at the same time they have failed to destroy my immense pleasure which I have derived from my leisurely existence in a tent on the sandy shore of the Mediterranean.

"Life viewed from such an angle can be singularly pleasant, for as far as the Present is concerned I haven't a care in the world, and even if I had, I couldn't be bothered to worry about it.

"However wrong this form of Philosophy may be, I find it best suited to modern warfare; one must just drift with the tide.

"At the same time, Jane, I find it rather difficult to express my thoughts clearly and logically, and only wish it were possible to talk to you instead of writing, for the main theme of this letter is one which I have pondered over a great deal, endlessly in fact, so much so that at times I feel I am losing all sense of proportion. Hence this letter for I have come to rely on your advice and mature sense of judgement.

"Your first letter was of course a God send, for never have I been in such dire need of reassurance as the time when I received it. So it is that while on one hand I must thank you for your first, at the same time I am hoping for yet another.

"The last six months, by far the most strenuous of my life, have left me rather tired and weary. So it is that for the second time in eight months I have had time for serious contemplation as I am spending my second spell in the surgical ward of an Army Field Hospital.

"There is very little wrong with me. I had a couple of septic toes so our Squadron Doc pushed me off for ten days rest. So it is that I have obtained this opportunity to write to you.

"My chief concern is of course, and always will be, Daisy. While it is true that of late I have found it necessary to contemplate what is going to happen today and the next day, at the same time I have subconsciously been ever striving to find the true solution to the problems of the future.

"Hamlet's 'To be or not to be' seems mild compared to my present quandary. I feel I have ignored the future long enough. Now that my mind is more or less acclimated to war, I am a little more stable and must therefore exert myself and make preparations for the future.

"The future is far distant but I realize that, not having heard from Daisy for such a long time, I must take steps now if I am to secure any happiness after the war. From her last letter, and from yours for that matter, it is obvious that neither she nor you have any true conception of what flying demands of one. To say that it is soul destroying is putting it mildly, especially so if one knows one isn't being provided with the best.

"In this latter respect, Jane, you misunderstood my bitterness toward in- dustry. Just imagine what one would feel like holding up a gangster with a water pistol and you realize how I felt when I last wrote in December.

"Even ignoring this, it is still necessary to acclimatize oneself to warfare. For unless one is lucky enough to have a reckless disposition, which I haven't, killing does not come very easily. When one is defending one's own land it is easy, but even then one has to be able to look a dead man in the face and learn and benefit from his mistakes.

"These are the reasons for my inability to write more often. When I was in the States I was too immature to realize what it all meant, and in any case you glamourise flying there which is a great mistake. Fortunately I learnt most of my lessons on my return to England, most of them the hard way, and having spent a rather soft and pampered life I suppose I was more than usually shaken, especially so last November for I saw the light in no uncertain manner.

"However so much for the past, I want to write to you of the future. As I find life in general at the moment, I cannot help but feel somewhat alarmed at what must inevitably lie ahead of me.

"I am inclined to believe that the world will be at war for another two to three years, and even then demobilization will be gradual. Also it certainly won't be all beer and skittles when it's over.

"First and foremost I can imagine myself in four years time while only thirty one, feeling more like forty five. I have realized during the last year or so, or at least have had a certain and ever increasing presentment, that while I have been reaching greater maturity I have lost what was my greatest asset as a youth, that ability to leap carelessly over every difficulty, that confidence which made me superbly sure of myself.

"I am aware also that I have lost a good deal of my conceit, which is a good thing, but with it has gone my terrific confidence. Somehow it feels as though, whereas prior to the war I felt as though I controlled my own destiny, nowadays I'm prepared to let fate run me.

"Thus it is that I wonder whether in the post war phase I should achieve enough to merit having Daisy as a wife. I cannot but help feel that my educational qualifications would not be worth the paper they're written on in the States, for after all an Englishman is really educated from the neck downwards.

"Added to this, I should take a year or two to get really acclimatised, possibly many years to become established. Money at times might be an unheard of commodity. Further I would be an outsider in a nation in which ten million men would be striving to return to civilization.

"A world wide slump is within probabilities, no jobs and food queues could easily be the order of the day.

"Do you really think, Jane, with all these probabilities it is fair to even suggest that Daisy should build up hopes for a future?

"The only logical answer seems NO.

"Maybe you will reply that no man who was really in love could logically consider his prospects of getting married. All I can then say is that I've been under such a physical strain during my training and operational flying that I'm temporarily devoid of any emotional potentialities.

"Please don't consider that because of all this I'm becoming a defeatist, partially perhaps for I must admit that because I'm not sure of myself I tend toward defeatism.

"My current mood is however the reverse, I am badly in need of a raison d'etre. This war has caused me to live aimlessly long enough, whereas before I lacked decision this is coming with maturity. I only wish I had it before, for then I would have swept Daisy right off her feet and married her there and then.

"However I didn't and now it does not seem cricket to ask her to wait. Lacking conceit and judging myself by my own standards I'm not so sure that I'm worth waiting for.

"To sum it all up in a nutshell, it seems that if I write and encourage her I'm asking her to wait for a long time without even promising her a prize."

In another letter to Jane dated July 26, 1943, Parsons wrote:

"This letter is by no means being written on the spur of the moment. In an endeavour to obtain full sincerity, I have been penciling my thoughts as the days roll by. I have been in hospital a week now so I have had plenty of time for contemplation.

"Yesterday morning they operated on my right toe, and incidentally have made a very good job of it. My dear, I thought I should be disfigured for life!!

"However to become serious again I wonder just how much more I can tell you and yet prevent you assuming that I've tended toward being theatrical. If you do think so after reading the next few pages it's just too bad.

"Also Jane, please don't confuse my present feelings with those of a penitent prostitute. Far from it for I feel I must say, somewhat glibly possibly, that this war has not shaken me morally, I've got too great a fear of disease.

"My whole trouble is that my mind is getting scarred by so many ghastly incidents. Also at times I've had the living death scared out of me. Thus I'm becoming a man of many memories. Not that I brood over them, but they do blot out some of my dreams.

"So that you will understand and therefore be in a better position to judge, I will sketch briefly a little of what has happened.

"It began over a year ago; we were a happy go lucky, fairly drunken crowd during training. We did mad things and somehow got away with it.

"In my case it was wings, wine, and song, until one day, being at the end of our training, Smithie and I really hit the high spots.

"Being the best of pals we threw discretion to the wind, in any case we had blind faith in our machine, and flew across England like madmen.

"He had a girl staying at the local pub, I thought it was his fiancée. Anyhow I entertained her that night while he flew alone and died.

"It is useless to try and conjure up words adequate enough to express the next few days. I was officer in charge of winding up his affairs. The lies I told his parents and fiancée. Where was his wallet and ring, there were a hundred such things.

"So the first and by no means the last military funeral I attended was that of my best pal and was a farce.

"Hundreds of gallons of gas had been aboard that kite and I had already seen the charred wreckage.

"For ten days I went to Cambridge—at least this was better than London—and on my return I recommenced flying with sanity.

"Of this there is little to say, save that I was often referred to in a humorous way as Widow Parsons if I became too critical of my new chauffeur.

"(I ought to mention here that it is the custom of Observers, or Navigator Bombardiers as you call us in the States, to refer to our pilots as mere drivers. Which of course is perfectly true in light or medium aircraft as it takes only one Observer to lead over a dozen aircraft. The Observer and the leading gunner are the only people who really count. Believe it or not, no man was more shaken than Major Hanna when he overheard me refer to him as just another bloody chauffeur.)

"That was a year ago, but by no means an isolated incident. Worst of all I don't have to delve in my mind for others. It's a bad thing when one's knowledge is based on dead men's mistakes.

"An Observer, especially if he is leading a squadron in formation on a day light raid leads a hell of a life. In fact the whole squadron is dependent on you profiting from other people's mistakes, and not others from yours.

"Unless you have been at an operational briefing before a mission you could never understand just what this means. Two score men stand around you while you with the leading gunner and pilot endeavour to explain what you hope will happen.

"Hope is by no means a strong enough word. I learnt to pray each day in the nose of our aircraft, not for myself but for those who followed behind.

"I doubt, since flying is so glamourised in the States, whether you can fully appreciate the tenseness of such an occasion.

"You aren't a bunch of heroes going out to defend your native land!! On occasions, especially if the ground troops are losing it's different, one does feel, to use that old expression, prepared to do or die.

"You can do this sort of thing once, twice, even a dozen times, but then you feel that the dice cannot always be loaded in your favour. You feel that in the end someone has to die.

"This is the real strain of flying, the strain that saps one's very soul. If you can understand what I am trying to express you will realize why I haven't written and why I feel as I do today.

"I had a grand time with my American squadron, we had our differences of opinion to begin with naturally, especially so since I was used to a batman and early morning tea in bed and dressing for dinner. For after all one doesn't have to look tough to be tough, also I can remember being most annoyed when I found one lined up with the men for one's food instead of having one's batman wait on one.

"In the end however we got on like a house on fire, we became all of what they said we were. We did a job and what is more always brought them back alive.

"I was sorry to leave them but after the fall of N. Africa I was transferred back to my old squadron. I don't fly much, thank God, but one must still endeavour to enlighten others and one can only do this by remembering all that has ever happened to you.

"It's a hell of a life, Jane, can you wonder that I feel tired and at times dispirited. I feel somewhat shopsoiled now, God only knows what I'll feel like after another two years of war.

"Jane, I feel I have been too verbose, however I felt it was the only means of expressing myself. To get around to the real point of this letter, today I am posting Daisy a letter admitting that I was utterly wrong and pointing out that in spite of all that I have written here I don't care how long we are forced to wait as long as we eventually get married.

"Do you think this is fair? I mean after all it may be a hell of a time. If you feel that I'm buoying her with false hopes, for God's sake say so, for though I am sensitive about the fact that it's certainly not cricket, I can take it straight from the shoulder if necessary.

"I heard from Daisy via Mother yesterday. I was sorry to hear that you and Henry have had your family down with chicken pox. That's damn hard lives. I do sincerely hope that Henry is not contemplating putting on a uniform. However irksome it may seem don't otherwise forget my lad you've now become the main pillar of the Wood family. I know you must be more than busy but what about dropping us the odd line on life in general.

"Must end now for I must finish my epistle to Daisy. Cheers for the time."

The sense of adventure and duty that pervaded the Wood family led Winifred to join the war effort as well. She shared much of Jane's strength and confidence but also possessed a great style and flair in her personal appearance. In fact, of all the Wood girls, Jane was the only one who showed a total absence of interest in fashion, even though she had started her journalism career by writing about it. Winifred had become the third family member to graduate from the University of Miami, attending school there from 1937 to 1941. When she first showed an interest in learning to fly, her mother disapproved and her father suggested she wait until she finished college. Deferring to her father's wishes, she took on a job as a German translator for the Bureau of Censorship after graduation. She got her start flying seaplanes through the Civilian Pilot Training (CPT) program, where two women were required for every ten men who signed up.

A friend of sister Daisy arranged for Winifred to get a job as a Link instructor in 1942, a program that trained would-be pilots in the earliest versions of flight simulators. The situation with pilots was desperate in 1942, as America frantically tried to play catch-up after years of military atrophy. It became apparent that the CPT program through which Winifred learned to fly would soon be unable to train any more pilots unless female instructors began taking the place of men. Every available male pilot and instructor was needed for the military.

In September 1942, some major advances took place to make use of the nation's untapped wealth of female pilots. Phoebe Omlie, one of the nation's great pioneering female pilots, got a program started in Nashville to train a select group of female pilots to be flight instructors for the military. She knew the program would be under major scrutiny, so she made the course tough. Ten hardened women graduated from the class, and any one of them could have been a combat pilot instead of an instructor. One of them was a young woman named Dorothy "Dot" Swain, whom Winifred Wood would meet the following year and form a lasting friendship with.

Jacqueline Cochran, a legendary female flyer, had been working with the Air Transport Auxiliary in England since the autumn of 1941 to recruit American female pilots to ferry military planes across Britain. Cochran pushed for the start of a program, with the help of General Hap Arnold, to engage women in the United States in more than ferrying activity. The Women's Airforce Service Pilots, or WASP, was born in early 1943. Dot Swain had originally wanted to fly for Cochran in England before joining the instructor program, and Cochran even visited the instructor facility in January 1943 to try to convince the entire group to come fly for her. Swain instead taught Navy men to fly in Portales, New Mexico, after graduating as an instructor in February, but she felt the tug of the WASP program. Many of her friends who had been employees with her at Piper Aircraft had joined the WASPs, and the lure of testing out real military aircraft rather than small trainers was hard to resist. One visit to her WASP friends in Sweetwater, Texas, was all it took. She found out they needed instructors and asked for reassignment from the Navy program, which she received in June 1943.

After gaining only about thirty to forty hours of experience flying seaplanes, Winifred Wood went down to interview for the WASP program in the spring of 1943, one of some twenty-five thousand women who applied nationwide. To her surprise, she got a telegram telling her to report in April. Unable to do so, she wired back that it was impossible, disappointed to miss out on such a great opportunity. To her further shock, they wired back that she could report the following month.

Once they completed training, the WASPs trained male pilots, towed targets, ferried Air Force planes to different bases around the country, and flew every plane that the Air Force had, from the B-29 Superfortress to the P-51 and P-47 fighters, as well as B-25s, B-17s, and other combat aircraft. Winifred Wood recalls: "I was never into whirls and turns and acrobatic flying, but I was a good instrument pilot. I loved B-25 school."

The WASPs were a shock to the male world of the US Air Force, and it took a lot of staying power to withstand the knocks that came with the territory. It wasn't too tough for most of the women. A more liberated, rowdier group of females had rarely been gathered together in America before, certainly not in the military. Like Jane Reno, the women of the WASP were never concerned with what men thought of them or with proving themselves to men. They joined up because they loved flying and they wanted to serve their country. Though the military was a much harsher awakening in regard to men trying to subjugate them than any environment Reno was to face, the WASPs were too confident to ever let male resentment affect them. Certainly it could be exasperating, as Winifred Wood discovered after graduating as a WASP and traveling across the country to Sacramento. She detailed the experiences in her book *We Were WASPs*:

"Dinner in El Paso was enlivened by a lad who sat at the next table and lectured us about planes, how they flew, what made them fly, how he had been up twice and how he had guessed maybe we had been up too because of the wings we wore.

"'What are you?' he asked. 'Radio operators or something?'

"'Not exactly,' we said. 'We are WASP's.'

"'WASP's?' he said, looking puzzled. 'I never heard of them. Are you a sort of WAC?'

"'Well, no,' volunteered Clayton. 'The WASP's are a separate organization.'

"'Oh, I know. They work on the planes and let you wear wings,' was his answer.

"What was the use? Flying was the last shining outpost of adventure, the epitome of virility to him. It wouldn't have been kind to tell him we flew."

At the Westward Ho restaurant in Phoenix, they came across a gentleman who had heard of the WASPs, and they were initially happy to find someone who understood them. That was until he asked, "Say, girls, did they ever let you go up in a plane alone?"

In Tucson, they tangled with an MP who wanted their papers, disbelieving their explanation that they were officially civilians who didn't have to carry military papers. His scorn increased when he asked why they were wearing the pink shirts and slacks of officers, and they replied that they had to arrive at the base in uniform despite not having their proper uniforms yet.

"You mean you're allowed to wear that uniform when you aren't even in the Army?"

"We're attached to the Air Corp," said Sara Ann "Sammy" Chapin through gritted teeth.

"I guess you've got your plane parked outside," laughed the MP. "Well, I never have seen your likes before and probably never will again. Women pilots! What's the Army coming to?"

The trip only got worse. In Los Angeles they faced an ass of a first lieutenant:

"'Do you girls really think you are helping this war?' he derisively asked. 'Good lord, I was at a ferry base with some of you WASP's. One of them ground-looped a 6 all over the field. Ship was a total loss.' He waved his hand magnanimously. 'Of course, if they had kept you on small stuff you probably would have done alright.'

"'But that's only one person. A lot of men have groundlooped too. We've got a pretty low fatality rate. Lower than the men.'

"'Yes, but there are a lot more men and they are flying bigger stuff.'

"'We mean in cadet training.'

"'Oh that,' he said. 'But all you do is fly straight and level. No formation work, no acrobatics, no crowded conditions.'

"'No crowded conditions?' the WASP's protested in unison. 'Listen, my friend, have you ever seen Avenger Field? No—we thought not. The men take each phase of their training at a separate field, but we flew all phases at one place. And we have yet to have a mid-air collision.'"[1]

They were fighting a losing battle. He believed the biggest plane a woman should fly was a Cub. To save him from having a heart attack, they demurred from informing him that they were all on their way to Mather Field in Sacramento to fly B-25s. As William Parsons noted, flying was glamorized in the United States, and American pilots would have been shocked to be treated like pilots in the RAF—"another bloody chauffeur." Former WASP Kaddy Landry Steele agreed: "Absolutely! It was glamorized, it was treated as so macho. Men couldn't get over women being allowed to do it."

The last letter Jane and Henry Reno got from Bill Parsons, during the mop-up of Italy in the latter half of 1944, suggested that he had reconciled himself to life without Daisy. Although the WASPs regretted that they couldn't have played a greater part in the war effort, Parsons suggested that he wouldn't have wished his war experiences on anyone. Like many combat veterans, he was troubled by his desire for someone to understand what he was going through, while viewing that understanding as such a tragic loss of innocence that he was reticent to inflict it on his friends:

"It is one of those hot and sultry days when the only thing is to get in a swimming pool and stay put, instead, however, I regret to say that I am penned up in a stuffy office trailer where I am due to be Duty Officer for the next 24 hours. As I haven't written to you both since heaven knows when I will endeavour to jot down a few memories to let you know how things have been going in this part of the globe. The most amazing thing to my mind seems to be that in spite of some two years of active flying I am still going around more or less whole and moderately sane, however that is beside the point I suppose. At the moment of writing, I am grounded on completion of my tour of operational duties, and am waiting transfer to a staff job in the Middle East. Being single I still have two more years to serve overseas before I'm due for the Boat Home for the odd spot of leave, and I must say that if the next two are as long as the first two, I've got one hell of a long time to wait. In a way, though one gets reconciled to service life [after] a time, after all while the war drags on it's just as well to be over seas, for it would be impossible to settle down to a sane existence until the whole shooting match is over. This war is a bloody nuisance, for apart from the odd few that get bumped off it does seem to be wrecking most people's lives. One learns a lot when one censors the men's letters, the more I read the dimmer is my view of women in general, the modern marriage just doesn't stand the strain of war when it entails long separation.

"I wonder if you can really appreciate just what war is really like. To get through as a member of a combat crew, one has either to kid oneself that you are one of the lucky ones, or else one goes to the other extreme and by using a little logic realise that in the end one is bound to buy it, and therefore endeavors to reconcile oneself to the fact. I have been weighing things up during my ample spare time of late and I find it more than interesting to remember some of the many psychological phases through which I have passed during the last two years. I can't think for the life or me, why I should hold forth at such length in a letter to you both except that by so doing you would understand why I haven't written you a really decent letter since I left you. My last two letters, the only two for that matter, were written when I was recovering from various spells in hospital. These were the only times that I have ever felt relaxed enough to turn to writing. At all other times one is too screwed up with flying to be at all logical and coherent in one's letters.

"Of late I have had the opportunity of finding out for myself that in the past Travel Agencies have been putting over one hell of a bum story about the beauties of Italy. I've knocked around through most of what we have got so far and it's more than disappointing. The country stinks, the Italians are a bug ridden diseased race with a much lower standard of living than existed in the real Arab villages, added to which they have no sense of decent relations among themselves. They really are the bottom.

"The time is now 9, and having had a most excellent meal plus the odd few drinks while my deputy stood in, I will now to the best of my ability, endeavour to continue without resorting to any form of British humour, for since Daisy seldom if ever understands my sense of humour, you may possibly be the same. In passing, I might say that it is surprising how little our two countries realise about each other, it couldn't be more annoying at times, still that's another story. Returning to Italy, it is beginning to pay dearly for its alliance with Germany. In a quiet sort of way the average British Tommy is getting his own back for the part the Italians took in the bombing of London and elsewhere. While army regulations prevent us from looting, they still allow us to accept presents from a conquered people, and in this respect, I have found the Italians most generous. At least half of the total camp equipment has been donated at some time or other by the local inhabitants. To the average American, this is most undemocratic, but then they do not know what it is like to have had their homes bombed.

"War, is war after all, and it is impossible to soft peddle at all. To me, it is amazing to think that people who fight expected to be treated as human beings when they are captured. I couldn't laugh more when I hear that view expressed, after all war isn't cricket, though there seem to be bags of people who think so. When I look back on those terrific days which I was so fortunate to spend with you in Miami, I invariably end up by thinking of my class mates, and at least I can be thankful of one thing, they too had a good time.

"You must excuse the many breaks in the trends of my thoughts, but every now and again the phones ring and I have to spend the odd half an hour attending to odds and ends. At the moment the war is going well, there is a real blood lust on, prisoners are few and far between, the Hun hasn't the guts of the Japs. Churchill's remark of a few days back, "We want them to stand and fight, our intention is to hold and annihilate" is the stuff to give the troops. This kind of fighting might not shake the Japs, but the average Gerry isn't so keen to die for the old fatherland. I've only flown once with a real lust up myself, though it was over a year ago I still have very vivid recollections of the occasion; I was somewhat precariously seated over a field trench latrine, some half an hour before I was due to take off when a bomb fell fairly near. To be caught with one's pants down is a rather shaking experience, I got cut and bruised in my fall, but it was not until hours afterwards when I had repaid in no mean measure the indignity which I had suffered, that I realised that I had pulled on my pants without any of the usual precautions.

"I've had a hell of a lot more than my share of luck, for I've had a very eventful flying career, and in addition while on the ground I have done a Billy Mitchell on more than one occasion and been involved in some most heated arguments with ranking officers. You can't fight a war with systems and paper and I really got myself in a jam prior to Sicily when I stuck to my guns and told a high ranking officer the truth by describing a trip which he had organised as a fucking shambles. His chest swelled so much that he nearly burst his medal ribbons.

"Apart from these incidents, I have had some most amusing times. As navigation officer, one of my duties has been to assist in the movement of the squadron when in transit from one field to another, and to map out the camp on arrival. This has always provided a welcome change from the daily sweat. The French in N. Africa did not impress me very much, their indifference, not having been under German rule, got my goat a bit; on the other hand, I took a very good view of the Arabs in the farming areas. On one memorable occasion, I landed in the desert well away from all trace of civilisation, and was received by the local inhabitants, who came in hordes on horseback and camel, as a demi-god. One of the priests, or village headman got down on his knees in front of the plane and called to Allah to get rid of us or something. This was the first time that I ever saw any of the Arab girls, and a really smashing girl came up on a white horse. Language difficulties unfortunately prevented any form of conversation, also she was provided with a suitable escort, so we contented ourselves by making signs.

"Memories of Africa call to mind meeting Capt Richenbacher [Rickenbacker], to my mind he was one of the few men who really understood what flying was like. I listened to one of his pep talks which was really grand for he was so obviously a real flier. None of us could understand why he was ignored when he got back in the States. In those days one was often addressed by celebrities and we had a grand talk from Churchill and Anthony Eden, plus the review by the King when we waited for some two hours under a boiling sun cursing him under our breath. The cheers which greeted his arrival were more or less an expression of relief than anything else.

"Sicily was the bottom, I haven't a memory of that stinking hole. We lived on nothing but bully or almost as bad American C rations. I believe that we once went for over a fortnight with nothing else but the same tin of C ration three times a day. The water was heavily chlorinated and by no means plentiful, while the whisky ration got sunk. The flies and mosquitoes were everywhere in hordes, then to cap it all I ended up in hospital for another operation on my foot, my third operation in eight months. I've had Sicily in a big way.

"Well so much for the past. What worries me most is the future. Quite candidly I hope to Heaven I don't end up in Burma fighting the Japs for I've just about had enough of this war. It's not that I'm getting nervous in my old age, for I couldn't care less whether I get bumped off or not, it's just that I've had my fill of discomfort and am quite content to sit back and let some one else do a bit for a change. In any case I feel that I have already killed more than my share of the human race.

"I'm afraid this has turned out to be a most disjointed letter, the many interruptions have distracted my thoughts. I'm sending these odd jottings in the hope that they might amuse you both and may cause you to appreciate an airman's moods.

"I do hope you two are not having too much trouble with your growing family. Really you do go in for things in a big way, I would have thought you had enough on your hands with four bouncing children without adding to your troubles with a miniature farm as a sideline. Give my love to Janet, and please remember me to the Wood family."

When the WASPs were disbanded and sent home, many of them were at loose ends. They loved flying with a pure passion that surpassed that of most of their male counterparts, and they didn't want to stop. Suggestions were traded about becoming bush pilots in South America and Alaska, or anywhere they could get paid to fly. The sheer variety of aircraft they had flown made them better pilots than most men, who in the military learned to fly only the type of plane they were destined to use in combat. Many of the women didn't have anything tying them down and wanted to stick together for a while longer.

Winifred Wood came home to live with her mother in Coral Gables, and other WASPs followed not far behind. Doris Gee, Mildred Caldwell, and Dot Swain all came to live in Miami, and Kaddy Landry and Caro Bayley ended up there along with Lela Loudder. Landry and Bayley were delivering a plane from Cleveland to a WASP in El Paso who had gotten married, when weather prohibited them from crossing the Appalachians. They flew down the East Coast and visited a WASP in North Carolina, hoping for a break in the storm. When the mountains remained socked in, they hopped down to Savannah to visit another friend. Still, the severe weather kept up.

Bayley suggested they visit Winifred and the other gals in Miami. Landry balked, pointing out that all their detouring to that point had been more or less on the way, and that Miami was considerably out of the way. But what else were they going to do? They knew their friend in El Paso was in no hurry to receive the plane, so Landry reluctantly agreed.

"Also, I was damn curious," Landry recalled. "All Winifred ever did was talk about her sisters, how wonderful they were, what a great family she had. I thought, I want to see this family."

Landry was not disappointed. Upon meeting Winifred's big sister Jane, with her sardonic husband and four little children, Landry recognized another woman of substance. She was also delighted to find that the other Wood women were wilder than Winifred, who had most inherited her mother's sense of decorum.

"Jane had a friend down on Key Largo who had a house they were letting us use for the weekend," Landry remembered. "We were stocking up on boxes of liquor, because we were planning to have a great time and we did a lot of drinking then. We had marvelous parties, everybody would get drunk and fall down. There were going to be some Air Force boys down there, too, from a nearby base. Winnie looked at our supplies aghast and said, 'You can't bring all that. My sister Dolly is coming.' Well, I thought, 'Gee, Winnie, is she an even bigger prude than you?'"

The trip was the beginning of a close friendship between Landry and Dolly Wood Denslow.

"She had the greatest sense of humor of all the Wood girls," said Landry. "She could keep you laughing and laughing. Jane and her weren't that close, not nearly so much as Jane and Winnie, but Jane always did respect how bright Dolly was."

After Landry and Bayley arrived in Miami, the WASPs began looking for a house together. Jane Reno took them over to her friend Mrs. Day's house—the blind woman whose welfare Amelia Earhart had been interested in—to see about renting it. The house was dark. Landry recalled that it seemed like no one was home.

"Mrs. Day?" Reno called out.

A voice replied from the darkness.

"I'm in here reading, Jane."

Landry thought it a thoroughly absurd statement to make under the circumstances, but there was Mrs. Day in the unlit room, fingering a text in braille.

The pilots all moved in, and the house at 3802 Little Avenue in Coconut Grove became known as the WASP Nest. Landry, the hardest drinker and the toughest talker, was outranked in seniority only by Dot Swain, the softest talker and most gentle-mannered of the group. Though Landry professed to have no use for children and "couldn't see the sense in anyone wanting to have them," the Reno children adored her anyway. If being raised by a mother like Jane wasn't enough to breed girls who wouldn't take no for an answer, the presence of the WASPs in their formative years clinched the deal. In a speech forty-eight years later, Janet Reno recalled the impact they had on her life:

"I was seven years old when the WASP's were disbanded and my Aunt Winnie came home from the war. And shortly thereafter, some other WASP's came to Miami and they became the part and parcel of our lives. We owned them. I owned Dot Swain, Bobby owned Doris Gee, Marky and Maggy had a fight between Lela Loudder and Caro Bayley and I think Marky got Lela and Maggy got Caro.

"I can still see Aunt Winnie coming home in the blue uniform. She was a heroine to me. And then Dot came down and she was Miss Ophelia Jones in the air show. She put on a funny hat and old lady stocking shoes and she went out and flew this plane like she learned to fly in this plane."[1]

The routines Swain performed were meant to provide a comedy filler within the air shows. They were based on a rural schoolteacher character called Miss Ophelia, whom the announcer was supposedly teaching how to fly by directing her as she went. While the crowds roared with laughter at the wobbling, looping, stalling and other near-disastrous antics of the "novice," anyone who understood aviation realized that it took a pilot of great talent to safely simulate such erratic flying. After an unplanned stall that almost led to genuine disaster at one show, Swain finally decided not to try her luck anymore and retired the routine.[2]

In a postwar society where women were being pushed back to traditional roles, the young Janet Reno found the outlook of the WASPs to be inspiring.

"I had the impression when I talked to one of them that I wasn't going to do anything bad," Reno said. "I wasn't going do anything disrespectful. And it was not so much that I was going to get punished if I did—except maybe by Kaddy Landry, and Doris Gee would tell me what she thought of me—but more important, I didn't want to disappoint them.

"These ladies grew up in a Depression. When you took a can of tuna fish and shared it between a family of five and made it go . . . and then shared with some more people along the way . . . and you don't feel sorry for yourself, you remember those times, those extraordinary times when people shared. You went off to war to help defend a nation against one of the worst tyrants in the history of the world and you remember it with pride and vigor, and you remember the fun stories along the way, and you remember those you lost with pride and honor.

"I thought, I can do that. I can do anything I really want to do, as long as it's the right thing to do and I put my mind to it. Because those ladies went and flew planes.

Winifred Wood and fellow WASP Caro Bayley, drinking outside the Bayview Bar and Restaurant in Tavernier in the Florida Keys, mid- to late 1940s.

Kaddy Landry engaged in fierce wrestling matches with the Reno children that left them either laughing or crying. Either reaction was fine with Landry. Her professed view on welcoming babies to the world was that you should snip off their heads as soon as they came out.

While living with her mother, Winifred Wood set to writing the history of her WASP experience, and in 1945 *We Were WASPs* was published. Her sister Jane was her editor, and Reno was thrilled to be a source of guidance again to

Winifred Wood with future general Bob Brown (*center*), circa 1944.

one of her siblings. Few of them had ever paid her advice much attention, but Reno relished the big-sister role, especially in the years she had abdicated journalism in favor of raising her children. Without other outlets for her intellect, she grew restless. A new literary magazine called *Maelstrom* launched in Coral Gables in February 1945, and Jane became its feature writer on books.

The plane that Landry and Bayley had been delivering to Texas sat idle, still awaiting delivery. The young newlyweds in Texas soon moved to Puerto Rico and told Landry to keep the plane until they were restationed. It became a plane for the Miami WASPs to use—which they dubbed "Private Willis"—and remained so until a hurricane later in 1945. Hurricanes were a constant refrain in Florida life in the latter half of the 1940s. Seemingly as many hurricanes hit south Florida in those years as in the entire second half of the century.

As the hurricane approached, people scrambled to get all the aircraft of south Florida safely stored in hangars. Landry remembered the fate of the WASP aircraft:

"The plane was out at Richmond Air Base. We spent one full day ferrying airplanes in there, they had 475 planes crowded in, because there was nowhere else for them. All the planes from Boca Chica, from Homestead Air Force Base, civilian planes . . . what they did, the single engine military airplanes they stood up on their nose, and the civilian planes in underneath them. The problem was they didn't drain any of the gas tanks, and all the gas tanks leaked. There was about a foot and a half of gas in the hangar. When the hurricane tore the roof apart, metal came crashing down and sparking and the whole place went up. My God, I've never seen anything like it, going out there afterward, it was just one big heap of ash."

Working on her sister's book and at the fledgling literary magazine *Maelstrom* rekindled Reno's desire to write again. In the postwar environment, however, there were precious few opportunities for women to do any kind of newspaper work outside the women's section. As the WASPs found themselves at loose ends, liberated by the opportunities they had gotten during the war, so too did many women journalists who had gained valuable newsroom experience while the men were away. Opportunities quickly disappeared when the men came home. In fact, there was a social overcompensation to cater to the perceived needs of men that negated much of the progress of the past two decades. Women were largely banished to traditional gender roles in the home and workplace for at least another decade to come.

Miami writer and historian Helen Muir, a friend of Jane Reno, was a women's section editor at the *Miami Daily News* during the war. Muir hired Dorothy Jurney as an assistant, who went on to help transform "women's journalism" into a more substantive medium. Jurney worked at the *News* very briefly before moving to Washington and getting a city editor job at the *Washington News*, available only because of the shortage of qualified men. She gained two years of valuable experience doing news there before her editor, John O'Rourke, told her he needed her to make way for a man returning from India who had never been more than a cub reporter in the sports section. Not only that, he asked her to teach him the job as city editor.

"Dorothy, you know, I would like to make you city editor," said O'Rourke, "but I just don't think it would work. You know why?"

"Yes, I'm a woman," replied Jurney.

"That's it."[3]

When her husband got a job in Florida, Jurney went back to work for the

*Miami Daily News* in 1946. She was rehired by Hoke Welch, who was the managing editor, and Jurney told him, "Hoke, you know, I've been working for two years in the newsroom of the *Washington D.C. News* and that experience was very important to me and I would like to continue in the newsroom."

Welch had an opening in the women's department, and Jurney said, "Well, if an opening comes in the newsroom, I would like to be transferred."

She didn't like the head of the women's department, and so she eventually went to Welch and reminded him of her desire to work in the newsroom. Welch told her he would see what he could do. Later that day he called her in: "Dorothy, there isn't anything I can do about it. I've talked to Dan Mahoney."[4]

Mahoney was the publisher of the paper, and his word was final. He was an unrepentant chauvinist who didn't believe that women could be taken seriously in an official capacity. Jane Reno's most memorable vision of Mahoney was meeting him in the elevator once, and Mahoney, chortling with pride about the latest young blond bimbo on his arm, said: "Ain't she a pistol, Reno? Ain't she a pistol?"

Seeing no satisfactory future at the *News*, Jurney moved over to the *Miami Herald* in 1949, where she took over the women's section. Jane Reno started writing for the *News* again herself in 1946 but managed, through a gradual backdoor approach, to navigate herself into a position of indispensable importance at the paper. Through her desire to write nothing more than the occasional *Florida Living* freelance article for the Sunday edition while her children were still young, she quietly began racking up article credits. So quietly, in fact, that almost no one at the paper was aware of her existence. From 1946 to 1951, she didn't write a single article under her own name. Don Reynolds seemed to be her earliest alias, soon to be followed by Richard Wallace as she became more prolific. She wasn't officially on the staff so not on Dan Mahoney's radar. Howard Van Smith, whom she knew as "Howie," became the Sunday editor at the *Miami Daily News* in 1945 and a good friend in the coming years. Reno's daughter Maggy remembered Smith being a guest at their house in the late 1940s and assumed that her mother worked out the plan with Smith to write under male identities to get stories published.

When the children were between the ages of five and nine, the Reno family began adventuring into the wilderness more regularly. They almost always ended up stuck in the mud, remembers Maggy Reno Hurchalla, or with everyone sopping wet, or both. The first memorable outing for the children was a trip down to Flamingo in 1947. Everglades National Park had not yet come officially into being, and the road was nothing but marl. Between episodes of getting the car unstuck, Jane and Henry showed the children how to catch a raccoon.

Later that year the family borrowed a horse van, put bunk beds in it, and spent three weeks discovering Florida. The horse van belonged to Eddie Padgett, a notorious gambling boss who had run the Miami Syndicate along with Merle Yarborough, Bill Bartlett, and Ace Deuce Solomon. Their organization had muscled out the Depression-era gamblers, controlling the mainland side of the action while the larger S&G syndicate handled all the gambling on Miami Beach. The presence of the Army on Miami Beach during the war put the S&G operation temporarily out of business, and as gambling took hold again after the war, competition increased from out-of-town gangs like Murder, Inc., and the Purple Gang of Detroit. Eddie Padgett found himself muscled out of the action in Miami and became one of Henry Reno's sources for the gambling exposés that Reno was working on at the *Miami Herald*.

"There was a brief consideration as to the ethics of borrowing the van from Eddie," daughter Maggy recalls, "but Mother found the idea so delightfully ludicrous that they didn't give it a second thought."

Their trusty old Jeep was the workhorse that carried them through most of their explorations, all six of them and their camping gear jammed into it for long trips. On a trip to the Smokies, they stayed in a hundred-year-old log cabin with a cookhouse that a hungry bear kept ransacking. Eight years after the Smokies trip, Jane Reno wrote a playfully ridiculous article with a great deal of tongue-in-cheek protesting of the introduction of black bears to Everglades National Park. She quoted the experience of a mythical Miami matron who was, in fact, herself. By the end of the piece, it became clear she'd been reading a great deal of Walt Kelly's *Pogo* and had taken her fancy to full flight:

"As this matron tells her story, she proves that park officials may really have to decide between the safety of people and the safety of bears in a few years. The woman must be nameless in print because she is a fugitive from the Smoky Mountains National Park service. 'Bears ruined what should have been a wonderful vacation for my family in the Smoky Mountains National Park a few years ago. We were there in a stout cabin in the woods for two weeks. I spent half the nights sitting up to drive away a bear. In the end, I shot that bear, which is very much against the law. Let me tell you, and see if that law-breaking should hurt my conscience,' she begins her story.

"The fourth night of their vacation, a bear discovered their food supply in the kitchen of the cabin. He yanked open the plank door of the kitchen, went in and plundered $10 worth of food. He mixed eggs, oatmeal, and honey together into one pool on the floor. He mangled the bacon and spilled the milk. He turned over a kerosene can in all this, and stirred the mess with a steak and few ears of corn. The sight was enough to break a housewife's heart. He didn't go out the door, but went out the window, breaking it in his passage.

"These bewildered Miami vacationists went down in the valley and bought a lock for the door, and rabbit wire for the windows. The next night, the bear wrenched the hasp off the door, walked in again and made a like mess. Cost, another $10 worth of food. They cut a stout sapling to bar the door and spoke to a ranger about their bear problem. The ranger looked sympathetic and told them to beat on a dishpan to drive the bear away. This worked for two nights. They would hear the bear attacking the kitchen, turn on their flashlight, and beat on the dishpan. It was a big black bear.

"On the third night they dozed off. That night the bear ripped off the rabbit wire over a window and went in that way, overturning and breaking the stove. It took an hour's scrubbing to clean the floor after that entrance, and another $10 worth of food was ruined.

"The next day they hauled up pine planks and nailed bars on windows. The bear came that night and ripped tar paper off the roof, while they beat on the dishpan. Our Miami matron, frayed with lack of sleep and almost at the end of the family vacation money, went down the mountain and asked a park resident, a woman, what to do.

"'Shoot the bear, honey!' said the mountain woman promptly.

"'But I haven't got a gun! It's against the law to have a gun in the park!'

"'I'll loan you my husband's gun,' replied the mountain woman.

"'Shoot to scare him?'

"'Shoot to kill him!' was the succinct mountain answer.

"That night, the family popped out of bed when they heard the ripping of boards. Somebody flipped the flashlight toward the kitchen, to see the bear outside methodically tearing planks off the wall. The Miami matron grabbed the gun, one of the family held the flashlight behind her, and she fired once.

"'That bear gave a moan like a big, old man dying, and dropped right there. I went inside and locked the door and began to shake and cry.'

"The one charge of No.2 shot had hit the bear just below his shoulder, right in the heart, they found the next day. The pattern of the shot was the size of a dinner plate. The bear weighed about 250 lbs.

"'It took the whole family to haul him and throw him over into a little ravine. He was a moth-eaten bear, with ticks. But it was afterward, when I heard tales of what a wounded bear can do, that I really shook.'

"The Miami matron shows no compunction about her law-breaking. 'We heard stories,' she said, 'of the injury or death of tourists in the park. Tourists feed the bears in spite of warning signs. Every year some begging bear comes to a brave tourist who stands his ground. Result—one less tourist. . . . Tell a ranger of bear troubles and he gives you a shifty-eyed, worried, non-committal look. That's all he can do, except warn you not to harm the bears.'

"'Fool around with a bear like that for a few days,' she concludes, 'and you'll realize why they speak of the "Russian bear." If Russia is half as thick, remorseless, strong, and cruel as the bears, I just shiver. It's not like they had a resident bear problem in the Everglades park. No, they had to go plant four of them on Cape Sable! Why did they want to put anything so like a Russian right at Miami's backdoor?' wails this unrepentant bear-hater."[5]

If the lifestyle at Sunnyside in Jane Reno's youth had been an anachronism, so too was the environment in which her children were raised at their South Eleventh Street house in South Miami. This part of the city was still lightly developed, with scarcely any traffic. The family had a buggy that they hooked up to Tony the Pony and used it to travel around on short trips that didn't justify the use of a car. Wartime rationing of gasoline had been the original impetus, but even after the war the children loved to travel in the Tony-powered buggy. One of their favorite destinations was the wading beach in Matheson Hammock Park, on the shores of Biscayne Bay.

"We came down Red Road, and across to Old Cutler," said Mark Reno. "A little before the beach there was a rickety wooden bridge across the canal, and Tony would stop at the foot of it without fail. Every time you got to the bridge, you had to get out and lead him across."

Tony had been a Christmas present to Janet Reno in 1945. She came running in from the yard on Christmas morning to announce her delight and

Bob and Mark Reno on Tony the Pony at the 111 South Eleventh Street house in South Miami, with Jane Reno standing next to them (nearly unrecognizable wearing her hair the longest she ever did in her life) and Henry Reno in background, circa 1945.

showed hardly the least bit of perturbation that all she had to show for her present was manure.

"Guess what!" she yelled. "Santa Claus brought me a pony. He ran away, but he left his droppings in the front yard, so let's go look for him."

After a mad chase across what seemed to the children like the entire southern half of Dade County, they finally caught up with the blue-eyed pinto pony.

"He made good time," said Maggy Hurchalla. "He kept running from field to field. We asked people if they had seen them, and that was how we followed him. One tomato farmer grumbled, 'Yeah, I saw the blankety-blank-blank, he tore up all of my tomatoes.'"

In 1947, the family moved farther south and bought twenty-one acres on North Kendall Drive for five hundred dollars per acre. They wanted more goats and another cow, and needed more space. They lived in a small yellow house at the front of the property, in an area that was far out in the country. Kaddy Landry remembered that friends and family thought they had gone mad moving "so far out into the boonies." There was nothing between the Reno family and the Everglades but a barren landscape of scrub and pine, and a lot of limestone.

The property housed a veritable menagerie. Peacocks, squirrels, goats, chickens, cows, dogs, and ponies had a home there, and the children brought home an endless procession of pets for temporary and sometimes long-term stays. Although she enjoyed the wealth of animals, Jane Reno could never accept the ubiquitous mice. The family dislike of cats exacerbated the problem, because the combined skills of the indigo snake and their dog Liza Jane couldn't keep up. One night Jane shook Henry awake to tell him a mouse had run across the bottom of the bed.

"You gotta hand it to 'em!" he said and went promptly back to sleep.

Wood rats were also common. Henry Reno described them in a letter to Jane while she was visiting her pregnant sister Daisy in New York: "The rats are having a Roman holiday in the house and Liza has traced one into the piano. I wake up in the middle of the night with Liza running the scale in pursuit of the musical rat. She pokes her head under the top cover, sniffs ferociously but vainly and lets her head go and the cover comes down with a bang."

Before Jane Reno began getting her feet wet in journalism again, her husband's star was already shining brightly with more than twenty years under his belt at the *Miami Herald*. In 1951, the *Miami Herald* won a public service Pulitzer Prize for their series of articles dating back to 1947 on the wide-open gambling of Miami. The *Herald* credited the award to Henry Reno and Wilson "Red" McGee, the primary authors of the articles. Although the stories seemed to do little to change the situation at the time, by the time of the Pulitzer Prize the city had attracted the attention of powerful figures in the nation. Senator Estes Kefauver came to town in 1950 to hold hearings and expose the corruption. Jane Reno later wrote of the era: "Police departments and the sheriff's office were riddled with corruption. What were the good people of Dade and Broward doing all this time? They were sitting with their eyes squinched as tight shut as they could squinch them. Both Miami newspapers exposed the situation, describing how and where illegal gambling was operating. The gamblers laughed and called the stories good advertising." In 1951, the Graduate School of Journalism at Columbia University wrote to Henry Reno asking him if he could share some of his methods and experiences. He replied:

"On one occasion I visited the plush Club 66 for dinner and the operators, who had been the butts of many of my exposés, invited me into the gambling room. To Mrs. Reno and myself they explained in great detail the operation, particularly as to the profit end. It was an amiable meeting and one of the operators confided in me that when the club first opened and *The Herald* printed every detail of the operation, they were worried as to whether they would ever get off the nut, which incidentally was a cool $250,000. He said later they quit worrying and considered the *Herald* stories good advertising. 'Everybody could read on your front page when we were open and they came in droves.'"

Though their journalistic paths rarely crossed, Henry was always generous with his knowledge, even if it meant his wife beating him to a story. The favors weren't limited strictly to Henry's deep understanding of the Miami underworld. One of Jane's most compelling stories, "Hurricane," was based on an account of the Labor Day storm of 1935 that Henry first wrote, as related to him by Captain Edney Parker. She described their relationship by saying: "He taught me what I know about newspaper reporting. We work on competing newspapers, but we don't compete. I do background articles, and stay off the crime beat usually."

That Henry Reno was a quietly formidable reporter was beyond question. The complex moral and journalistic issues the crusading crime reporter faced were extensive, and Henry Reno managed to balance them well. Taking on gambling in a town where the police were assumed to be in the gamblers' pockets was no easy task. Reno wrote of his work that led to the Pulitzer:

"The early stories, run once a week and sometimes oftener, told factually as possible of places operating and men behind them. I took full advantage of factional strifes and ambitions within the various police departments; feuds between various law enforcement agencies and above all, of the inevitable feuds between rival members of the gambling fraternity. All of this, in a sense, was playing both ends against the middle. In this system there is the danger of being used or of becoming the whip of one faction against another. But I overcome this to some extent by striving for accuracy and getting around to exposing all of them one time or another.

"For example: One of my early sources of information was a police official who was out as the head of the police vice squad and who was striving to regain the power that went with the post. He was delighted to use me as a whip for all the gamblers operating, of which I was entirely aware. His information was entirely accurate, however, and he was in position to get facts which I could not have gotten. The net result to the *Herald* and to the public was that the gamblers did get whipped.

"When this police official gained his goal, there were other dissatisfied personnel to take his place as informers. As a matter of fact, the further we went along, the more I came to depend upon certain members of the gambling fraternity for much information.

"This was possible because of feuds between the gamblers, and while this meant being partial to one element at times to expose another, this partiality never weighed heavily, nor consistently. Many of these contacts were made possible by the inroads of outside gamblers into the Miami scene, which up to that time had been virtually closed to outsiders. One big factor in one's favor in this kind of reporting, is that it is virtually impossible to libel a known gambler and in all the scores of stories I wrote, only one threatened libel resulted."

The police official to whom Henry Reno referred was Lieutenant Huttoe, whose falls and rises in grace within the police were legendary within the force and within the gambling fraternity. A decade earlier, in 1939, Henry Reno had already written of Huttoe—"whose ups and downs as the head of Miami's police vice squad almost parallels the classic example of Mayor E. G. Sewell as in 'in again, out again, gone again, Finnigan.' And because Huttoe has previously staged comebacks in the face of what seemed to be the impossible, Miami's vice front with its hundreds of bookies, gamblers, numbers agents, and women, is wondering whether the little man is down this time for the count of 10."[1]

Clearly, at that juncture, Huttoe wasn't. He regained his position as head of the vice squad yet again and was forced out one more time in 1947, whereupon he became a source for Reno while filing suit against the city to reclaim his job. Although Reno wasn't averse to Huttoe regaining his job, he personally thought Huttoe was a disaster. There were almost no "good guys" among Miami public servants, Reno had come to learn, just a steady rotation of a lesser of two evils. On the gambling side, Henry Reno's main source was Eddie Padgett, whose gambling syndicate had been muscled aside by more powerful northern organized crime groups (and who loaned the Reno family the horse van for the trip around Florida in 1947).

Jane Reno had a simple formula for a happy marriage. If asked what kept Henry and her so close while raising their children, she would say, "Sex every night for eleven years straight." Their relationship shifted when the intimacy abruptly stopped. No reason was given, but Henry began to spend every night out in bars, and his drinking increased substantially. The marriage was strained as Jane adjusted unhappily to celibacy. She responded angrily, and Henry sulked. At the same time in 1948, Henry went deaf in one ear, which contributed to his unhappiness. The affliction was one of the worst things that could happen to a reporter. A frustrated Jane went to the family doctor, John Dix. He told her that it was possible that Henry had suffered a minor stroke and become impotent, thus explaining the loss of hearing, termination of sex, increase in drinking, and sulkiness. Rumors spread among her siblings, though, that Henry was having an affair and that she had put an end to it.

One day in 1949, a strange man covered in mud walked into the driveway of the little yellow house. With his odd way of talking that Jane Reno would come to love, he announced that his swamp buggy was stuck. He introduced himself as "Sippi" Morris, and he was curious about these people who had a jeep and lived so far out on Kendall Drive. He could talk longer and faster than Reno, and he never ran out of stories. Reno described him as "a white man, small, plump, fabulous, a joker. Anybody loves Sippi because he makes them laugh."

The Reno property was as close to the Everglades as any Miamians lived at the time. Still, they knew very little of the sawgrass wilderness to the west of them. In the next few years Morris revealed the mysteries of the Everglades to Reno, who had held a distant appreciation for the "river of grass" ever since she was a schoolgirl.

Milton "Sippi" Morris was a Firestone tire salesman, and one of the most

interesting characters of the Florida wilderness. The Reno children fondly remembered him as a great storyteller who came and went randomly for decades,
his appearances always a joyous surprise. Excited cries of "It's Sippi!" would fill
the air when his Jeep rolled down the Reno driveway. During the 1930s, Morris lived near the winter residence of Al Capone on Palm Island. The legendary
gangster had a goldfish pond on his property, and Morris had a pet raccoon
that would sneak over and eat the goldfish. Until Capone headed back north
to Chicago in the spring, Morris lived in dread of the gangster linking him to
the missing fish.

On a deer-hunting trip Morris took out of season with Dade County sheriff
Jimmy Sullivan, game wardens caught the pair while Morris was dressing a
deer. Someone had to go to jail, and the sheriff wasn't going. (The crooked
Sullivan had been friendly with Henry Reno up to the point Reno's gambling
exposés began to hit him hard, but by 1951 he was making public statements
blasting Reno.) To save face for the sheriff, Morris volunteered to take the rap.
He was covered with deer blood when he sat down for a jailhouse breakfast
across the table from a murderer. Morris looked at the man and said, "They say
I killed three, but I only killed one." The murderer gave Morris his breakfast and
moved away.

It was Morris who led Jane Reno to her first award-winning story, during
one of their adventures in 1949. Reno wrote a dramatic retelling of it for her
Pall Mall *Big Story* script.

"We were lost somewhere between the Devil's Garden and the Big Cypress
Swamp, a few miles north of the Big Cypress Indian Reservation. Our two
swamp buggies pushed into a night as black as the pit, through hub-deep water,
in and out of pot-holes. All the stars were in the wrong places.

"We were headed for Sam Jones Old Town, a site of a long-gone Indian en-
campment. We had a mine detector along, and planned to do some exploratory
digging in Indian mounds. (Something happened to the mine detector bouncing around on the trip, and it wouldn't detect anything smaller than a swamp
buggy.) Sippi announced we were lost, circled around on cattle tracks that went
nowhere for half an hour, and brought us out on a deeply rutted road. It was
about 11 p.m., and along comes a truck full of Indians. I was a little more scared
than when we had been lost. Some of the Indian men got out, somebody hol-
lered, 'Look who's here, Josie! It's Sippi!' All the Indian men then piled out,

crowded round Sippi laughing and joking and slapping him on the back like a Rotarian convention. I found Seminoles like Sippi because he likes them, and because he makes them laugh.

"'What are you doing out this time of night, Josie?' Sippi asks a sturdy, elderly Seminole.

"Everybody stops grinning, their faces looked lined and grieving in the headlights. From behind the truck wheel steps a six foot white man, wearing a battered Stetson. From the truck cab steps his wife, a stocky, graying little white woman. They are introduced to us all as Mr. and Mrs. Raymond Henderson. Henderson is camp manager of the Big Cypress Reservation.

"A half-dozen Seminoles are introduced to us by Sippi. Everybody looks worried, depressed.

"'Whatsa trouble?' says Sippi.

"'Oh, Mr. Morris, if the world only knew what was going on here, people would do something about it, it's just terrible!' says Mrs. Henderson.

"It was one of the most sincere and dramatic cries out of the night I ever heard. The hairs on my arms stood on end. I knew this was my big story.

"'We're coming back from taking 21 sick babies to that hospital in Clewiston, and they're more sick back in camp. The hospital is so little, and nobody else is doing a thing, and those children are running a temperature as high as 105. It's been going on for two weeks, and I'm at the end, I don't know where to turn!'

"Says Sippi, like a magician, 'This is Mrs. Reno, of the Miami Herald, she'll write a story about it, and somebody will do something.'

"Everybody looked relieved, like they had expected as much of Sippi—that he would turn up in the night with a newspaper reporter to tell the world about their troubles. We asked Josie Billie to take us to Sam Jones Old Town where we would pitch camp that night, and promised we would come on into the reservation next morning."

Reno hadn't written for the *Miami Herald* in twelve years. Morris's pronouncement seemed so assured, however, that there was nothing else for it— she wrote a story for the *Miami Herald* as Jane Reno, one of the only times she ever used her married name as a journalist. She didn't exist as a woman yet at the *Miami Daily News*, where she was still writing freelance as Don Reynolds and Richard Wallace. Only a few months before she had written a Sunday feature on Sippi under the Richard Wallace pseudonym.

"Josie led us like a cat, through the dark two or three miles off the road, through the flooded grassland. He steered us into a black clump of palmettos and vines—a hammock. 'This Sam Jones Old Town.'

"Josie helped us get a fire going, warned us not to tramp around too much for fear of rattlers, helped pitch the two tents, and had hot dogs, apples, coffee, and graham crackers with us.

"Sippi: 'Josie and I are old friends, many's the time we been drunk together.'

"Josie, smiling fondly at Sippi: 'No drink no more, Sippi; no smoke no more. I'm a Baptist minister now.'

"After supper Sippi asked Josie to say grace. 'Seminoles,' said Sippi, 'say grace after a meal, not before.'

"We bowed our heads, and Josie's deep resonant voice rolled out, 'For God so loved the world that He gave his only begotten son that whosoever believeth on him shall not perish but shall have everlasting life.' Then he switched into the Seminole language, and in that deep rolling voice of his, Seminole is a wonderful language for prayer.

"The firelight flickered, and you could fairly feel Josie's spirit move us all.

"Afterward we talked about Sam Jones. He was a Seminole, a lieutenant of Osceola, the great Osceola who led his tribe in the war more than a hundred years ago. When Osceola was captured under a flag of truce in 1837, Sam Jones took up the leadership and retreated into the swamp.

"'Sam Jones made a camp here about ten years after the war,' Josie explained.

"'What war, Josie?' I asked.

"'The Seminole war,' said Josie matter-of-factly, like there wasn't any other. 'That happened about 1840.'

"Josie said he had been born near Jacksonville, and his mother was born in Alabama. 'White people,' he explained carefully, 'call us Seminoles. That means "outsiders." We call ourselves Mikasukis.'

"'Spend the night with us, Josie,' Sippi invited.

"'Can't do it Sippi, got to preach a sermon tomorrow morning.'

"Sippi took Josie off through the night to his chickee in the reservation some ten miles away. On the way Josie pulled Sippi deep into a tangled hammock to show him where Sam Jones was 'buried.' The Indian hero had been 'buried' on a platform, covered with brush, beside a tremendous live oak tree. That was before 64-year-old Josie had been born, but his people's memory marked that spot.

"Early Sunday morning we went on into the reservation. We saw sick babies, in a coma with high fever. They lay listless under palmetto-thatched chickees. Each child's mother sat beside the sick ones, kept flies away with palmetto fronds. There were no stoic Indians there, and the expressions were of gravest concern.

"Mr. and Mrs. Henderson live in a small wooden cottage. That cottage had the only pump on the whole reservation, with its tens of thousands of acres. They are good people, and the Indians like them. Little groups of chickees, each belonging to separate families, are sprinkled through the swamp, several miles apart. Mrs. Henderson was frantic, and the Indian men and women were deeply concerned. These Seminoles have a reputation among everybody who knows them of being devoted to their children. They treat them with an obvious deep affection and composure, take them everywhere with them—the fathers have the same loving devotion as the mothers.

"We did a quick check-through of most of the families on the reservation. We drove way in, through the property, until water was over the floor-boards of the Jeep.

"'This is getting to be air-boat country,' Sippi said when we turned back.

"We tore back north up the rutted track that was then the road to the reservation, to the small sugar-cane raising town of Clewiston. There we found a tiny hospital in an old frame residence full of sick babies and their concerned and grieving mothers.

"The nurse on duty was in high praise of her patients. 'They are fine people. It is hard on them. They have no money. We haven't enough food for the mothers, but we need them to stay here and help with the sick children. The men drive 75 miles back and forth to the reservation each day, bringing pots of sofkee for the mothers who are staying here to eat. They sleep on the floor. There are not enough beds to go around.'

"We tore back down the road to Miami. The next morning the story of sick children was on page one of the Miami Herald, and it stayed there for several days. Money, food, blankets, and clothing came in. The people of Miami came through right generously all that fall with money clothing, and food. Sippi and I took two jeep loads of stuff in, most important of which was probably pumps.

"We helped them over a rough spot, a little, I think. Courageous, dignified, even gay among their friends—their qualities have moved me mightily. I know what it is to camp in the night, among the mosquitoes. Josie Billie's grandmother was born in the same Southern highlands that my grandmother had been born in. I wondered if my people could have lived if we had been driven south into that swamp a hundred years ago, without mosquito nets. I wondered if I would have had good manners and good humor and a tremendous faith in the Son of God if I had been born in a chickee beside the swamp pools."

A few years later, in 1953, the *Big Story* radio and television series aired Reno's story of the Seminole sicknesses. Her role was played by radio presenter Lucille Wall, who a decade later began a thirteen-year stint on the television soap opera *General Hospital*. The *Big Story* was sponsored by Pall Mall cigarettes to recognize the best journalism in the nation, offering a cash prize of five hundred dollars as well as national exposure. Though Reno welcomed the money, she was leery of how the Seminoles would be portrayed in the dramatic presentation.

"Be careful what you say about Seminoles, if you can use my *Big Story*," wrote Reno to the show's producers:

"Anthropologists, hunters—whoever knows them at all well—are all impressed with their honesty. It is an honesty about statements of fact, an awareness of the importance of being scrupulously accurate. Every now and then local newspapers use some outlandish story on Seminoles, and some of them come boiling into town to say 'White man *locksie ojus*,' which means, 'White man lie very much.'

"It is hurting my conscience somewhat to entrust my friendship with the Seminoles to a script writer—*National Geographic* did a 'factual' story on the Seminoles about 1935, and for 15 years thereafter the Indians wouldn't speak to anyone from *National Geographic*."

The trust of the Seminoles was notoriously difficult to obtain. Reno was fortunate to have Sippi Morris as her introduction, and to be on the spot at the right moment. That got her inside the *chickees*, but she had to continue earning their trust throughout the next decade. One of the greatest lessons the extroverted Reno gained from her friendship with the Seminoles was that there was a time for humility and an art to listening.

The little yellow house no longer seemed large enough for the Reno family, and Jane decided to design her ideal home. She wanted space to accommodate the whole family and visitors, and a wide, open design fronted by a screened porch half the size of the entire house. Life was not meant to be lived in closed-off rooms; the spacious porch was to become a gathering place for generations.

Jane went out one day in the summer of 1949, bought a pick at the local hardware store, and began chipping away at the limestone on the "east ten" of their property. Her husband, Henry, didn't quite know what to make of it but didn't question her plans. Very little that Jane did took Henry by surprise at that point. Still, most of their property was composed of the formidable limestone that comes to the surface at the lower end of the Everglades and throughout the southern end of Florida. If he had been a bookie instead of a crime reporter, he would have put down nearly even odds on his wife versus the limestone. The nod went to the limestone, though, because it seemed a feat worthy of John Henry to break through enough of the rock to pour a foundation.

Janet Reno remembered the day that her mother picked the children up at school and announced:

"I'm going to build a house."

"What do you know about building a house?" the children responded skeptically. They knew better than to question their mother's will, but it was fair game to question the little details like "how."

"I'm going to learn," she said simply.

Every day her husband came home from work at the *Miami Herald* to find that a little more progress had been made. "The damn woman is serious," Henry marveled. He sold enough acreage for her to be able to afford materials, content to indulge her but not sure that the time or money was there to complete the project. The architectural plans had been made up in June 1949, and it took Jane months of arduous work to break through the limestone. For fifty cents per hour, the children dug out the sand from between the rock.

Though the children's mumps, PTA meetings, and Christmas festivities slowed the work, by March 1950 the foundation was ready to pour. Reno learned the building trades as she went along. Every time she came upon an unfamiliar task, she would visit building sites to pick the brains of workers or hire someone for however long it took to learn their skills. Usually it took her no more than a day to learn the basics of a trade. In an accounts ledger, she kept track of the costs in meticulous detail. One entry noted an expense of $1.80 for nine beers for the plumber. Her son Mark recalled: "The plumber was an old drunk that H. O. [Henry] found down at the Spotlight Bar. Didn't even do the job right. We had to fix up the mess he made."

After receiving the building permit in March, Jane worked steadily throughout the rest of the year. By Christmas of 1950 she had finished much of the base of the house, including the porch, part of the chimney, the plumbing, and much of the adobe walls. Her friend Travers Ewell, an engineer with a bristling white mustache, was the owner of the Adobe Brick Company, and it was his house in the Florida Keys that she was attempting to emulate. Travers advised her on many of the structural matters of the house, and she bought her adobe from him.

When funds ran low, she would write an article for the *Florida Living* magazine in the Sunday edition of the *Miami Daily News*. The articles were, for the most part, the standard home and design features she'd started doing for the *Miami Herald* before getting married, or do-it-yourself articles born out of all the new building trades knowledge she was absorbing. Many of the articles reflected her love affair with the wild and wet places to the west of her. In the summer of 1949, she wrote a Sunday magazine article called "Timber" about the brutal work harvesting cypress trees in the Big Cypress Swamp, and, as her friendship with Sippi Morris grew, she wrote an article about him. Both were written under the pen name of Richard Wallace.

"I'd write a story and get twenty-five dollars for it," she recalled, "then I'd buy more block for the house."

After the holidays were over, she took on the house with renewed enthusiasm. By the end of January, she'd finished much of the house's wood frame, which consisted of sturdy cypress posts and tie beams. At this point, Henry said, "By damn, she really is building a house," and he took two weeks off to put up the roof beams. His eighty-five-year-old father, who had brought his young boys over from Denmark forty years earlier, helped out.

When she was done with the structure of the house, in February 1951, Reno wrote to her sister Winifred:

"Henry finally got sold on this house proposition, cashed some insurance, increased the mortgage, and we are in funds to almost complete it. All I have to do now is settle down and run it up. Copper screen, electrical conduit, plumbing fittings, flashing, and such like rare and valuable things fill our living room. Mother's garage is filled with a pump and water heater, toilet, sink, tub, and basin. We've got the stuff now, all we need is the muscle. We're making enough spare jack along as we go with extra articles for the *Weekly* and me from the *News* to get the rest of the material by the time we need it—shingles, sheathing, and windows is all we don't have. So it is clear sailing, and we think we should be in my dream house before the year is out."

Working relentlessly through the spring, Jane Reno put the roof on and had it shingled by early summer. The cedar shingles were planed to such exact specifications and nailed on to battens by her so precisely that a tarpaper and plywood base wasn't necessary. The original roof came unscathed through Hurricane Donna a decade later, and the shingles were replaced by family members in twenty-year cycles, a task passed on from generation to generation. Each time the shingles were put on the way they were done originally. Her pride and joy was the chimney, made of old, soft, orange brick. She bought the bricks for ten cents apiece from the owner of a burned-down house, picking them out of the rubble and cleaning them one at a time. Helped along by federal pamphlets on how to build a fireplace, she carefully designed it so that it would draw properly.

The house was finished in late October 1951, at a total cost of $7,217.39. In the course of constructing it, she and Henry changed the plans from a two-story to a one-story house. The money was not there for the barn-like structure with two huge porches that she had initially envisioned, and her family all came to agree that the scaling back of the house was for the better. It ended up consisting of two large bedrooms, a kitchen with a fireplace, and the large red-brick porch.

Family remained the most essential part of her life. To Reno, home was not an address but rather any place in which her extended family gathered and put down roots. Throughout her childhood, Sunnyside was as much that home as Macon, and she provided her family with a Florida equivalent to Sunnyside when she built their new house in Miami. From the rich, dark piece of mahogany driftwood that formed a mantelpiece over the fireplace, to the chimney bricks she scavenged and lovingly cleaned, to the giant cypress beams that her eighty-five-year-old Danish father-in-law helped lever into place, there was a story to be told behind almost every corner of the house.

After the family moved in when the first stage was finished, there was never a precise sense that the house was "done." The breezeway and two-room addition were added a couple of years later, and Jane and Henry committed as much money as they could to finishing bits and pieces. When the impending college costs of the children confronted them, they forgot about doing any more. A few of the interior walls were left unpaneled, as well as the ceiling in one of the bedrooms. The house maintained a rugged, frontier look, and the porch became the centerpiece of living that it was intended to be.

Henry Reno had been doing regular freelance pieces for the *American Weekly*, a New York–based magazine that paid quite well. Though Jane thought the kind of true crime and sensationalist pieces that her husband was writing were somewhat tacky, it was hard to argue with the supplemental income. It was also relatively easy work for Henry, who was a master of letting characters tell a story. The stranger-than-fiction cases he presented were often just a matter of sifting through hilarious trial testimony for the best quotes and artfully piecing them together.

Looking into a possible story on the twenty-one-year-old heir to the Pulitzer fortune, Herbert "Petey" Pulitzer, Henry found no special drama in the young man's Palm Beach life suitable for *American Weekly*.[1] Henry passed his findings along to Jane, who did a "how the rich are living now" story for the *Miami Daily News*.

Between house building and feverishly producing freelance newspaper stories, Jane Reno tried out ghostwriting. Her Sunday editor at the *Miami Daily News*, Howard Smith, asked if she wanted a ghostwriting job, saying he would get her a contract if she produced two chapters. Reno jumped at the chance and wrote to her sister Winifred in 1951 of her first meetings with the subject:

"So now I have started ghost-writing the autobiography of Dr. Sarah Sidis, who is a small, plump, 76-year-old Russian Jewish version of myself—and quite the most delightful and exciting person I have met in years. You may remember years ago much newspaper publicity on her son William James Sidis, who graduated from Harvard at 16, and was lecturing on higher mathematics at 11. Her husband was highly respected as a psychologist by William James and the brilliant school of men who flourished around James at Harvard in the 1890's. She could not speak English or read or do anything but simple addition when she was 14 years old. When she was 18 she passed entrance examination for Boston University Medical School, and graduated from there in three years. She has a beautiful daughter, now 40, who never went to any school until she was 15. All Helena ever wanted to do, her mama says, 'was ski and play football with the boys until she was 15.' Then Helena took Smith entrance exams, passed with highest honors, and went to Smith, at 15.

"I go over and listen to the old gal talk for three hours straight, and she feeds me port wine and an invention her own consisting of coffee ice cream with Pepsi-Cola poured over it. What we want to do in the book is not only to tell how all her family could learn so quickly that they were called geniuses, but also to show that such people get one hell of a lot of more fun out of life than the rest—and the kind of fun that the rest call fun, love and laughter and variety. She says they weren't geniuses, a million bright boys in this country could do the same thing her son did. And we want to do a very powerful and subtle sale on the idea that it is a good thing to do. Of course, Dr. Sidis could hardly have found anybody more in sympathy with her than me. When she says, in a manner very reminiscent of Madame Lenander at her best, 'I can do anything!' I say, 'I can do anything, too, except sing soprano.' [2]

"Howie and I think we can write a best-seller. If we don't, even if the book is never published, if I never get anything but the Pepsi-Cola invention and the talk, it will be far more fun, Winnie, than anything I have done since I started the house. Only two people have shown any sympathy with Dr. Sidis, as I describe her to them, and that is just as I have described her to you. They are Maggy and Janet. They think she must be marvelous. But most people resent her acutely from the moment they hear that about her son. Janet says confidently, 'I couldn't do what her son did, but I could do what her daughter did.' This resentment is a challenge, because I have known—and met it a little for much of my life. Dr. Sidis is very cognizant of it, but it doesn't bother her, she is so gay, and so affectionate. Nobody who knew her personally could fail to like her. So we want to change this resentment against the 'smart' into one of complete sympathy."

Unfortunately, Reno's book project with Dr. Sidis lasted no more than the first two chapters before it was abandoned. More than a decade before, the abrasive national columnist Westbrook Pegler accompanied a fellow journalist on an assignment to find what had become of the former child genius William James Sidis. Discovering that Sidis was a recluse who never talked to anyone and rarely ventured from his decaying brownstone on West Fourteenth Street in New York, Pegler and his friend were ready to climb down the rain gutter if necessary to gain access to his apartment. The landlady said that he was unlikely to talk to them and that he was out at work. She told them that when he was home he never read, didn't have a phonograph, and did nothing but sit in his apartment until he went to bed. When they came back, however, the landlady got Sidis to meet with them. Pegler described him as a "grim, almost frightening fellow, small but formidable in his somehow hateful bearing."

Sidis repeated in a robotic monotone, not moving his teeth or his lips: "You will not get a word out of me. You will not get a word out of me."

He stood there resolutely repeating this until they left. The landlady was waiting for them on the stoop and explained that Sidis had told her that he was never going to think again. He was resentful that his father had pushed so much upon him at an early age, and he vowed that he was done with thinking. His job was working an adding machine—which saved him from performing any mathematics himself—so he had perfected a thoughtless routine. The only hobby he had of any sort was collecting streetcar transfers. He had a collection of thousands of them, which he traded with other collectors. Sidis died at the age of forty-six in 1944.

When Dr. Sarah Sidis died in 1959, Jane Reno's son Bob wrote a story about Dr. Sidis and her family for the *Miami Herald*.

"She went through Boston with a brilliant record and was graduated from the medical school to become one of the first woman doctors in the U.S. Boris graduated from Harvard and entered the pioneer field of psychiatry. Together they founded the Sidis Institute for Abnormal Psychiatry at Portsmouth, NH. For Sarah, education had opened up a whole new world. Boris became world famous in the field of psychiatry. The girl who a few short years ago had been an illiterate immigrant began to move in the circle of the bluebloods in New England. President Wilson appointed Sarah to make a world tour and report on modern trends in education. The world traveling Sidises taught in the great learning centers of Europe and America. . . .

"The Sidis method of teaching, authored by Boris Sidis, had three basic parts: Love, understanding of the child to help him to avoid fear, and a willingness to help him develop his reason. Sarah and Boris saw no reason they should not push their son ahead in his studies. After all, hadn't fame and intellectual attainment opened up a whole new world for them? They thought fame and attainment would give Billy the keys to the world just as it had for them. The burden of fame began to repulse Billy from public life. Boston newspapers decided since he was a genius he must be weak and eccentric. Reporters said he had nervous breakdowns. They said that he hated dogs. (He had always had dogs as pets.)"[3]

Sadly, as Jane Reno found, there was not a great deal of sympathy for extraordinarily bright people or their children who become prodigies. History judged the Sidis parents harshly in the wake of William's "failed" adult life. Boris died in 1923, and Sarah Sidis made enough money on the stock market to move to Miami in the 1930s and live there until her death. Interest in the Sidis teaching system evaporated because of William's fate. Daughter Helena, a more modest success of the method with whom Jane Reno's daughters felt a kinship, was forgotten about entirely.

Evidence suggests that it was environment and outside forces that caused more of William's problems than his parents' ambitious teaching system. It wasn't quite Jane Reno having to fight every boy on the block when she was eleven and declared a child genius, but it was similar. He was an outspoken pacifist during World War I, and his parents arranged a teaching position for him at the Rice Institute in Houston when he was seventeen, after students at Harvard physically threatened him. He lasted only a year at Rice, feeling unsuited for teaching and frustrated by the treatment of him by students who were his seniors. He gave up on graduate mathematics and tried law at Harvard but soon gave up on that. In 1919 he was arrested at a violent May Day rally in Boston on charges of sedition and given an eighteen-month sentence. His parents kept him out of jail by putting him in a sanatorium for a year and threatening him with an insane asylum, and then taking him to California for a year. By the age of twenty-three, the damage was done. Too much unwanted attention from too many directions in his young life caused him to commit as an adult to living a nonthinking, reclusive life, a plan he stuck to until his death.

As a freelancer with no guaranteed salary, Jane Reno began producing as many articles as the *Miami Daily News* would print. Howie Smith finally gave her the green light to start writing some of the articles under her own name in early 1952, though she continued to also use Richard Wallace, John H. Reynolds, Don Reynolds, and Don Renold in place of her regular nom de plume, Jane Wood. When she wrote an article on carpentry, she employed her trusty tradesman name of Hal Hand. Many years later a friend and colleague at the *Miami News*, Howard Kleinberg, remembered that in the sports department someone named Dick Reynolds regularly got a free set of tickets from the Hialeah race track. (Kleinberg was misremembering, as the tickets were always for Don Reynolds.) It was a mystery for quite some time since there was no staffer by that name. "We could never tell who the hell was Dick Reynolds," Kleinberg said.[4]

No one ever saw Messrs. Wallace, Reynolds, or Renold in the office, so no one knew they were all the same journalist who was penning columns as Jane Wood. Sometimes the paper forgot to maintain the façade, such as in one issue of *Florida Living* where the front page of the section listed an article by Hal Hand in the contents, but when you turned to the page, the byline read Jane Wood. It wasn't unusual to open *Florida Living* and find three of six articles written by Jane Wood, Richard Wallace, and Don Reynolds.

On North Kendall Drive, the new Reno house became more of a menagerie than ever. Maggy Reno Hurchalla remembers: "Daddy would come out of the bathroom and say 'Would somebody come get this'—and you can interject pelican, otter, boa constrictor—'out of here so I can take a bath?'"

The year Jane went to Colorado with the Boy Scout troop, taking daughter Maggy with her, they brought back a chipmunk from the mountains. Upon loosing it in the house, Reno regretted the choice, as it began "eating on my precious Encyclopedia Britannica and Henry's mattress. Yesterday he fell in the shrimp soup."

To lighten the handful at home and to give her children the exposure to the world that she had had at an early age, Jane offered her thirteen-year-old daughter Janet the chance to spend a year of school in Germany. Roy Wood,

Jane's uncle, was a judge in a new Germany being reconstructed under the Marshall Plan, and the family thought it would be a good opportunity for Janet to see Europe. Unlike her mother's happy exile in Greece, Janet's trip was not a result of her becoming uncontrollable. Although they were taught to be opinionated, Jane rarely encountered in her children the discipline problems she had presented as a teenager. In part, this was due to her being a much more forceful mother.

"People always ask how Mother got us to behave," her son Bob said. "She beat us with a bridle. But we always deserved it."

When she thought the children had overstepped, she had no hesitation in taking a belt to them. Reno was feeling a deep sadness still over the change in her previously idyllic marriage, but the children's only exposure to the sadness was in explosions of anger at their misbehavior. Her daughter Maggy

Jane working on her house 1950–51. The trusty Jeep and Jane atop the ceiling beams.

remembered it lasting up to the point that she was big enough to take the belt away from her mother—the girls were six feet tall by age twelve—and then Reno never did it again. Because the new house had only two bedrooms, there were rather cramped quarters until the extension was done. Having Janet away while they built the extension made life easier.

While America was showing no effects of the war by 1952, Janet wrote letters home describing the immense rubble and devastation that still existed all over Germany. The country was a depressing place for a schoolgirl, and though Janet enjoyed the experience, she was also homesick much of the time. She wrote an article for the July 13, 1952, issue of the *Miami Herald* about her experiences, and the newspaper's editors were surprised at the perceptiveness of the fourteen-year-old's impressions:

"Of all Germany, it was Berlin that most quickened my heart, and was the most exciting city, and Berliners were the Germans who moved me to respect and admiration. You could see the terrific Russian propaganda in the Eastern sector of Berlin, and there I first in all my life felt Russia as very menacing. There I felt that Russia was afraid of us, was a frightened country grabbing everything she could out of a grab bag, and in her fright she is dangerous.

"But I could see and sense that the Berliners had stood up under the worst bombing, had gone down fighting to the last ditch, and then had held just as staunchly with the West in the days of the blockade. It was a very exciting city because of this character and pride of its people, and the drama, and the knife edge I could feel.

"The rest of West Germany didn't seem to me to have that character. I came to think they will follow just anybody—Hitler, America, Communism—anything that offers to lead. And when we pull out I think they will fall right in the arms of Communism. But most Europeans are not nearly as afraid of Communism as Americans are—they laugh at us a little over all our fears."[5]

When, a few years later, Winifred Wood was planning to spend a year in Germany teaching, her sister Jane warned her against falling for the cheap seduction of northern Europe—"the virtue of cleanliness." The distrust of this virtue explained a great deal about Reno's housekeeping habits, as well as her larger view of life. Not only did she have her doubts about people who did not obey the priorities she shared with Steinbeck, she thought it was evidence of a deep-seated fault.

A thirteen-year-old Janet Reno being greeted by her parents, Jane and Henry, upon returning from Germany in 1952.

"You will not understand," wrote Jane to Winifred, "that the clean and orderly Teutons and Scandinavians can—as many clean and orderly people do in this country—hide a basic sluttishness of spirit. The hostess pre-occupied with dishwashing misses the conversation. I, too, can remember when I try, the excrement in the gullies leading up to the Acropolis, but what I do remember is the Parthenon on top. You notice what you cultivate the habit of noticing.

The scatological German humor, a particular heavy sniggering about human functions, is the other face of their pre-occupation with cleanliness. Another disorder that the cleanliness and order of the North European races covers is a prizing of melancholy—known to more sensible and Southern races as the sulks."

Here she was expressing her disgruntlement over some of her husband's Danish characteristics. She went on to lambaste the failures of his countrymen in World War II.

"You will learn, intellectually, to walk and to march in a disciplined way from German culture. But you will never learn to fly. I do not approve of racial prejudice, but I find it entirely unnecessary for me in this lifetime to forgive the Germans for Jew-hating and Hitler—and the brave, blond Aryan Scandinavians of Denmark and Norway for being round-heeled pushovers. I find it entirely pleasant and salutary to remember my dirty, undernourished, unsanitary, talkative, undisciplined Greeks were the race of all the world—except maybe the Yugoslavians—who fought hard in the face of absolutely certain defeat for the honor of the matter. Those months when the German drive toward the Suez Canal bogged down finally in the mountains of Greece proved for this generation that our childhood concepts of honor and courage are best. But it is a terrible thing to me how our sluggish myths will ignore facts of history that do not fit. It is the habit of most Americans to respect North Europe, but have a fastidious contempt for the Mediterranean.

"I go to Athens still, Red, in beautiful dreams, and it feels like going home. There is no land whose mountains, curves, slopes, and seas ever seemed so beautiful to me."

# 12 | The Miccosukees

Throughout the 1950s, Reno became ever more involved with her Miccosukee Indian friends, gaining their trust and respect. She was one of the rare journalists who would take the time to hear what they had to say and report it accurately. She was allowed to attend their ceremonies, and she brought her children to Green Corn Dances, an important yearly gathering of the tribe for purification and rite-of-passage rituals. The lifestyle of the Miccosukees appealed immensely to her. Family was extremely important to them, and it was a matriarchal society where the women quietly ran everything. When men got married, they went to live with their wives' people. Miccosukees were proud but didn't carry a trace of conceit among them. Their history was an oral one, and as a collector of stories, Reno could listen for hours to their legends.

From her first introduction through Sippi Morris in 1949, she began learning a great deal about the Seminoles and Miccosukees. She realized how lucky she was to have been taken to the grave of Sam Jones, some ninety years after the great Miccosukee leader's death.

"Unless you had become a Baptist like Josie had," she recalled in a 1971 interview with historian Marcia Kanner, "no Indian would ever take you back to a hammock that another Indian had been buried in. Because they devoutly believe in ghosts.

"I remember around 1957 I happened to be over by Doctor's Hospital when I saw a bunch of Indians at a stoplight and someone waved and said 'Hey, Jane!' William McKinley Osceola was at Doctor's Hospital in Coral Gables for some illness, and I mean a serious illness. They cut open his chest and got his heart started again, and he lived for several years thereafter. But he said to his sons while he lay in Doctor's Hospital, 'I have ghosts.' Well, they went out to the medicine man and got some medicinal things, and they came back and pinned them on his pillows. He said, 'Thank you. The ghosts are away.'"

Louise Tiger told Reno another time: "They all believe in ghosts. The time my daddy was in the hospital and then he died and then I fainted because I was pregnant; my husband Bobby Tiger came in and said 'That old man's come back to get you. That old man's come back to get you.'"[1]

In the time she spent at the Big Cypress Reservation investigating the problems of the children's sickness, Reno met a character that fascinated her.

"He was absolutely coal black," she said, "and he didn't speak any English. He was in his eighties. And Sippi said to me, 'That's the Black Sheriff of the Seminoles.'"

Many years later she asked her friend Howard Osceola about the man.

"You remember that old black man that lived in the Big Cypress in 1950?"

"Yeah, sure," replied Osceola.

"Sippi Morris told me once he was the Black Sheriff of the Seminoles."

Osceola snorted and said:

"That's ridiculous. That sounds like Sippi! That man was a slave of my family. That was a black slave of my family, and my relative—somewhere back there—had a wife who was unfaithful to him. And the first time she was unfaithful, he cut off the tip of one ear. The next time he cut off the tip of the other ear. The next time he cut off the tip of her nose. And then he thought 'Hmph.' And so he said to this black slave of his, 'My wife's no more use to me. Look, if you will kill the man that she's been being unfaithful with, I'll give her to you as a wife.'

"And so that black man"—that was long, long ago, said Osceola—"got a shotgun, and the guy that was being unfaithful with her, he picked up a shotgun and killed him, and so she was his wife, and so he got to be a member of the tribe."

Oral history sustained Seminole culture, and Reno loved the stories that had been passed down through generations. The relations between blacks and Seminoles in the nineteenth century had been intriguing and complex, as for that matter had been the history of the Seminoles. As Josie Billie had noted, the entire grouping of Miccosukees and Muskogees had been branded with the name Seminole in the early 1800s, and it still caused confusion. The remnants of the Muskogees accepted the name over time and took up reservation life along with some Miccosukees. The rest of the Miccosukees living traditionally in the Everglades refused to accept the white man's label and were the only Indian tribe in the United States that could proudly point to the fact that they had never surrendered and never signed a treaty giving up their rightful claims to the lands of Florida. Howard Osceola explained his understanding of the meaning of the word "seminole" to Reno:

"My daddy told me that back yonder when they were chasing them all, when they were chasing all the Indians, some white soldier said to one of our fellas, one of the Miccosukees, 'Who are those Indians we see out there way away, out on the horizon? We can never catch up with them, the ones that are always running away. Who are they?'

"And our fellow said 'Seminolay!' It's a word of our language, the Miccosukee language, that means wild, a seminolay pig, a seminolay horse, wild, not fenced in, feral. It doesn't really mean run away, it means a wild hog, a wild horse—a free man!"

The origins of the word are almost as open to interpretation as the clouded history of the tribes that came to be known as Seminole. The word "seminoli" (spelled many different ways by white historians, since neither the Muskogees nor Miccosukees ever had a written language) is supposedly a Muskogee word that translated as "people of the distant fires." In turn, the Miccosukees imported the word into their own language with a different meaning. There is a theory that the word was originally a bastardization of the Spanish word *cimarron*, for maroons, or runaway slaves.

The Muskogees used their translation to describe the standoffish Miccosukees, and the latter translated it however they pleased, depending on who they were applying it to. While the Muskogees had accepted the name "Seminole" with which the white man had branded their tribe, the Miccosukees never accepted being branded with the name. Jimmie Tiger, a Miccosukee, explained it in this context to writer Peter Matthiessen when Matthiessen was researching his book *Indian Country*. Tiger translated it as a slur against the Muskogees.

"*Siminoli*—that means wild, okay," Tiger told Matthiessen. "To us, it means *scared* wild, like a rabbit. In the wars, them Seminoles run off like rabbits all the time—they was so scared, you know."[2]

The descendants of the great warrior Osceola—Howard Osceola and his many siblings—explained to Reno the relations between Miccosukees and Muskogees at the time of the Second Seminole War, when the tribes had banded together to resist the encroaching whites. Reno remembered:

"I was told by Homer or Howard that in the last Seminole wars, when in effect they had become a group working and fighting together, 'the Muskogees gave us the songs and the Miccosukees gave us the leaders.' Osceola and Coacoochee, or Wild Cat, were Miccosukee, and they were the leaders in fighting, but the Muskogees gave them the songs. And by the way, I should tell you something about leaders. Leaders are not chiefs. These men have been more democratic than you and I could ever imagine. My own theory is—I feel it in my bones, I've read it since I knew—that they taught white American people democracy. They didn't have any chiefs. They said to Osceola, 'You lead us, you fight better.' There was delegated authority."

When Osceola was forced by General Thomas Jesup to trade in seventy-four runaway slaves in exchange for the freedom of a great Seminole leader named King Philip, the general dishonored himself terribly. Though they came to him under a white flag, Jesup took them all prisoner. Coacoochee—who was the son of King Philip—escaped, but Osceola remained imprisoned. Buffalo Tiger, a descendant of Coacoochee, told Reno:

"The story we know is that Coacoochee and Osceola were captured under that flag of truce when they went in, and they all went in to that place in St. Augustine, and they went in that fort. They sang a song and they made magic, and they got the dogs quiet and they got the white soldiers asleep. And all the Indians. Coacoochee got out through those narrow little slits."

"You know how narrow they are?" Tiger added.

"Yeah," Reno replied.

"Osceola was too fat to get out."

Reno related the anecdote shortly after to Howard Osceola, suspecting that Tiger was being mischievous.

"That sounds like Buffalo!" exploded Howard irately. "That wasn't true at all! Osceola and Coacoochee made a deal that Wild Cat would get out and Osceola would stay and try to reason with the white people."

Faced with a hail of criticism throughout the nation for his dishonorable conduct, General Jesup, undaunted by this shaming, sent out more troops to fight. As his officers confronted the Seminoles farther to the south, the terrain increasingly favored the Indians. There was no way his army was going to succeed in the hostile muck of the Everglades. His officers came to him with this view, and agreeing, he wrote to the US secretary of war to suggest that the war be ended, with the Indians allowed to live in peace in the Everglades. At a camp on the Loxahatchee, he invited many Seminoles in under a truce while awaiting a response. Secretary of War Joel Poinsett replied that the war was to go on until the Indians were defeated. This was the policy of President Andrew Jackson and had been since Jackson waged the First Seminole War as an aggressive general in 1818. He hated Indians passionately and did not want to let up until every last Indian was removed from Florida. Jackson had nearly faced censure for his conduct in the First Seminole War, and against strong national sentiment to the contrary, he demanded his generals employ the same disreputable methods during the Second Seminole War.

General Jesup once again rounded up most of the Indians and their black allies and shipped 680 over to Tampa to be sent west. Of the 165 blacks, 150 had been born free in Florida and spoke only Muskogee. Since then, the Lox-ahatchee—"lie river"—has represented the most egregious event in Seminole legends in which *loxa-dot-chay*—"white man lie."

"During the years I have known the Miccosukees," Reno wrote, "I have come to realize that they have a long, strong verbal tradition, a fund of stories, a great history. It has made them excessively proud, and brave, and honorable, and free. Also, accurate reporters. These are my cherished virtues. People whose history is transmitted verbally are more outraged at the little and big decorative lies and half-lies indulged in by some writers than are people who read": "And there is the way they feel about the sunny wet wilderness in which they have hunted for a century or so—that land cannot be owned, and men should die where they are born. Thoreau could feel this way. Property owners can't. But because of this feeling, I have another wonderful window on a freedom I shall never enjoy."

After the betrayal at the Loxahatchee, General Jesup worried that his fort—the ancient Spanish fortress Castillo de San Marcos—in St. Augustine would be overrun. He ordered all the Seminoles he was holding to be shipped to a North Carolina prison. Most of the great leaders were in custody, including Osceola, Micanopy, and King Philip, and Osceola died in North Carolina, a broken man. The war dragged brutally on, and the embattled Jesup was replaced by Colonel Zachary Taylor, who achieved a temporary sort of peace by refusing to let slave owners come to Florida to claim black Seminoles. Then the Seminoles attacked again, drawing new calls for their final slaughter. By now, however, the Seminoles were becoming experts at guerrilla warfare, launching lightning raids and withdrawing back into the Everglades. Taylor resigned, and another leader came in to battle the Seminoles to a standstill in 1842. Three hundred or so were left, under the leadership of Osceola's lieutenant Sam Jones, and they were still proud and undefeated. The Everglades was their home.

In the late 1850s, their numbers were diminished even more when the United States unsuccessfully waged the Third Seminole War. Jefferson Davis was forced to admit that the Seminoles had baffled "the energetic efforts of our army to effect their subjugation and removal." Though more than one-third left voluntarily, one or two hundred remained, still led by the ancient and resolute Arpeika, aka Sam Jones. Even nearly a century after the fearless leader's death, his spirit lived on. When Josie Billie showed Jane Reno the burial site in 1949 in the place called Sam Jones Old Town, they saw the imprint of where a panther had laid down to rest the night before, right beside Arpeika's grave. The remaining Indians were mostly Miccosukees, able to adapt to the Everglades because they had always been hunters. The Everglades Indians had steadily increased in number to more than one thousand strong when Reno first met them, and she reflected on their incredible adaptability:

"I had understood that after the tragic removal to Oklahoma from Tampa—the ones that did leave, and so many died, it was a trail of tears for Seminoles as well as Cherokees—there were about three hundred that fell back down into this swamp. I think one reason that I respect and love them so is because these people came from the high, clay hills that I know well, where I was born, the Appalachian hills of Georgia and north Florida, Tallahassee, those pretty high, clay hills.

"They fall back down into this endless saw grass, that was so different from their home, and to live it all seems to me a hell. Could I have done it? Live they did, and change their way of life they did."

Congressman Joshua Giddings of Ohio, a fierce abolitionist and defender of the freedoms of runaway slaves whom the Seminoles had taken in, wrote in 1858:

"Florida was purchased; treaties with the Florida Indians were made and violated; gross frauds were perpetrated; dishonorable expedients were resorted to and another war provoked. During its protracted continuance of seven years, bribery and treachery were practiced toward the Exiles [runaway slaves being harbored by the Seminoles] and their allies, the Seminole Indians; flags of truce were violated; the pledged faith of the nation was disregarded. . . .

"Men who wielded the influence of Government for the consummation of these crimes, assiduously labored to suppress all knowledge of their guilt; to keep facts from the popular mind; to falsify the history of current events, and prevent an exposure of our national turpitude."[3]

One hundred years after Giddings issued his protest, the facts were still known to but a few. Surprisingly, when the claims were brought to their attention, the federal government and the State of Florida were quick to recognize the validity of the claims and begin negotiations. Most newspapers and the general public, however, didn't have the slightest clue about Miccosukee/ Seminole history.

When Reno first met Josie Billie and the Big Cypress Reservation Seminoles, they were not yet part of an official tribe. There were the Big Cypress, Brighton, and Dania Reservations of Seminoles but no unifying body or official tribal council. Many of them had converted to the Baptist religion like Josie Billie, whereas the Miccosukees living along the Tamiami Trail in the Everglades followed their traditional pantheistic religion and lived their traditional hunting and fishing lifestyle. As the reservation Seminoles began to organize in 1950 as a tribe and stake a roughly $50 million claim against the federal government for lost lands, the Miccosukees began to organize in 1952 to stake their claim for the land that was still rightfully theirs by treaty. The Miccosukees wanted only land, not money. By having accepted reservation life, the Seminoles on the reservations could fight only for monetary compensation.

In 1954, a Miccosukee delegation brought a buckskin declaration to Washington and presented it to President Eisenhower, asserting their rights. The tribe sat down with the US government and tried to work out a solution. President Eisenhower appointed Indian Affairs Commissioner Glenn Emmons as his special representative to work out an agreement with the Miccosukee General Council. As the general council had a treaty on its side and an undefeated, free-living status, the federal government recognized them as a unique case that had to be dealt with separately from all other Indian claims. The initial claim for one million acres was compromised within a year down to four hundred thousand acres, which would also allow the Miccosukees to still go frogging

George Osceola, one of the Miccosukee elders, carries a message on buckskin for President Eisenhower on a trip to Washington, 1954. *Left to right*: Jimmy Billie, Buffalo Tiger, George Osceola, attorney Morton Silver.

and fishing—but not hunting—on the newly formed Everglades National Park lands from which they had been abruptly ejected in 1947.

Seminoles from the reservations worried that the land claim would trump their money claim in importance and began complicating the efforts of the Miccosukee General Council by trying to dissuade the nonreservation Miccosukees from pursuing the land claim and urging them to join the reservation Indians in a money claim. A group from the Dania Reservation went to Tallahassee in 1955 to present Governor LeRoy Collins with a Seminole shirt, calling themselves "tribal authorities" for the Seminoles. Just before their visit, however, the superintendent of the Dania Reservation had written to the governor to make sure he understood they were *not* tribal authorities. As Jane Reno explained in one of her newspaper stories: "All this seems trivial, unless you are a Seminole. Then it becomes as important as whether—during the last war—you recognized Free France or Vichy France as the French government."

When Josie Billie became a Baptist minister, he gave up his "medicine bundle"—which by tradition made him head Medicine Man and chief of the Miccosukee General Council—to his younger brother Ingraham Billie. Thus, it was Ingraham Billie who became the recognized leader of the general council, through his status as head Medicine Man. However, meetings were not directed or ruled by Billie but rather were communal forums where everyone was free to speak and decisions were come to by common counsel. The feeling of the Miccosukees of the Everglades who followed the Miccosukee General Council was that the reservation Indians who called themselves American citizens and Florida citizens and sought money had accepted defeat by the white man and abandoned Indian ways of life and as such had no rights to benefit monetarily from lost lands. The Miccosukees saw themselves as a sovereign nation, free men never incorporated into the United States of America.

The Seminole Indian Association (SIA) that "interested" itself in the welfare of the reservation Seminoles was a group of white cattlemen who often tried to speak for them, and who insisted that the Everglades Indians were kidding themselves if they thought the US government was negotiating in any kind of good faith. The SIA men said, not without accuracy, that the US government had only ever negotiated with Indians in monetary terms. Nevertheless, there did seem to be a genuine interest on the part of the Eisenhower administration to come up with a different kind of settlement for the Miccosukees. No other undefeated tribe remained with a legitimate claim like they had.

Governor LeRoy Collins took office at the beginning of 1955 in Florida after a special election was held to fill the final two-year term of Governor Dan McCarty, who died in office. In 1956 Collins appointed a state commissioner on Indian affairs, Colonel Max Denton, to study the Seminole land claims question. Denton got off to a bad start with the Miccosukees by stating a wild misunderstanding of their claims before even meeting with them.

"They want," Denton said, "an acre or two right where they are living to call their own."

Miccosukee interpreter Buffalo Tiger and Bill McKinley Osceola came into Miami upon hearing the news to visit Jane Reno and express their indignation. Tiger contrasted their experiences with the federal authorities versus the state ones:

"Commissioner Emmons, the President's representative, knows very well what we want. The leaders of our tribe and our lawyers have met with Commissioner Emmons and his lawyers in our camps and in Washington. Emmons understands the way we live, our problems, and our claims. He knows that if my people are going to live as game and frog hunters that they must have a great deal of the Everglades grass and hammock land as their own, where the oil well, and the cement plants, and rock-pits and other such things of the city cannot reach.

"He has spent much time and trouble coming to learn about my people and to talk to our leaders. We think Emmons is a fair and honest man. Now the governor of Florida has appointed this man Denton in Tallahassee who does not know what he is talking about and will not even come down to our camps. None of my people who live along the Tamiami Trail and in the Everglades want just one acre of land. We need many thousands of acres where deer, wild pig, and frog can also live."[4]

Chastened, Denton came to visit with the Miccosukees a few months later in February 1957, at Jimmie Tiger's camp at Forty Mile Bend on the Tamiami Trail. He sat under a willow the Miccosukees had named the "Promising Tree," after Commissioner Emmons and US congressmen had made them great promises there. Denton made more promises. After Denton spoke, Jimmie Tiger asked through Buffalo Tiger, "Are you sincere? These people have heard things like this before."

"I've got four years to help you try to settle your rights," replied Denton, "and I'm sincerely going to try."

Denton sympathized with their occasional problems with game wardens and desired to preserve their hunting rights. He told them, in what would be a steady refrain the Miccosukees would hear from the government concerning the idea that white lawyers were misrepresenting their interests:

"You have too many white people talking for you, well-meaning people who go around saying that they know what you want. You need one group to speak for all of you, but I know that White men have kept Indians disorganized deliberately. You are good people, with a fine background. There's a good history in back of you. You are to be commended for your peacefulness with which you have taken your treatment from White men. If it had been on my side, I wouldn't have done it.

"You can accept whatever religion you want. My intention is not to try to do anything at all about your religion. I promise to make no effort to change your way of life. I want to help you help yourself in the way you want to help yourself. I think Seminoles should have the right to live and hunt in the Everglades National Park. The state should have insisted on hunting and fishing rights from the first in the park. The state of Florida put far more into that park than the federal government has done, through its land gifts."

Some of the Miccosukees wanted to know what had been done in Washington about their desire to secure land north of the Tamiami Trail in the water conservation area. Denton explained that the feds had done nothing to his knowledge. All the water conservation area was state land, between six hundred thousand and seven hundred thousand acres, and Denton said he didn't see why an "Indian preserve" couldn't be set up on part or all of it. He also suggested that a hundred thousand acres of private land was for sale for twenty-five dollars per acre in the Big Cypress Swamp and that he thought the state could possibly buy it for the Seminoles.

Denton clarified that he didn't think the state's negotiations should have any bearing on the council's negotiations with Emmons and the Eisenhower administration and also recognized the intractable differences between the reservation and Trail Indians:

"If all your claims against the U.S. were satisfied, we feel the state still has an obligation. Get the federal government to do what they will, then we will come in. I agree with you that there should probably be two tribes set up of Florida Seminoles, representing the two factions that don't see eye to eye. Any land agreement reached will be for all Seminoles to use, not just one group or faction.

"I don't think you are asking for claims against the state of anything unreasonable. Your claims against the state of Florida should have been settled when Jessie Willie was a little boy, fifty years ago. It is heart-breaking to me that we have waited so long. Governor Collins recognizes that the problem with the Seminoles should have been settled long ago."

Not only were the Miccosukee claims to Florida land clearly established in the Treaty of Moultrie Creek, but the US Supreme Court reaffirmed that those lands belonged to the Seminoles in 1835, ten years before Florida gained statehood. No decision had ever been made since then to overturn that ruling. The Seminole Wars didn't settle the matter, however largely victorious the US government may have been in them, as no official surrender ever occurred. Undefeated Seminoles remained in the Everglades, and their heirs retained the rights to the treaty lands.

It was for this reason that the Miccosukees were primarily negotiating with the government of the United States, as the treaties that deeded their lands and their battles had been with the federal government. They were arguing from the position of a sovereign nation. Although the State of Florida owned most of the land the Miccosukees wanted, the Miccosukees viewed the state's claim to ownership as invalid. They saw it as the federal government's job to get their land back for them regardless of whose land it had eventually become.

This situation inevitably produced a political football that was kicked back and forth between the federal government and the State of Florida. The federal government seemed amenable to the demands but didn't own the land the Miccosukees wanted. The state wanted to grant vast tracts of land to the Miccosukees but needed them to get a legal agreement settled first with the federal government. On top of that, the lower half of the Everglades had just been turned into a National Park in 1947, which, as Colonel Denton noted, had come about largely through the granting of state lands. There was not a lot of political stomach to turn over more of the Everglades to the federal government so that it could make good on treaties violated before Florida statehood. Hunters were a powerful political constituency in Tallahassee, and even if their numbers were small in the Everglades, there was still great concern after the closing of National Park lands to hunting that more hunting lands would be taken away from white hunters if the Miccosukees were given land. The Miccosukees astutely recognized this political reality and offered early in negotiations to open up the proposed lands to white hunters.

Jane Reno later reflected on the Miccosukee negotiating efforts:

"I admire good politicians, more than any other professionals, and I found

The Miccosukees meet with a delegation from the state government while Jane Reno (*far left*) takes notes, circa 1954–57.

the Miccosukee negotiators splendid. They were polite, patient, never ill-tempered, and deft in their discussions—with an expert ability in exposing hollow promises as hollow. They would not be conned. During all the long land discussions in the mid-1950's, these Miccosukee council members seemed to me to have that quality that makes great statesmen—complete loyalty to their people and to the goals that seemed best to those people.

"In the variety of inter-tribal problems that came up, I admired the way that these Indians didn't try to push each other around. You sit in on a number of discussions of such problems, and you see that they keep talking until they all agree on the way. And, in the end, fellows that don't agree move off somewhere else, down river it used to be, in north Florida a century or two ago. They don't have any of this tyranny of the majority—which frightens me more and more, as much as dictators. Sure, it weakens them politically, but it makes U.S.A. freedom look pretty shackled and circumscribed."

What was aiding the Miccosukees in being taken seriously in their land claim battle, when the US government had only ever been interested in offering money and reservations in the past, was the Eisenhower administration's push to throw out the whole system of reservations. The idea was to grant Indians throughout the country full, independent status as landowners to do what they wanted with their lands, and remove federal support. Though the idea seemed to have merits on the face of it, in fact it was primarily a way for mining and oil interests, developers, and the like to get access to reservation lands that were off-limits to them. If they could divide and conquer Indians into groups of individual landowners, anathema to the traditional Indian view of the land, it would be easier to buy them out. A bill in Congress was rallied against and defeated by Indian groups in 1953, but the notion was still being pushed.

For reservation Indians, clearly the notion was a bad one. For the last undefeated tribe in the United States, who didn't have anything to call their own, the change in government policy was an opening to secure their land claim.

Shortly after the meeting with Denton, Commissioner Emmons notified the Miccosukees that he wanted to send a representative to sort out the issue of the rival reservation and nonreservation factions, echoed the sentiment that it seemed the only solution was to create two tribes of Florida Seminoles. Until there was a legal tribal entity—or two separate ones—with which the government could clearly negotiate, it was hampering progress. The Miccosukees distrusted this notion, though, of the white man's laws determining who was "legal" or not, especially given that the federal government by law recognized only reservation Indians as being able to legally constitute an official tribe. The Miccosukees stuck firmly to the idea that they were a sovereign nation and as such could constitute themselves any way they cared to. They wanted the land claim to be addressed first on behalf of all Seminoles, and for the reservation money claim to be dealt with later and separately.

# 13 | Osceolas and Tigers

As Reno became progressively more absorbed with the Miccosukee Indians, she began working on a book with Miccosukee interpreter Buffalo Tiger. She was all too aware how great a challenge the Miccosukees faced in their battle for land and how easy it was for modern culture to overwhelm Indians. It was a vanishing moment in history, where many of the Everglades Indians were living relatively untainted by outsiders and still speaking their own language. She wrote of Buffalo Tiger to her uncle Bal:

"He is a unique person, in my experience. He never went to school, can't read or write to any extent. But he was married to a white woman for a few years, until their divorce, and speaks English much better than any other Seminole alive. He has that curious quality, so rare in the world, of being the perfect interpreter. He can make of himself a vessel to carry one man's meaning to another, without adding anything of himself but acute perception in what he is trying to interpret. He is not a Seminole living in their traditional way of life himself, but he was raised in that way and is enormously interested in understanding and seeing it all in his own mind. For example, the traditional Seminole religion is a formal, intricate ritualistic pantheistic religion, rich in stories and myths. And they have kept a verbal history of their people alive around their campfires and in their council that goes far back beyond pre-Columbian times. A few hundred, perhaps 500 of them have lived, right up to now, integrated in a way of life to which we are quite alien. They have in literal truth a culture almost untouched by White men.

"Now Buffalo has that curious temperament that makes the very greatest historians and poets. It is the impulse that makes writers, for they say it must not be that after these people die there will be no memory of them. It must not be that the world will lose all record of their dreams and stories and myths and existence as a separate people. It is the impulse first to perfectly understand, and then to write it down. Now, this man has the scholarly frame of mind. He quite understands that just because he was brought up among these people, and is one of them, that he does not know all about them. He is trying on week-ends, for he runs a little workshop in Hialeah to make a living, to—as it were—sit at the feet of the old men.

"Though I am not sure he has the word research in his vocabulary, he is doing research. He has, however, a good and flexible English vocabulary, and is enormously aware of the importance of the right word, the shade of meaning, accuracy. This is somewhat the way of small children, who live with a verbal history, and want their stories told them just exactly right. Now there will come a day, in a year or two maybe, when this man will feel he does know that story in the way he wants to tell it—the story of Seminole culture, it will be. And he is going to have a problem of getting it set down. What I want to see happen is some foundation, like the Rockefeller or the Guggenheim, give him a small grant of money. That way he can buy himself a wire recorder and hire a typist to transcribe what he says. And he can take a few months off and dictate a book. It would be quite a thing for anthropology and history, and because of his individual temperament I think the book would also have real literary quality, Now, you are familiar with my enthusiasms, which do not dim. But the Bureau of Indian Affairs, and various extremely scholarly people and lawyers whom I know are just as much impressed with this project as I am. When the day comes Buffalo feels he is ready to try to get a book written, are there any Rockefeller Foundation grants for such a project and how does one go about getting them? Let me know about this sometime please. If I cannot see lost causes win, I at least do not want the record of their very existence lost."

Unfortunately, along with many of her hopes for the Miccosukees, the book was never able to materialize. A half century later, Tiger finally worked with another writer to commit a memoir of his life to print. In one passage from Reno's notes for it, Buffalo Tiger explained to her what life had been like as a Miccosukee child growing up in the Everglades.

"I was born in the Everglades in 1920," said Tiger. "At that time the Tamiami Trail had been built about as far as William McKinley Osceola's camp. About twenty-five miles west of Miami. My grandfather had a nice little village about two and a half miles west of where the Blue Shanty [a bar] lay on the Tamiami Trail, about ten miles west of the road end. My grandfather bought skins from Indians, took them in to Miami and sold them, bought groceries to take back.

Jimmy Tiger (*left*) and Buffalo Tiger, circa 1954–57. They were two of the primary spokesmen for the Miccosukees in the 1950s in their interactions with the state and federal governments.

He had a store in the swamp. The families of my mother's two sisters lived there, so there were many children with my sisters, and brothers, and cousins.

"My mother had ten children, five boys and five girls. Eight are still alive. Two died when they were about twelve years old. One had appendicitis, but I don't know what the other died of. My grandfather built the camp, but it belonged to my grandmother because all villages belonged to the wife. The only thing that belongs to the husband are his gun and his traps. All the children are members of their mother's clan, or family. When a man tells his wife, 'I'm going to my camp,' she knows he's going to his sister's camp or his mother's camp.

"This is the first place I know as home. Sometimes families get together, go on visits to each other. During the visits they always tell what happened in the war between the Indians and the white men, but we never see any white men. The first thing we're taught when we're little is to watch where we step, so as not to step on a snake. The next thing we're taught is to be quiet and good and mind the older people. They pointed out why we should be good. White men were the reason. They told us about the wars and how the Indians had to run off the islands in the saw grass in the Everglades, through the swamps, away from the white soldiers. A child who wasn't quiet and wasn't good might be left behind. And he would be carried back to the white folks by the soldiers.

"I can tell you, this scared you! The little ones all felt the same way at that time. They had no warm feelings toward white folks. The first white man I ever saw had stopped at William McKinley Osceola's camp on Tamiami Trail. I thought if I talked to him I would get shot or taken away from my mother. They shot guns all the time, they were always shooting something! When I was a little boy we liked to watch white men. But we were afraid to let them see us, so we'd sneak around half a day in the saw grass, just watching a man fish in the canal or watching hunters shooting guns.

"My father's work was hunting. Most of the menfolks in the village would go away from two weeks to a month on hunting trips. You know, I was so scared of white men, and then I went off when I was about twelve or thirteen to Hialeah, where my uncle had an alligator wrestling camp, you know, showing off to the white people how you wrestle alligators. I went there, and I went to school there, and I discovered that white people are just like any other people: some good, some bad."

Hialeah Race Track had a moat in the center around a small island, upon which was an Indian *chickee*, and camping there was paid employment for Indians during race season. Flamingos also paraded around the island. Since they had already all but disappeared from the Florida Keys, the racetrack was one of the last places in south Florida the birds could be seen.

"Wild Bill [Osceola] camped there sometimes," remembered Reno. "That's a job. You go into town and camp out, cook, and pay no attention to anybody. You live there for a month or two and get pretty well paid."

Reno noted that the Indians also made money by letting tourists view their lifestyle in villages along the Tamiami Trail but laughed at the idea that the Indians were being exploited: "The Indians treat the white people like they were chickens. I once took an aging Britisher, and he said, 'It's appalling that people should exploit themselves so that we can see their way of life.' I said, 'Honeybunch, they think of you as a chicken. Look at that chicken. They don't pay any attention to what that chicken is doing, just like you. They don't think you're important at all.'"[1]

Buffalo Tiger explained the Miccosukee usage of names to Reno, which was radically different from how names were used in white society.

"When it comes to names," Tiger said, "that was one of the things that I found hard to understand when I came to know white men."

"Indians don't teach their children the names of their fathers and mothers. I don't know the Indian names of my parents. Indian names are very private things. My mother's white name is Sally Willy, and my father's white name is Doctor Tiger, but these are just names for white people to use. A baby is given a name when he is born, but he is never called by this name. He's called by a nickname.

"When I was little they called me *Mamusek*, 'old man,' because they said I talked like an old man. When a boy successfully passes through his first Green Corn Dance he gets another name. Girls keep their same name, but they're always called by their Indian nickname. It is impolite to call anybody by their real name, though it is alright to use that name when you talk of them to some other person. You can see why I find the names of white people, the way they use the names, confusing."

Coming from the newspaper business, where everyone wanted their name known, Reno found the concept refreshing. She kept her maiden name among the Miccosukees because she first got to know them using her *Miami News* reporter byline. The mention of the name Jane Reno would have drawn a blank to most of her friends on the Tamiami Trail, but everyone knew Jane Wood.

While Reno was attracted to the justness of the Miccosukee land rights cause and their rich history, the Seminole ritual dances cemented the bond between them.

"They have the greatest parties!" she recalled. "The drinkers get to pass out, without being viewed censoriously thereafter. What they say afterward with a big happy grin, is: 'You sure did have a good time at the Snake Dance, Jane Wood.' And the adolescents pursue amorous occupations in the bushes, with giggles. Oh, modern civilization in the U.S.A. is poorer because it doesn't have the equivalent of the Snake Dance! The Green Corn Dance is great, too, with medicinal and judicial overtones."

Reno described the rituals in an interview:

"They are two beautiful parties. The Snake Dance is later in the summer, it's late in August. It doesn't have all the religious connotations the Green Corn Dance has. It's just a beautiful party. It's somewhat like the Green Corn Dance, which occurs around the first of June. Everybody's gathered on this hammock, this island, with old dead pine trees that I can still see, for a week. And they came not from miles around, but from hundreds of miles around.

"The last night of the Green Corn Dance—there were chickees set up, whole big families, seven sisters and all their brothers—nobody is allowed to go to sleep once they begin dancing. Nobody is allowed to eat. At every stop in the chanting—it's a snake-like kind of dance, hand-holding like you did in college in the Twenties—they would line out the dance, three old, old men sitting there, they would line out the dance and everybody would go around.

"I said to Howard:

"'Who's the little, little guy on the end?'

"'He's my sister's son. We call him Weepers.'

"'How old is he?'

"'Three.'

"This is around midnight.

"'What do you mean "Weepers"'?

"'Don't you know finders keepers, losers weepers? We call him Weepers. That's his nickname.'

"Men, women, and children are chanting around, and in between every dance the Indian sheriffs walk around carrying a long, slender cypress pole, about ten feet long with a palmetto spine circle tied on the end. There are two poles, the other with a deer tail on the end.

"'What do the Indian sheriffs do, Howard?' I asked.

"'The Indian sheriffs make sure that anybody who gets in the dance has to take a drink when the dance stops and cannot go to sleep.'

Howard Osceola, circa 1954–57. He was one of Jane Reno's closest friends among the Miccosukees, and one of their primary spokesmen in dealing with government officials.

"So you pass down a ritual bottle of wine, beer or whiskey. Alice Osceola was dispensing beer that night. Along towards dawn at the Green Corn Dance, everybody, not having been allowed to sleep, and not having had anything to eat for the last twenty-four hours, and having had these ritual drinks, is pretty damn drunk. It gets really pretty out there, the light, light, lightness of dawn, that pretty color.

"Then what comes is a ritual scrape. They use a block of wood that's about the size of a book of matches and through it is stuck about six needles, just plain, sewing needles. They stick out about one-sixteenth to one-eighth of an inch. The medicine man goes around and he scrapes them. He scrapes their arms, their chest, and their back. Howard said they used to have a mean old medicine man that really scraped them deep. It scrapes, and they bleed.

"Then they go off into small tents, where there are hot rocks, on which are thrown water. The guy sits in there and he sweats. He's been scraped, and he's bleeding. He comes out and he's covered in blood and sweat. If you walked in there at about that moment, at dawn, and hadn't ever seen it before, you would cry if you didn't know that everybody was drunk and that it didn't hurt, didn't hurt at all.

"'What is this for?' I said. 'Is it for health, or punishment of sins?'

"'It is for health,' Howard said. 'A woman loses blood, but a man doesn't lose blood, so a man gets impurities. This is health. He needs a bloodletting and a sweating once a year. The punishment of sins comes later.'

"'What about the punishment of sins?'

"'We got one here we're going to talk about tonight. There are some fellas here from that clan, fellas here from this, and one of their fellas killed one of our fellas. We're going to decide what to do.'

"'What might you do?' I said.

"'We might take one of theirs.'

"'You mean you might kill the man who killed your man?'

"'No,' he said. 'Look. This guy that got killed in our clan was a big man, he was a good man. This guy that did the killing from the other clan. You know about poor white trash,' he said, 'you know about poor nigger trash. Well, this was poor Indian trash. And he did the killing. So we could take not him, but one of their good guys. He killed one of our good guys.'

"'That's Indian justice?'

"'Right.'

"'What are you liable to do?' I asked.

"'We're liable to talk about it all night and not liable to do anything, and we'll leave it so if one of our guys takes one of theirs, he'll be, in effect, home free.'

"I'm one of the only persons I've ever known that walked out of the Green Corn Dance at nine o'clock in the morning, drove home, got dressed, and went to a Jewish wedding at noon at the Seville Hotel. The bridegroom's mother got drunk, the men danced, and I thought, boy, I've seen it all.

"The Snake Dance is the same thing, but no punishment, no scraping, and just larking, just fun.

"'What's the Snake Dance all about?' I asked Howard.

"'Well, you know the water's high and the snakes are high. They get over the road. It's to keep the snakes quiet.'

"It's purely for fun. They are the most beautiful parties, and then these beautiful Indian friends of yours like Alice Osceola and Mittie Jim bring you hominy grits, fried bacon, and biscuits for breakfast the next morning, baked over a Seminole fire."[2]

Reno's son Mark remembered the wee hours of the morning at one Green Corn Dance, when his brother Bob was passed out nearby and he was about to pass out himself. Alice Osceola, a large and commanding member of the Osceola clan and sister of Howard, turned to Mark and said: "You sleep with me." There were few things that daunted the six-foot-four Mark, but this was one of them. A bold invitation from a peer of his mother was confusing enough, but he also had no idea how consenting or refusing would affect relations with the Miccosukees. He looked at Alice with some trepidation, wondering if he understood her right. When they entered Alice's *chickee*, he glanced toward the bed and mosquito net. She shook her head and said firmly: "I sleep here. You sleep over there," pointing to the floor. He was greatly relieved.

The entire Osceola family became dear to Jane Reno and provided much of her insight into Miccosukee daily life.

"I became very good friends with William McKinley Osceola's children and Tiger Tiger's children," Reno said. "William has eight children, and very devoted, all of them. Homer, and Mittie Jim, who doesn't speak any English but makes the prettiest shirts on the Tamiami Trail, and Wild Bill Osceola, who has a daughter named after me, Jane Wood Osceola, and Howard, and Alice, who's married to a nice white man who's a stock car racer, and Ethel, who's married to a nice white man. And John, who is a charming man, and drinks! Douglas, who's the handsomest Indian in the Everglades . . . those are eight of William's children. He has another son, Mike, who none of them speak to, because Mike, many years ago, sued his daddy over land, and that's considered as bad taste among Indians as it is among white people. But the Osceola family, William McKinley Osceola's children, I love them all. They have helped me out when my car was broken down, helped me through waters and swamps, I love them."

"The nearest we came to success was under LeRoy Collins," Reno remembered years later about the land claim battle of the Miccosukees. "He came down and

Jane Wood Osceola, five-month-old granddaughter of Chief William McKinley Osceola, named in honor of Jane Wood by her father, "Wild Bill" Osceola.

met with the Indians, and they came darn near to setting aside this sixty thousand acres that the Miccosukees of the Trail wanted.[3] Except they wouldn't do it in perpetuity. They would do it thirty years, ninety years, I don't remember

what. They almost did it, but the Indians said, no, no term on it, it must be forever. And all ours. But LeRoy came nearest doing it, and the Indians liked him."[4]

In July 1957 Collins came to tour the Everglades and try to further an agreement with the Miccosukees. In his typical moderate fashion, he deftly refused
to take sides in the fight between the reservation and nonreservation groups.
He repeatedly urged that they try to reconcile their differences and said that
progress could be made once the Indians displayed a unified front. He recalled
that the last Florida governor to meet the Seminoles on their home ground had
been Dave Scholtz in the mid-1930s. When Scholtz asked what they wanted,
they curtly told him they wanted to be left alone.

"But, we are asking you to help the state," Collins said. "I know you have

Jane Reno (*right*) with Florida governor LeRoy Collins (*center*), during LeRoy Collins's 1957 tour
of the Everglades and meeting with the Miccosukees.

been beset over many years with various factions. Now, nobody can come up overnight with a plan in which all Seminoles can be united."

Speaking on behalf of the reservation Seminoles, Miami lawyer O. B. White pressed the governor that the Seminoles needed to unite as one tribe, to which Collins countered, "I doubt it is a part of the duties of the State of Florida to take an aggressive part in establishing unity."[5]

(White was a familiar face to Reno, as twenty years before he had worked with her father on the divorce trial in which both White and George Wood had physically assaulted the insult-hurling witness.)

A basic premise of the reservation Seminoles' lawsuit for money against the United States government was that they spoke for all Seminoles. They desperately wanted the nonreservation Miccosukees of Tamiami Trail to abandon the land claim and join forces for money under one front. While the reservation Seminoles had a greater chance of being legally recognized by the US government, they also were keenly aware that they lacked any traditional Indian authority. The Miccosukees held that authority, as the Miccosukees of the Trail lived far more by the old ways than the reservation Seminoles did. Also, the federal authorities had made it clear that they would have preferred to take care of the whole Seminole problem all at once with the formation of a single tribe.

Mike Osceola was a former Miami Senior High School football player who became a de facto spokesman for the Dania Reservation Seminoles and was terminally at odds with the rest of his nonreservation Tamiami Trail family. At the meeting with Governor Collins, Mike showed up uninvited and demanded to be allowed to sit in on it. He was nearly physically ejected by his siblings until Collins asked that they let him stay. Buffalo Tiger agreed as long as Mike kept his mouth shut, which, to everyone's surprise who viewed Mike as a compulsive troublemaker, he largely did. Collins refused to be pinned down on a position by any side, and the 1957 meeting left things in a further state of limbo.

A week after the meeting took place, on July 21, 1957, the reservation Seminoles formed a constitution and legally became the Seminole Tribe of Florida. They declared their group as the sole existing tribe of Seminoles in Florida. This had little impact on the state negotiations, which still viewed the Miccosukee land claim as the problem they needed to resolve, because the reservation Seminoles weren't asking for anything from the state. It seemed to set the stage for a path forward, as the federal authorities now had a duly recognized tribe with which to negotiate a money claim, and the State of Florida had the Miccosukee General Council with which to negotiate a land claim. Still, the endless sticking point would be exactly what legal form the Miccosukees would take and how land would be deeded to them. The State of Florida couldn't negotiate with a sovereign nation.

One of Reno's amusing memories of the Osceola clan was from one of the few fights she witnessed among the Miccosukees, and the family reaction to it:

"John Osceola got into a fight with Homer Osceola at the Green Corn Dance early in the dawn. John was drunk as a skunk—well, everybody was drunk, but John was a little riotous drunk, and he got in a fight with Homer. Alice and Mittie Jim rushed out and said, 'Stop it! Stop it!' They tied his legs together, they tied his hands together, they tied his arms together in back of him, and they tied a cord between him and his legs. He was lying there and saying something. I don't know what he said because I don't understand a lot of the Indian language. He lay there for an hour or two and sobered up, and some gentle, young Indians came out and cut the cords, and he crawled off into the bushes and went to sleep. But when an Indian gets drunk, his wife or his sister or his mother, or both sisters if they are living, are entitled to go out and tie him up. He does not resist this. He may be fighting drunk, but they tie his hands behind his back and his legs together, and he doesn't resist."[6]

Reno had been seeing Seminoles coming into Miami since the 1920s and was always impressed by their colorful dress. She soon learned that the origins of the outfits were more recent than most people realized. As they had adapted themselves to a new environment, they also adopted modern technology in the form of the sewing machine to add a new wrinkle to their culture.

"These sewing machines came in this part of the world about 1890 with the Brickells," Reno explained.

"Not long thereafter the Indian women were making these beautiful quilted patterns which require a sewing machine. It was pedal operated then, actually it was hand operated. Now they're doing it with electric ones. I took a very perceptive writer out there once, and she was especially interested in that. She said: 'I think these shirts and skirts are the only authentic Seminole craft.'

"My own thesis is—I don't know where they got the quilting, it was probably circa 1900, Mary Brickell or something like that—that they made them initially so they would not be Jim Crow-ed. Here are these Indians coming into town, and they're dusky skinned. Our Seminoles have a pugnacious chin, and full lips, that might be Negroid. Their Indian features, the features they carried over from Mongolia, are black eyebrows, and straight black, black hair.

"But they are by no means red skinned. Any fool Ku Kluxer or southern immigrant might have thought they were 'niggers,' and treated them badly. So they made these shirts which said, in effect, *I am Seminole and I am an Indian.* Every little Ku Kluxer that ever came to Florida was pretty scared of Indians. The shirts had no basis. They were based on the sewing machine. They were what the Indians gave the sewing machine. There's an art, and a creativity, that goes on from the sewing machine, right?

"My justification is that Indians off in Big Cypress and such don't wear this stuff. They wear blue shirts and dungarees, and the women wear blouses and skirts of some description. Actually the young women wear blouses and dungarees. I remember in the Twenties when we saw them in town, and I think we saw them in town more when we first came, they said in effect by the costumes and those beautiful blouses the Indian women wore, and the skirts, and the shirts of the men: *We are Indian.* And nobody put them down or made them sit in the back of the bus, or gave them any trouble."

Though the Miccosukees usually had a legend to explain most things in their lives, even they were at a loss sometimes. (To Reno's occasional exasperation but usually to her delight, Sippi Morris would make one up for them if they were lacking.) At one Green Corn Dance, two to three miles north of the Tamiami Trail, Reno was sitting with Howard Osceola and the tribal attorney Morton Silver. It was a beautiful hammock—an island in the Everglades—with a dead pine tree, and they were sharing a bottle of whiskey and a bottle of wine, watching the dance.

"There's Alice Jones," said Silver. "Have you ever told Jane Wood about Alice Jones?"

"No, I didn't," replied Osceola.

"What about Alice Jones?" Reno asked.

"She's ambidextrous," contributed Silver obliquely.

"What do you mean?"

"She's a hermaphrodite, Jane Wood," said Osceola.

"Really? How do you know?"

"Well, she's a woman and she used to date our girls and she knocked them up."

"My goodness, she was a man."

"No," Osceola said, "she had breasts on her."

"My goodness, where does she live now?"

"She lives with an old, old Indian woman."

"What does Indian legend say about this?"

They had been talking about Seminole legends, and Howard sighed: "We never knew it before. When the world gets old, you see strange things, Jane Wood."[7]

Among the things that Jane Reno shared with her children in the early 1950s were learning to wrestle small alligators with the Seminoles, exploring springs and rivers, and taking part in the pioneering of scuba diving in Florida. Loving the reefs as she did, Reno embraced the notion of breathing underwater. Jacques Cousteau and Emile Gagnan had invented the Aqua Lung system in France some eight years before, which was the first self-contained underwater breathing apparatus, or SCUBA. A whole new way of exploring the ocean was born. Shortly after its introduction to Florida, Reno went on a dive outing with the Cub Scout troop for which she was den mother and was fascinated by the device. Even though she didn't try it herself, she wanted her children to learn. They became guinea pigs the next time they were out on the reefs, going by what instruction she could give them. Maggy Reno Hurchalla remembers: "I sank to the bottom and was unable to breathe. This was all new to me so I was sure I was doing something wrong. I sat there for as long as I could, but with no air I finally had to swim back to the surface. I found that they hadn't turned my tank on."

After some false starts like this the children picked it up quickly, and Reno tried it herself. Maggy, at the tender age of twelve, became a scuba instructor in the summer of 1953. Working in conjunction with the Dive Corp. of America shop, Maggy got a call on the rare occasion that the dive shop sold a scuba regulator. Many of the regulators were bought by wealthy South Americans shopping in Miami, because scuba diving was so new that few locals were engaged in the sport. The dive shop would arrange an appointment for Maggy to show up to demonstrate the equipment in a swimming pool. She took the customers through a brief course that covered most of the basics that a professional dive certification today does, showing them how to clear their masks and regulator, and to always breathe out on ascent. The demonstration concluded by having them leave all their equipment at the bottom of the pool and diving down to put it all back on.

"I got paid ten dollars a lesson," remembers Maggy, "which was real good money back then. We're talking dollar an hour days, so that was good. In fact, it was probably better money than I ever made as a teenager."

Because she was six feet tall, no one ever thought to question Maggy's age. The issue did come up embarrassingly once, when a South American gentleman assumed she could drive one of the cars to shuttle his party back and forth somewhere. To his disbelief she declined, saying: "I can't drive. I'm only twelve."

Having explored the reefs of the Keys since her first snorkeling trip, Jane Reno got to know many of the area divers. She wrote the story of Hope Root's fatal attempt to set a depth record, and after his death followed up on a frightening discovery of his in the Florida Keys. In the summer of 1953—Root died in December—Root and Reynolds Moody were diving for grouper east of Angelfish Creek. Just before their air ran out, they spied a group of cylinders lying on the ocean floor. Thinking they might be naval ordnance, they wrote to the Sixth Naval District in Charleston. The Navy wrote back, expressing doubt that the cylinders were their property.

This got Root and Moody thinking that they might make some good money off of salvaging their find, if they were chemicals or something else of value. Their brief look had revealed an enormous number of the cylinders. A follow-up dive shattered that hope, though, when they discovered that they *were* in fact Navy property and that they were depth charges. No fewer than 260 drums were sitting on the ocean floor, with the potential for creating a staggering explosion. The Navy eventually removed all the drums but was slow to do so, and it took a letter from Reno to a Navy admiral to finally get the job done. Reno wrote: "During the years they lay off Key Largo, the corroding cylinders of TNT could have been blown by a nosey shark, and the noise would have reached Miami 50 miles away. Nobody on a nearby ship would have lived long enough to pray if the deadly pile had been accidentally touched off, said a Navy demolition expert."[1]

On the day that Hope Root died in December, Reynolds Moody had done a preliminary dive to check the currents and warned Root that diving was not feasible. Moody was probably the most seasoned diver in Florida aside from Root at the time, but Root chose to his disregard his warnings.

"Hope had set an unofficial record before," Reno wrote, "on November 27,

1953. He had reached a depth of 350 feet. Paul Arnold was the only witness to that feat, although Ed Fisher above them took underwater photographs of the deep dive."

The front-page stories on Root's final dive in the December 3 and December 4 issues of the *Miami Daily News* were some of Reno's most prominent articles for the *News* to that point, and they resulted in an increasing number of her hard-news stories being published going into 1954. The belated *Big Story* award in 1953 for her 1949 *Miami Herald* article also was a wake-up call to *News* publisher Dan Mahoney that one of his best writers was a woman freelancer. Managing editor Hoke Welch had a great relationship with Reno and was happy to assign her more newsroom work.

Ed Fisher was another of Reno's friends and was one of the best underwater photographers in Florida for decades. The elite crowd of enigmatic characters pushing the limits in the early years of scuba diving often ran afoul of each other's bullheaded attitudes, though they usually had an enormous respect for their peers. Fisher recalled being on the fatal Root expedition aboard the boat of Jordan Klein, who opened the first dive store in Miami and became a legendary underwater cameraman and inventor over the years. *Life* photographer Peter Stackpole was also onboard, and they encouraged Root to put a safety hitch in his dive belt in case something should something go wrong. Root ignored them. On the only dive Fisher did with Reynolds Moody, he remembered Moody breaking their plan and diving off by himself to the bottom at 270 feet. Fisher was outraged at what he saw as Moody's arrogant irresponsibility and never dove with him again.

Jane Reno jumped on any excuse to mix work with play and covered every diving story she could. When Ed Fisher decided he was going to set the record for the longest stint underwater with scuba, she wrote about it for the *Miami Daily News*. The desire for Fisher's oddball accomplishment came out of the development of the first rival regulator to the Aqua Lung. Up to that point, Cousteau's company had a corner on the market. When a new regulator called Dive Air came out, Fisher joined Jody Summerall and Paul Arnold, who owned Dive Corp. of America, to come up with a way to promote it. What better way than a twenty-four-hour dive, they thought?

Fisher designed the dive because he was fascinated by the possibilities for the future of man living underwater. When the original diver slated to carry

Hope Root diving to his death, 1953.

it out withdrew because his wife didn't want him to do it, Fisher stepped in to take his place. He was confident that he could manage the endurance feat.

The first annoyance that Fisher had to overcome was the difference in how he and Arnold conceived of the dive. While Fisher had envisioned the challenge as one involving a man alone in the sea, Arnold was trying to get as much publicity out of the stunt as possible and had people floundering around in the water during the daytime.

"What pissed me off," Fisher remembered, "was that Paul sent spearfishermen out to protect me. A barracuda came up and one of them speared it, which was just going to attract sharks. I was furious and communicated to him to get the guys the hell out of there. The whole thing was too much like a circus for me, which was spoiling the essence of the dive."

At three in the afternoon he entered the water and rolled out a knapsack and set up camp on the ocean floor. Fisher had made up special liquid foods and devised a system where he could suck them through straws. Helpers came down and replaced his air tanks every hour. He rested much of the time but occasionally walked around the reef with the help of heavy lead weights holding him down. At dinnertime he set out on a spearfishing expedition of the reef and speared an eighteen-inch snapper, which he ate raw. He noted that he couldn't taste it while holding his breath, so concluded you need to breathe to taste. At 8:10 p.m. he wrote in his log book, which was a series of white plastic tiles he wrote on with grease pencil: "Pitch dark. See tentacles like arms of brittle star out of coral. Worms all over my light." At 9:30 p.m. he wrote: "Struck severely by wandering sea urchins." At 2:30 a.m. he reported: "Getting extremely cold. Eating candy and exploring reef."

The worst was yet to come. He had on a thin wetsuit that began to compress him uncomfortably, and heat loss began to catch up with him after more than a dozen hours in the water. He was getting hypothermia and felt like he was going to die. One of the factors that had not been adequately planned for was that even in relatively warm tropical water, immersion for such a long period of time could result in hypothermia. Though the onset of hypothermia made him progressively more loopy, he endured on through the night as the moon and waves caused shadows to dance around him in the clear water. At 8:10 a.m. he recorded:

"Friday. Was much too preoccupied to keep log at night. Tired but couldn't really sleep. 2 times I went off for a wink but the noise of my exhale brought me out of it. All the problems I thought would be paramount turned out to be minor. Big problem dehydration. My skin on hand look like prunes. Feel slightly dull witted. Overall feeling of dehydration yet wet. Last night I was very cold. Shivers. Still slightly cold. Somehow lack enthusiasm to do any of the things I planned."

Forty minutes later he wrote on his slate to Paul Arnold, "I don't think can last more than one hour."

"There is no substitute for victory," wrote back Arnold, oblivious to the depths of Fisher's suffering.

Periodically Jane Reno donned a tank and swam down to see how he was doing. She had her own unique achievement as a journalist, recalling: "I did the world's first underwater interview, as far as I know. You interview underwater by writing on a slate with a slate pencil."

After Fisher had been down for twenty hours, she dove back down to check on him. A log entry from a half hour before had noted he was feeling better and confident, though the eighty-two-degree water felt like it was freezing to him.

"Think you can make it?" she wrote on the slate, handing it to him.

"I can make it," Fisher wrote back.

Jane Reno interviewing Ed Fisher underwater during his record-setting twenty-four-hour dive in 1954, thought to be the first underwater scuba interview ever conducted.

When she came back to the boat with the news, Paul Arnold wryly commented to general relief and laughter, "Arrogant son-of-a-bitch."

At 2:03 p.m., his last log entry read: "One more hour. I feel like a dehydrated salt cake. Can think of nothing but fresh hot water and steak. What did we prove? There's no place like home!"[2]

In the years to come, Fisher was amused by various successful attempts to break his record and improve upon it. The stunts were invariably in warm-water tanks at dive shows and the like, and bore few of the hazards and challenges of diving in open water on a reef. Four years later the record had stretched to more than twenty-eight hours, but a diver nearly killed himself in the process despite doing the marathon in the controlled environment of a tank at the Miami Seaquarium.

Because of her enthusiasm for scuba diving and the amount of news coverage she dedicated to it, when Reno went into Dive Corp. later during the 1950s to rent some tanks, her friend Ed Parnell said, "Jane, you have done so much for scuba diving I would like to give you free air as long as I work in the shop."

"I thought about it," she recalled. "Knew some newspaper writers were on the take. Then I thought if I were ever asked, 'Were you ever on the take?' I could honestly answer: 'Yeah, I took free air.' I did, about forty dollars' worth that summer, until Ed quit to become a school teacher."

Looking back at her own involvement more than fifty years later, daughter Maggy Reno Hurchalla marveled at the company she was in as a result of her mother getting her into scuba diving in its earliest days. Like her mother, though, she was in it only for the thrill of being able to stay underwater and loll happily about without a care in the world. The men who were pioneering the sport were like an underwater version of the astronauts and pilots of *The Right Stuff*, bold heroes who had no fear of dying, relentlessly pushing the limits of how far they could go. Hurchalla remembered merely being an "air junkie," enamored with the small pleasures of studying the creatures of a reef as closely as she wanted for as long as she wanted. Jane Reno described this sort of bliss in an article she wrote about undersea sledding in the Gulf Stream, an adventure on which she brought Maggy along. Another useful aspect of using her maiden name as a journalist was that Jane could involve her children in stories without people knowing they were related. While Reno enjoyed scuba diving, she was not as comfortable with it as her fifteen-year-old daughter. The plan was to use Maggy as the model for the underwater photographs, and Jane Reno confessed to being initially terrified about taking a turn on the undersea sled herself:

"Looking for a cool weekend trip? How about a ride down the Gulf Stream twenty feet beneath the waves in an undersea sled? You won't forget it. If you can breathe, swim a little, and stay this side of panic, you can make the trip. The water streams past you in a cool caress. Blue is all around to infinity. There is no horizon, no bottom, only a scalloped ceiling above. You have an undersea chauffeur for company, plus some dolphins. You seem to move at terrific speed, but quite smoothly, with never a bump.

"The ultimate horror of being way down under the water in the open ocean turns out to be completely beautiful. As you drag in the air from your aqualung in fast little gulps and hang on tight to the sea sled, you feel just two things in equal proportions—delight and terror.

"When your chauffeur manipulates the controls of the undersea sled so that you tilt and weave from side to side, you are not slung over suddenly. The water supports you in a much kinder fashion than air does. When the sled rolls completely over and the bubbles from your breathing apparatus are streaming to the surface, you feel that the bubbles have suddenly started going down. Head down, you feel like you are right side up. The wave-scooped surface of the water seems like the bottom. The sled rights, and you are dizzy.

"If you do not care to do this, you can get something of the effect from several glasses of champagne. You come out when you suddenly realize the greatest danger is that you could learn to love it under the water, want to stay. Back in the boat you are disconsolate. Air is such a sleazy product to have wrapped around your body.

"We went out from Whale Harbour on Matecumbe Key with Captain Hugh Brown in his forty-four-foot cruiser, Reef Corsair, for our undersea ride. Paul Arnold, president of Diving Corporation of America, and Maggy Reno, diving instructor, were to ride the undersea sled for photographs by Jerry Greenberg.

"His is the toughest kind of photograph. The cameraman puts his foot through a loop in the tow rope, wraps the taut rope around his body, hangs on with one arm, and grapples with the camera in its underwater case. The cruiser towing the sled is going at very slow speed, five miles an hour, but that seems terrifically fast when you are being hauled under the water like a piece of live bait.

"As the cruiser wallows slowly up the Gulf Stream, pitching through the cresting waves of the deep blue ocean, it is strange and disconcerting to watch the taut tow rope and know three people are down underneath the water out of sight at the end of the line. After the experts each used up a tank of air in photography, and that takes an hour, the time comes for the novice diver to take an undersea ride. For this exhilarating trip, you strap five pounds of lead weight around your waist and firmly hitch a tank of compressed air to your back. You put on a face mask, bite down on the mouthpiece of the aqualung to check the flow of air, then slip your feet into long swim fins.

"Thus attired, you realize that the most dangerous part of the trip is the waddle across the cockpit of the pitching cruiser, because so weighted and shod you can easily fall and break your bones or spirit. You consign yourself to the forbidding waves only by pulling a complete blank and going over like a zombie.

"Once you are over the side and under the water, everything changes instantly and completely. You are weightless, balanced between the buoyancy of the air tank and the lead weights. You kick with the swim fins and go back fast and easy to the sea sled, where chauffeur Arnold waits. You gulp hungrily for air, and air comes streaming into your lungs. Everywhere around you is a cool, kind, perfect blue. The water is smooth below, no matter how rough it is above. You grab the sea sled and are off on your terror-filled, beauty-filled ride.

"You discover that the way fish probably communicate with each other is by the look in their eyes and the expression on their faces. Your chauffeur, perched beside you on the rods of the sled, is much magnified by the water, and you can tell instantly by every grin and grimace what he feels.

"The sea sled has practical uses. Professional salvage operators find the device invaluable in locating wrecks. The Florida Game and Wildlife Service uses it for underwater surveys. The president of Venezuela has such a sled, and he reportedly uses it as your president has used the golf course—to get away from it all."[3]

Reno had a small cervical cancer scare in 1954. A routine pap smear came back "highly suspicious," and a biopsy revealed metaplastic cells most likely in the process of changing into cancerous cells. She had her cervix removed, and her gall bladder as well while they were operating. The pathologist then reported that they got everything suspicious and Reno should be good for an-other forty years.

"I am devoted to today's medicine," Reno wrote to her sister Winifred, "which has you walking down the hall on the fourth day and no bandages on a clumsy looking piece of stitching in the stomach. The children are minding me beautifully—I am as coddled as a communist."

By Janet's senior year of high school, it was apparent that she and her sib-lings had inherited their mother's intellect, and that they were likely to cost more than Henry and Jane made to put them through top colleges. Just as her parents had wanted for their children things that they themselves had been denied due to poverty, Reno felt strongly the same way when it came to education. Whereas she had never been able to pursue her dream of attending Columbia University, Reno wanted her daughters to attend any school they desired. (On the other hand, daughter Maggy noted, she did offer a car to any of them who wanted to stay home and go to the University of Miami. Volun-teers at saving money were welcome.) In 1955, Jane wrote to the Balfours about Janet's college plans:

"Janet is at present enmeshed in the throes of sending off applications to various colleges. She has applied for admission to Swarthmore, Cornell, Stan-ford and Scripps. The two California colleges are because she fell in love with them last summer. I secretly hope they turn her down—it is so darn far away.

"We can see our way, if things continue with us now, to four years in a state college for each child, financially. But the total costs of good private college are about double the Florida universities. However, Janet prefers to take a chance and start at a good school and hope that by work, loans, and scholarships she can make up the difference over four years. I am all with that way. She is a smart, nice, kind, strong, level-headed girl. She has been voted the most intel-ligent senior in her graduating class, and will finish among the top three or four seniors in grades. (Do not delicately imply, as Nina once did, that that is because Southern high schools are inferior. Nina suggested once that might be true of why Caroline Hunter and I made such good school records, and my reply was, 'I would have looked good anywhere, darling!') Anyway, Janet is capable of doing very good work in this world, with her head, her heart and her hands. She claims she is going to have eight sons, which will be great work and you need a wonderful education for that."

Watching Janet progress through schools was always heart-wrenching at first for her mother and then exhilarating. The pattern each time was that Janet started off timid, lonesome, and unknown but within a few years became one of the most prized students and popular among her classmates. Her brother Bob, on the other hand, was rather lazy in his approach to schoolwork, though he was showing a tremendous gift for oration and writing.

Every once in a while, Jane Reno's soft heart and open-door policy at the North Kendall Drive house would backfire. Her daughter Maggy attracted an unwanted suitor by the name of Bob Heineman, whom her mother initially described as a "tall, sweet young man."

In the Christmas of 1955, Heineman was riding his motorcycle down from Florida State University to camp out in the Florida Keys, and the fifteen-year-old Maggy met him through a friend. He was a marine biologist who had come over from Germany in 1940 when he was six years old. At first Maggy didn't mind his attentions because he had a motorcycle. Her mother appreciated that he unstopped the septic tank for the family, but she told Maggy she "might make her next conquest less total." Having quickly matured into a six-foot-one beauty, Maggy was relatively unaware of just how smitten Heineman had become with her.

She met up with him while she was in Tallahassee on a high school trip, and he took her on her first cave dive. Heineman was one of the pioneering cave divers who charted the underground passages 240 feet below Wakulla Springs, a short distance from the places Johnny Weissmuller had frolicked on the *Tarzan* sets. She learned all too well about his infatuation later, though, when he showed up again at their house in Miami.

"We all got pretty tired of him," Jane Reno recalled of the first visit, "except Marky at that age, who was always looking out the window when you were telling the rest the facts of life.

"So we were all horrified to find that Bob had dropped by one afternoon shortly after college was out in June, given Marky a five-foot boa constrictor he had left over from biology lab, and been invited by Mark to live with us for an indefinite visit during the summer.

"He was a moody *Weltschmerz* German boy, a poor, broke fellow, and his mother had a beautiful, loving German voice. She worked hard in domestic service somewhere up around Hollywood. So, when, after about two weeks

Maggy said she was going to move up to her grandmother's unless I asked him to leave, I said, 'Gee, I know, but I just can't, the poor stupid jerk is so poor, and he's got nowhere to go.'"

Heineman managed it himself. On the next Sunday morning, when Jane Reno was feeling her "usual fragile Sunday morning self," he said with a certain Teutonic lordliness, "Mrs. Reno, I wonder if I might have a talk with you."

They walked out to the adjacent pasture together, and he said, "What I'd like to ask, Mrs. Reno, is: How do you feel about your daughters having sexual intercourse before they are married?"

"Well, Bob, I don't approve of it," replied Reno with equanimity, "certainly if they don't like the boy."

About three days later he moved out without leaving a message. Mark took the five-foot boa constrictor down to the local pet store, added some money, and swapped it for a seven-foot boa. Jane Reno said the larger constrictor "was probably the best snake we ever had living with us, because it didn't sneak or surprise people, or hide."

Spring-hopping adventures though north Florida became a family ritual. On a hot summer day, nothing was more refreshing than playing in the waters of the Ichetucknee River or countless other cool, spring-fed rivers.

Jane Reno's cousin Peter Hunter was attending college at the University of Florida, and the springs of the Ichetucknee were only about an hour's drive from Gainesville. He wrote to her shortly after one excursion, reminiscing on the joy the gathering had brought him:

"I compare the feeling to the one Bemelsman says he experiences whenever he passes the *Normandie*'s old slip along the Hudson, and also to the farewell reviews of an army at the close of its service—Catton uses some good phrases to describe it at the end of *This Hallowed Ground*, ' . . . and they moved to the far-off sound of music and laughter.' Anyway, we shared a grand time yesterday, and I regret that we can't play together every day, and that, noble and generous and cultured and wonderful people that we are, there are so few of us left nowadays, and that 'Time allows in all his tuneful turning so few and such morning songs.'

"Thank you again for driving all the way up here this weekend and springhopping. Twas an experience whose pure serene I had never breathed till I heard the Reno's speak out loud and bold, and it was utterly wonderful."

Maggy Reno at what is now Gilchrist Blue Springs State Park with her mother, Jane, in the background, May 1956.

During the mid- to latter part of the 1950s, Jane Reno's journalism reached its peak. As much as she enjoyed being an extrovert in her private life, as a journalist she was a good listener. The Miccosukees had reinforced her belief in the importance of complete and total accuracy in reporting, and her husband had also been a great teacher. In the conservative society of the era, she had to overcome the tendency of men to avoid discussing complex issues with a female reporter, believing she was incapable of understanding them. Those who saw that Jane understood their issues opened up. When it came to investigative reporting, the ones who underrated her came to despise her for fooling them and to despise themselves for being fooled. Few journalists in Miami were ever able to bring to their reporting the wealth of detailed knowledge about the history of the community that Reno did. Her husband knew more about Miami than anyone, but within the scope of crime reporting he had limited use for his knowledge. Instead, he freely shared the information about Miami's power brokers with her, and the scope of her reporting allowed her to make great use of it.

The Kefauver hearings in 1950 had stripped away the veneer of respectability that covered gambling and corruption in Miami in the previous two decades, and Senator Kefauver kept up his Senate Special Committee to Investigate Crime as a running concern. Miami might not have been the most important place in the country for the senator from Tennessee to root out crime, but it was one of the sunniest places to do so. In 1955, Jane agreed to take part in a special investigation of the illegal adoption market, or "black-market babies." She could not have enjoyed herself more. Playing the part of Mrs. Frederick Zimmerman, she got to flash a fake diamond ring, drive a Cadillac, and invent a whole new socialite persona in pursuit of the story.

"It is the manner of money, Win," she wrote to her sister of the experience, "that turns the trick, more than the Cadillac and the phony diamond. White gloves and an air of being sheltered and protected. As a tour de force,

THE WEATHER
Fair through tomorrow. High today, 78 to 82; low tonight, in low 60s on Beach, low 60s inland. Gentle to moderate northeast winds.

Extremes Past 24 Hours: 75-66
Weather Report and Map on 6-B

# MIAMI DAILY NEWS

HOME EDITION

60TH YEAR, NO. 185   TELEPHONE 2-6211   MIAMI 30, FLORIDA   TUESDAY EVENING, NOVEMBER 15, 1955   FIVE CENTS

## News Reporter Exposes Racket

# YOU CAN BUY A BABY HERE

## $1,000 To $3,000 Is Asking Price

*How she shopped for babies on Greater Miami's black market is told here by News Staff Writer Jane Wood. She was subpoenaed by Sen. Kefauver's Subcommittee on Juvenile Delinquency to testify at today's hearing about her experiences.*

**By JANE WOOD**
Miami Daily News Staff Writer

Driving a borrowed Cadillac, wearing a phony diamond ring, I went out to buy babies on the black market for the Kefauver committee.

No baby sellers that I found here have any ready for immediate delivery, but I have the promise of a new-born infant next April for somewhere around $2,000 to $3,000, with a $500 cash down payment right now.

Another cheaper baby dealer promised to call me when he gets an unmarried mother, and his price will only be a little more than $1,000.

Among the baby sellers in Miami is a little mild-mannered, grandmotherly woman, Dr. Katherine Cole, who has left behind her a trail of death. The man selling babies cheap is Dr. Eduardo Suarez.

Wild comedy, sheer terror, death on a Sunday afternoon—all these you find among the strange baby-sellers, who have flourished here for years. They are the products of a city—Miami—that does not give enough help nor kindness to unmarried women who find themselves pregnant.

"Take my Cadillac," said Ernest Mitler, special legal counsel of the Kefauver committee, when he asked me to buy babies for him. "You drive up in a Cadillac, people's thoughts fly out the window, they forget they might be investigated."

**Convicted Of Murder**

Mitler gave me names. One of them was Dr. Katherine Cole, a naturopath. I looked up her record and found that she has been convicted of murder in the third degree in the death of a woman following an abortion. The conviction was reversed by the Supreme Court, because of insufficient evidence, due to the fact that when the woman who died said Dr. Cole performed the abortion, it was not proved that the woman knew she was dying.

Dr. Cole was also, I found, once charged with failure to file a birth certificate in a case where she arranged to have two babies born in different places, of different mothers, registered for a birth certificate as twins. This case was nol prossed.

I drove the Cadillac to Dr. Cole's clinic at 4765 SW 8th St. It is a very long car. The little wire-recorder in my pocketbook, a thing called a minifon, makes a whirring noise and has to be handled as gently as a sack of eggs. Both made me so nervous my hands shook and my voice trembled. Dr. Cole was very kind and gentle to me.

"I'm Mrs. Frederick Zimmerman," I told her, "and I was down here on a fishing trip with some friends, when my husband wrote me that we might be able to adopt a baby in Florida. His name is Jersey people gave him your name. My husband, Zimmy, is perfectly wonderful, and he can give me anything in the world I want. But we can't have a baby. And the social workers won't let us adopt a baby."

**Story Of Desertion**

Dr. Cole showed me a picture of her five children, and told me she was deserted by her husband, a brilliant man, and her professor in naturopathy, when she was 24 years old. Her husband ran off with his secretary. Her family wanted her to bring the children back to the South Carolina farm where she was raised. But she would not, and then, and there she resolved that she would never let any baby she delivered in her obstetrical practice be put in an orphan's home.

"I just placed a lovely baby with a New Jersey couple recently," she commented.

I took off my white gloves, her glance brushed

Continued on Page 6A, Col. 1

JANE WOOD SOUGHT BLACK MARKET BABIES
Minifon Wire Recorder Was In Her Handbag

## Miami Baby Racket In Probe Spotlight

**By HAINES COLBERT**
Miami Daily News Staff Writer

The Kefauver committee investigation of juvenile delinquency turned the spotlight on the baby adoption racket in Miami today.

Testimony of Jane Wood, Miami Daily News reporter who negotiated for the purchase of two babies, was scheduled for the second day of the hearing before the senate subcommittee.

Miss Wood was to take the witness stand after Judge Harry Woodward of the Richmond

County, Ga. (Augusta) juvenile court had completed her defense of his practice of sending hundreds of babies from Augusta into homes across the nation.

**Judge Defends Role**

The chubby, bald judge, speaking easily and clearly under the rapid-fire questioning of Sen. Estes Kefauver and his aides, insisted during hours of testimony yesterday and today that there was nothing "monstrous" about his role.

The committee began yesterday, and ended today the effort to investigate the families in which he sent the children.

**Given To Alcoholic**

The attorney cited one case in which Judge Woodward had placed children from a mother who was charged with drunkenness and gave one of them to an alcoholic who died shortly thereafter.

"I didn't kill him," the judge replied. "It was a natural death."

The grandmother of the child from Mrs. Ella Mae Parrish, of Augusta, had testified that she and her husband wanted to take one or two of the children and place the others with members of the family. She said she never saw the four tots after Judge Woodward took them from the custody of their mother in November, 1954.

**Rumors Stopped Practice**

Mrs. Evora Epps, operator of a child boarding house in Augusta, testified that she boarded the wards of the court at $25 a month between the time they were taken from their parents and placed for adoption. She said she began boarding the children in 1948 and stopped in 1951, explaining:

"There was a rumor going

## Son Describes How He Blew Up Airliner

Associated Press
Denver, Nov. 15 — In dispassionate tones, John Gilbert (Jack) Graham related last night how he rigged 25 sticks of dynamite to explode aboard an airliner carrying his mother and 43 other passengers.

All 44 were killed Nov. 1 when the big United Air Lines DC-6B blew up near Longmont, Colo., and crashed 11 minutes after it had left Denver.

Graham, a 23-year-old convicted forger, did not reply when asked whether he felt remorse.

U.S. Atty. Donald E. Kelly said the Denver construction and restaurant worker signed a "written admission" earlier that he killed his mother Mrs. Daisie E. King, 54, to collect her $37,500 air flight insurance.

Ironically, the insurance was invalid because his mother had

**In Line For Estate**
Graham who also is in line for a fourth of his mother's estate, estimated at $150,000.

Details of Graham's plot were begun Oct. 18 at St. Graham and his mother left here Nov. 1.

Construction of the bomb was begun Oct. 16 or 17, Graham said. Parts of it included the dynamite, a 6-volt battery, an electric timing device

## Early Vote Slow For City Offices

### Balloting Is Less Than 1953 Rate

**By CHARLES F. HESSER**
Miami Daily News Political Writer

Voting in Miami's city primary got off to a slow start today.

A sampling of 15 precincts by City Clerk Frank Correll at 8 a.m. indicated that only 2,000, or about 2 per cent of the 105,000 eligible voters, had cast ballots in the first hour.

Correll was sticking to his pre-election prediction that no more than 40,000 or 43,000 will vote by the time the polls close at 7 p.m.

During the first hour of balloting in the 1953 primary, approximately 3,000 persons had voted.

The weatherman had promised "fine weather" throughout the day, but the campaign has failed to generate much voter enthusiasm.

Miamians are voting for a mayor, two commissioners and on the question of whether to permit the sale of liquor by the drink.

**Some May Face Runoff**

Unless candidates in each group receive a majority of the votes cast in the group, the two high men in each group will enter a runoff next Tuesday. It is possible that mayoralty and the Group 2 commission race might be decided in today's primary.

Mayoralty candidate Joseph J. Orr and Christmas appear to be by far the leading candidates in the Group 1 contest, but William W. Davenport may pick up sufficient support to force a runoff.

Commissioner H. Leslie Quigg is given a good chance of

Continued on Page 2A, Col. 6

## Adlai Tells Plans Today For Seeking Presidency

Associated Press
Chicago, Nov. 15 — Adlai E. Stevenson was expected to formally announce today that he is a candidate for the Democratic nomination for president in 1956.

These close to the 1952 Democratic presidential standard bearer said the statement — which was trusted that she boarded the wards of the court at $25 a month between the time they were and placed for adoption. She began boarding the children in 1951 and stopped in 1951, announces that he is a candidate.

The statement will reveal his political plans and outline briefly

## BOB HOPE ASKS FOR RED VISA, WOULD LAUGH CURTAIN AWAY

Hollywood, Calif., Nov. 15 —(AP)— Bob Hope wants to go to Moscow and try to laugh the iron curtain away.

The comedian made a formal application yesterday to visit Russia for the purpose of filming a television show there with Russian stars. The application, seeking visas for 19 people, was delivered to the Russian embassy in Washington. The U.S. State Department has already cleared Hope.

"I understand there are some very good comics in Moscow," Hope said. "There have been cultural exchanges of farmers and journalists between the two countries. Why not an exchange of comics?"

## Magazine Lured Winchell Plugs

*Third of a Series*

**By JACK OLSEN**
Special to The Miami Daily News

In the chit-chat bars along New York's Madison Ave. the bright young men of the publishing industry discuss the magazine Confidential.

Almost to a man, they are convinced that they know the "inside story" about the magazine.

The inside story, they tell you with knowing nonchalance, is that columnist Walter Winchell is the hatchet and the guiding hand behind Confidential. A typical explanation:

"Winchell was getting a lot of hot information he couldn't use in his column, see? So he got this guy Bob Harrison to front for him and start Confidential. Gave Winchell an outlet for his stories.

"You want proof? Look at all the Winchell stories in Confidential. Winchell Was Right About That and 'Winchell Was Right About That.' And why do you think Winchell is always plugging the magazine on his TV show and in his column?"

**Story Logical But Untrue**

That explanation is commonplace only because it has been achieved with wide acceptability. Despite the neatness of the logic, the truth is not in it. The facts:

Robert Harrison, a well-to-do publisher of cheat and studdy, long had his eye on the idea of a "fact" magazine which would give the "dirt" on famous people.

WALTER WINCHELL
Plugs "Confidential"

His thinking on the subject was first influenced by a New

it fascinated me to be able to sell myself as the rich Mrs. Zimmerman, and I fell in love with the fictitious Zimmy before I was through. (He was Jewish and I was Gentile and that was why the social workers would not let us adopt a baby.)"

In 1956, she won the *Big Story* award again for a June 1955 story exposing a robbery gang that counted two Miami motorcycle policemen among its members. The police officers were suggesting the targets and taking a share of the profits, and some New Jersey drifters did the actual robberies. One of the gang, LeRoy Horne, got caught and sentenced to ten years in prison, and the unusual kindness of the judge to his wife—along with an article Jane Reno wrote for the *Miami Daily News* about her situation—led a year later to him fingering all the other parties involved. His wife had been pregnant at his sentencing, and the judge had helped raise money to send her to live near him at the prison.

As a result, Reno found information dumped in her lap one day from an anonymous source that described the workings of the gang. It was suggested to her that if she went up to the state prison camp in DeLand to talk to Horne, he might be willing to confirm all the information. She worked in conjunction with the police—normally her husband's beat at the *Miami Herald*—and drove 280 miles to DeLand to get the scoop.

The less-than-warm reception she received from the "banty rooster of a man" who headed the homicide division and accompanied her to DeLand, Lieutenant Eldredge, was one that women reporters were soon to face with regularity throughout the country as they entered realms of journalism that had up to that point been men-only clubs. Not fond of reporters to start with, Eldredge was extremely dubious that her information would lead to anything, and he tried to scare her with the gravity of what she was involving herself in. Reno wrote: "I assured Lt. Eldredge that I was not going to dye my hair red and call myself Brenda, that I was scared of armed robbers, that I realized that this was no TV program, and that I would not breathe down his neck or joggle his arm while he investigated, and that I would keep him informed of everything I knew and did, and would help where I could."

To Eldredge's surprise, Reno proved him wrong. LeRoy Horne laid out the story for her, phone calls were made, and the gang was rounded up. Patrolman Pete Balma was arrested, along with holdup gang members Jerry Casselli and

Ralph Tango. Later other gang members Nicholas Sottile and Arthut Kiefer were arrested as well. Horne said Balma's former partner, Patrolman Lewis Womack, had also been an accomplice during the time Horne was involved with the gang from February to October 1954. Womack had died in a mysterious explosion in his sixteen-foot boat, though, in July 1954. After Womack's death, Balma divorced his wife and remarried Womack's widow. The members of the holdup gang were convicted, but a criminal conviction was never secured against Balma, as Casselli refused to testify against him. However, Balma was dismissed from the force.

Reno got a one-hundred-dollar bonus from the *Miami Daily News* for her second *Big Story* award, and she loved the city more than ever for being a place "that has so many things to holler about and criticize that I shall never run out of story material for years." She was most gratified by the small wave of affection from fellow workers—"elevator operators, secretaries, proof readers, and many people in the *News* whom I do not know by name, expressed by touches on the shoulder, and hand shakes, that were more sincere than words can be."

She remained on freelance terms with the *Miami Daily News* until 1956. At the beginning of that year, this finally changed, and the forty-two-year-old Reno was given a guaranteed salary of one hundred dollars per week.

"It is not quite such a rat race as it was when I pushed myself to produce all they could use," she wrote. "Now, in 23 years I can retire."

A *Miami Daily News* blurb announcing the airing of the television episode of her second *Big Story* award read:

"You'd think that she would have little time for writing—living on the edge of the Everglades as she does with her husband, four children, eighteen peacocks, and four beagles. But writing comes as naturally as breathing to Jane Wood, Miami News Staff Writer, who'll appear on television tonight for her second Big Story appearance and award at 8:30 over Channel 7. Walter Headley, president of the International Police Chiefs' Association, will present the award for Jane's Miami News stories last summer that cracked a hold-up gang and sent three members to jail.

"Of course, no other woman has won this important recognition twice, but that's typical of Jane. What other woman would ride a sea sled twenty feet below the Gulf Stream to get the story—or get lost in Big Cypress swamp, and

Jane Reno with actress Lesley Woods, who portrayed her in the *Big Story* episode titled "Fingerman" that aired on NBC on September 21, 1956.

through this accident, come up with a story on Indian babies suffering from a mysterious malady that won her the first Big Story award in 1950.

"Jane could go on and on about awards and honors—from the Florida Bar Association . . . the Florida Daily Newspaper Association . . . the Miami Chamber of Commerce . . . But you'd have a hard time getting the information. She's modest and unassuming, and between homemaking, raising peacocks, and writing award winning stories for The Miami News, she's plotting and planning how to achieve her two favorite projects—a way to overcome the tragic need for facilities to treat mentally disturbed children—and a more adequate flood control levee system for Dade County."[1]

The start of the last sentence was where anyone who knew her well usually dropped the newspaper while choking with laughter. The strictures of the day still required the newspaper to pass her off as an unassuming homemaker who managed to knock out amazing journalism in her spare time. That nod to convention was reminiscent of the description of her as a childhood genius, when she had also been called modest and unassuming. Women of exceptional abilities had to be characterized as such so as not to threaten men. On the other hand, it was true that she never bragged of honors and awards, or placed much value in them beyond their monetary value.

During the previous years she had a desk at the offices of the paper but was paid only for what she produced. Breaking down the resistance to women in the newsroom was no easy task. Dan Mahoney, the publisher, knew she was one of the best reporters at the *Miami Daily News*, as did her managing editor, Hoke Welch. Mahoney had a hard time admitting to the public that there was no basis for his chauvinist biases, though. By late 1954 she was increasingly doing hard-news investigative stories that ran on the "Views of the News" page of the paper, and by early 1955 that had morphed into her *Special Report* feature.

The thought was somewhat comforting, because as she watched her father approach seventy and continue his legal work, she knew he had no safety net. Only within the next year or two did lawyers become eligible for Social Security, and Reno was finagling a way for him to pay income tax so that he would become eligible. In the meantime, with Mr. Wood's increasingly poor health and his meager law income, George Jr., Daisy, Winifred, and Jane were contributing fifty dollars per month apiece to make up for the shortfall in their parents' living expenses. While Reno's father still felt strongly about maintaining his independence, his wife, Daisy, was beginning to sway him to the idea that it was okay to accept help from his children. The care of their parents eventually became an acrimonious issue between the siblings, leading to some difficult confrontations in the upcoming decade.

If there was any doubt as to the source of such family battling, Reno had only to look to her father. While he and his sister May carried on their long-standing refusal to speak to each other, relations degenerated between him and his younger brother when Roy Wood came to live with George and Daisy for the first time since the Depression. Having returned from working as a judge in Germany, Roy showed up in 1957 with only a tiny income of his own, looking to land on his feet in a legal practice. Within a week it became obvious that the situation wasn't going to work out. Roy's wife, Helen, came down from Georgia on a weekend, and Daisy Wood gave her some "miscellaneous and under the circumstances, inappropriate advice," according to Reno. Roy Wood became furious, and the couples ceased speaking to each other. Reno could see both sides but wanted a part of neither. She had sympathy for her uncle Roy because of his wife, whom she described uncompromisingly:

"I consider Helen a disintegrating, neurotic slob who gives me the creeps. I consider her drinking simply a symptom and a mask for a profound neurosis that is going to destroy her. Most people don't realize that alcoholism such as hers is not the cause of such a disintegration of character, but a simple symptom. On the water-wagon she is as bad as off. Unfortunately, I am always kind to neurotics of that type, and don't give the useless advice, because I consider them quite hopeless and beyond me. I feel compassion for them because I consider them generally, with few exceptions, irretrievably damned. Because of this attitude, Helen thinks I am very wonderful, and understand her."

Though Reno was to engage in family battles over her own alcoholism, the savagery of her disdain for Helen Wood was primarily because she thought her aunt gave alcoholism a bad name. Reno came from the school of drinkers who believed that while alcohol might exacerbate some of your less flattering qualities, you should never use alcoholism as an excuse for them. Nor was she particularly fond of neurotics. Empathy was her stock in trade, but not necessarily sympathy.

In her new salaried position and established investigative news feature *Special Report*, Reno was assigned in the spring of 1956 to talk to a source who was leaking material from a grand jury that was investigating Circuit Judge George Holt. The source of the leaks mysteriously identified himself to Reno only as "Banquo's Ghost." Reno found him to be sleazy and untrustworthy and questioned his motives for offering the information. Reno's keen sense of fair play and justice, seeing beyond the obvious, was a healthy counterbalance to the increased trend toward crusading. In an extraordinarily detailed seven-part series that ran in the spring of 1957 on the deeply flawed grand jury system of Dade County, Reno revealed how the reputations of Judge Holt and State Attorney George Brautigam had been ruined.

Officials who were victimized often had their own array of faults, such as Brautigam's obsessive anticommunism during the McCarthy era. Judge Holt was also an ardent anticommunist who committed fourteen people to jail for refusing to answer questions about affiliation with the Communist Party. The Florida Supreme Court had to free them all in November 1954.

Jane Reno's belief in crusading against crusades was directed equally at what she saw as the "poisonous and insidious paranoid conformity" that was the hallmark of an America still reeling from the excesses of Joe McCarthy, and of crusading newspapers and select citizens overzealously trying to exert a moral influence on the community. The Kefauver Committee was driving a wave of crusading that Henry Reno had helped launch with his reporting and Jane had aided with her black-market baby story, but Jane was beginning to see the dark side of it. The grand juries were a symptom of this overzealousness.

The curious character whom Reno first came to know as "Banquo's Ghost" was one of the major players in the grand jury investigating Judge Holt. The antipathy of the grand jury for State Attorney George Brautigam began when the grand jury demanded that Brautigam let them appoint an assistant state attorney of their choosing to aid their investigation. When Brautigam explained that he was the only person vested with that authority, they suggested a candidate whom he might be willing to appoint. Brautigam met with their choice the next day, attorney Sam Weissbuch, with whom he was not acquainted and on whom he had not had the chance to run background checks. He explained the limitations of the position to Weissbuch and that funds were not available to pay him, and asked whether the attorney had any knowledge of the matter under investigation. Weissbuch assured him he did not and that he would sign an affidavit to that effect, but the state attorney told him his word would be sufficient. In a record check two weeks later, Brautigam discovered that Weissbuch had lied. Weissbuch had testified in front of the grand jury two weeks before Brautigam first met with him.

In fact, Weissbuch—who was leaking the doings of the grand jury to Reno as

"Banquo's Ghost"—had a decade-old grudge against Judge Holt. According to a statement by the judge released after the grand jury report was made public:

"This attorney was biased and personally prejudiced against me because during the war, after he had received a commission in the US Navy, he applied for the intelligence division thereof, and a naval intelligence officer came to see me as circuit judge, and asked for my recommendation, which was refused. I refused because I knew this lawyer S. D. Weissbuch too well and valued the safety of my country above his personal ambitions. However, his influence was so great that he secured from the Under Secretary of State, Sumner Welles, the entire file in this matter and found my objections therein, and came to me (and others, I am informed) and demanded that I withdraw it, which was refused. He thereupon threatened me that for the rest of his life he would exert every effort to 'get me.' All of these matters are of record."

The focus of the grand jury investigation was on whether Judge Holt had handled a case improperly involving a rich, elderly New Jersey man whose wife lived in Miami. Both had been deemed incompetent and curatorships had been set up to handle the estate. The grand jury's belief was that Holt was making his attorney friends rich at the cost of the estate. A long-running criticism of Judge Holt was his liberal awarding of attorney's fees, along with his propensity to name "Special Masters" in cases. The latter was a system whereby private lawyers were paid to hear cases and report back to the judge on their findings. It was a system that had allowed Reno's father, George Wood, to put food on his family's table during the Depression. Judge Holt made no secret about his belief that attorneys should be well rewarded, but it didn't always sit well with the public.

After Brautigam appointed Weissbuch to assist the grand jury, the state attorney paid the case no more attention until March 1956, when the jury foreman requested that Brautigam be present at a day's hearings. Brautigam was surprised by the hostility Weissbuch displayed toward a witness, striking a young attorney named Daniel Neal Heller at one point, and Brautigam warned Weissbuch and other grand jurors about their conduct.

The jurors sent Heller from the room and proceeded to berate Brautigam for interfering. The jury invited Brautigam back the next day, but when he was waiting in the anteroom, a juror came out and shouted at him through the glass that he "would not be needed, and was excused from any further ap-

204 THE EXTRAORDINARY LIFE OF JANE WOOD RENO

pearances in the Grand Jury room." That was the last that Brautigam saw of the grand jury until he was summoned to read their interim report on April 28. With the support of the newspapers there was a mood in the air of mid-1950s Miami that the legal system was constrained too much by procedure. Only two decades before, lynch mobs had still been taking matters into their own hands in south Florida. Newspapers convicted people in public, and grand juries demanded powers that would make them a law unto themselves. Mob justice operated under a new veneer of respectability, but it was still more or less the same thing. The Florida Supreme Court recognized this.

Brautigam was disturbed by the interim report of the grand jury, as it contained many defamatory accusations yet issued no indictments. He moved to expunge the report, but a judge denied the motion and had it released. Brautigam's stand proved unpopular, and he was defeated in the fall elections in 1956. The following year, a month before Reno wrote her seven-part series, the Florida Supreme Court upheld Brautigam and expunged the report from the public record. The court wrote: "Unlike Pilate, he did not yield to what at the moment appeared to be the popular side of a controversy, but performed his duty according to the dictates of his own conscience, as he had the right to do. Subsequent public events indicate that he paid a high price for his devotion to duty. Such courageous public service is worthy of this commendation."

Of the grand jury report, the Supreme Court railed:

"The parties here are not in agreement as to whether the report in question discloses the commission of a crime by the principals. But it at least convicted them—without indictment, without published evidence, without trial, and without due process of law—of wrongdoing little short of a crime, inevitably blackening their reputations and destroying them in their profession. Such a conviction by a grand jury is not far removed from and is no less repugnant to traditions of fair play than lynch law. The medieval practice of subjecting a person suspected of crime to the rack and other forms of torture is universally condemned; and we see little difference in subjecting a person to the torture of public condemnation, loss of reputation, and blacklisting in their chosen profession, in the manner here attempted by the grand jury. The person so condemned is just as defenseless as the medieval prisoner and the victim of the lynch mob; the injury to him is just as fatal as if he had been charged with and convicted of a crime."[2]

The problem with the grand juries was just one of the hundreds of *Special Report* features that Reno filed from 1955 to 1957. She wrote to her sister Winifred in the spring of 1957, describing the work:

"I am enjoying my newspapering pretty good right now. I had to regretfully give up working for Hank Meyer[3] for awhile—too crushing a load. But Hank is darling. We have been having some fine lively issues and events and cases this winter for the Special Report I write three or four times a week. I am certainly the best known and best newspaper woman in Florida, having become twice blasted in the current session of the legislature. (Blasted by villains whose displeasure it is an honor to incur.) The nice thing about my job is that there is in one way no ceiling to it. I can tackle the big, the complex, the difficult and the hot stories, and be so controversial I move from hot water to warm to boiling, with the blessings of my bosses.

"The challenge is to grasp and to communicate, fairly and accurately, in the most important local issues. For example: second mortgage racketeering and regulation, small loan shenanigans, the case of the brain-washed grand juries, the Seminole peace treaty (proposed), the U.S. Army Engineers flood control policies, hurricane research, a great feud over the Jackson Psychiatric Institute, the Puerto Rican farm labor camps. These are issues on which there have been a number of widely separated viewpoints in recent months. They take a degree of research, legwork. They are complex, and must be presented lucidly and vividly, but without over-simplification or distortion. I write something that is like a short magazine article, but it is specific, pin-pointed and local. I don't do a column, it is not that rigid or personalized. But it has a lot wider range of subject and of personalizing permitted than the regular reporter.

"This feature has sort of evolved in the last two years, and is cherished fairly highly by my bosses as well as by me, and is peculiarly congenial. It would be hard to go stale on, since it is always new and varying and demanding, and since I have a fair control in the tacks and tangents I can go off on. You can't coast on it, either, or get stupid. Last month I went to Gainesville for a two-day seminar on nuclear energy, consorting with a lovely bunch of scientists, and last week out into the Everglades to sit in on a Seminole council meeting where I am the only reporter in the world really welcomed. (Probably because I am the only reporter in the world that will bother to go to most all of the important council meetings and be extremely careful to get it all accurately.)

One real beauty about this particular thing, in case you think I sound stuffy and vainglorious is that I get a good deal of hammering in return on some of these things, and am subject to plenty of acid criticism within and outside of my office—things that begin with, 'You and your goddamn vain hyperthyroid, look what you did now . . . ' It's a lot of fun, and I wouldn't be doing anything else though I wish I could make twice as much money.

"Looking deeply into the workings and life of a big city is a very fascinating way to spend your time. Miami is very exciting to me, a true metropolis, an adequate education. I have developed a feeling for it of the type and magnitude that some of the really great city lovers have had for the really great cities—like Proust had for Paris, say. Miami with a ring of mountains could be, to me, the world's greatest city, always with a few hundred thousand things about it to clean, straighten, polish, or erase. You can curse it so, too—there is nothing piddling about its flaws. My current long-time crusade is against a poisonous and insidious paranoid conformity and malicious and vicious pseudo-reform-ing: i.e., I am crusading against crusades. You can't believe how this subtle corrosive has eaten into the old go-to-hell and tolerant town you grew up in. I hope to see the day we turn back toward the mean that lies somewhere be-tween the old free and easy wide open Miami and now."

Conflicts between Reno and her siblings could be especially caustic, especially between Jane and Winifred because of their implacably stubborn natures. Furthermore, Jane's attitudes confounded her sister. Whereas everyone else in the family had inherited their mother's sense of decorum to varying degrees, and her fashion sense, Jane had never shown the slightest regard for clothing or convention. A fierce argument occurred during one of Winifred's visits after Jane refused to take off a dress that Winifred had been ironing. Reno taunted her little sister with her disregard for its importance, and the episode culminated in Jane striking the enraged Winifred with the ironing board.

Winifred had married very briefly, settled down to be a schoolteacher in California, taught overseas in Germany, and returned to California. Around the time of the following letter, Wood had just moved back into the mountains east of Los Angeles to the small town of Idyllwild, where she joined fellow WASP and old friend Dot Swain Lewis.[1] Finding the mountains to be the perfect inspiration for her art, Lewis built a house and remained in Idyllwild ever after, most of the time sharing the house with Wood. In the same letter to Winifred in which she described her *Special Report* work, Jane wrote to her younger sister:

"The days are getting long, the wonderful rose and gold clouds are piling up in summer sunsets, and all about me is that delicious feeling that has come to signal summer: They are coming home! Janet and Mark and You. My chillun go away and come again most in summer, even ere now, so it has come to have that exciting feeling in it that used to be in Christmas.

"Janet will leave Cornell June 11th and come home by bus, perhaps stopping for a night and a day with Nina Balfour in Washington to see Washington. Markie will leave Bangor shortly after June 15th, by bus, and also perhaps stop over at Nina's. They decided regretfully in Bangor that Mark's 1948 Ford couldn't possibly make the trip, so he is going to sell it, for about $75 I gather. You will probably be glad not to ride with them in $75 worth of Ford. I sure as God would be.

"Janet has a job in the City of Miami communications promised, $60 a week. She also has a job for Cornell next year that will pay her the equivalent of $960 in room and board, so we are right proud of her. In her chemistry pre-lim, she made the highest mark in the class, 95, and the class average was 65. She adores Cornell, and has had some indication that Cornell loves Janny Baby.

"Bob has registered at Tulane, which should be quite perfect for him. He had rather hoped for one of the Eastern colleges to which he applied, but his grade average C blocked his admission there. It is very tough the last two or three years, and from now on indefinitely, to get admitted to good colleges. There are about seven applications for every opening. However Tulane is good and more solid scholastically than the University of North Carolina, which might have otherwise been his choice. New Orleans will be a wonderful city for him, too, he and I both think. He is quite happy. He is having a fine time winding up high school with proms and banquets. You never saw a smarter 17 year old in a tuxedo than my six foot three inch Bob. He is still headed for the law, in a totally relaxed sort of way.

"Maggy is reaping honors in school with an even slightly wider swath than Janet. As of now she will be valedictorian next year, though that could change. She has won the Biology medal and the History medal and the county United Nations $50 contest prize, and some debate honors. She has a literary style I consider gifted and is a fine mathematician. She is also six feet one inch tall and a raving beauty, and reminds me more of you when she wakes up in the morning than anybody I ever knew. Sunny disposition otherwise. She plans to spend the summer teaching aqua-lung diving as a teacher for Diving Corp. of America.

"Mark I am very homesick for. He has had a wonderful time in Bangor, been sweet and helpful and loving, they say, at the George Woods, and dotes on them. He was on the Bangor High football team, right tackle. Does lousy school work, can't read worth a damn. He is 6 feet 4, weighs 190, is the most gorgeous hunk of young man you ever saw and has all the emotional maturity of a little yellow duck."

By the middle of 1957, Jane Reno was in an enviable place for any journalist in Miami. She showed up at the office when she wanted to, reported on what she wanted to, and had racked up a series of prestigious awards in hard-news reporting that would have been the envy of any local male journalist, and unheard of for a woman. The slings and arrows came at her from all directions,

Teenage Mark Reno, 1957.

and she relished the attention from "villains whose displeasure it is an honor to incur." A *Special Report* feature in late 1956 discussed a University of Miami researcher's analysis of the development plan for the Everglades agricultural area, which suggested that the massive system of levees and canals rushed into construction for south Florida drainage was something of a not-well-thought-out pork barrel project.

Although any questioning of drainage plans that aided south Florida development was considered heresy at that time, the concerns of UM researcher Robert Ford proved extremely prescient. The agricultural area south of Lake Okeechobee that had been drained earlier in the century was treated as a sacred cow that had to be not only extended and developed further but worked around in planning drainage of Lake Okeechobee and south Florida. This faulty assumption was the basis for the booming future overdevelop-

ment of south Florida and subsequent environmental nightmares that ensued from cutting off the natural flow of water into the Everglades from
Lake Okeechobee. Ford noted that sugarcane was subsidized but limited
from expansion by quota, and vegetables were limited by market factors,
but pointed out that fattening of beef cattle had increased substantially in
the agricultural area. Still, his argument applied wholly to sugarcane as well,
which would eventually become the largest obstacle to the restoration of
Everglades water flow. The study by Ford also poked holes in the wildly optimistic and arcanely caluclated cost-benefit analysis—and public benefit—the
Army Corps of Engineers used to justify massive flood control expenditures
in the Everglades agricultural area. Reno wrote: "It is clear from his study
that from an economic standpoint that new industry couldn't survive if it
had to bear the full amount of the real cost of production. The current development is marked by huge corporation-type undertakings, he points out.
Thus, he says, the heavy federal subsidy of a questionable agricultural project
involves relatively few people."

Both of Florida's US senators, Spessard Holland and George Smathers, fired
off letters to the *Miami Daily News* in outrage, and former governor Fuller
Warren chimed in as well. In the state legislature, her articles on mortgage
rackets, life insurance, and small-loan shenanigans drew heated rebuke from
state senators who were supporting the industries. Her articles on the mess
of the Dade County juvenile courts drew angry rebuttals from some involved
in the court system. But time and again, her stories drew fulsome praise from
average readers who enjoyed the civics lessons in the workings of government
and business, and her pulling back the curtains on those long accustomed to
operating in secrecy to expose unsavory practices.

In testimony in May 1957, Judge Vincent Giblin lashed out against the brochure distributed in Tallahassee by Judge Holt—who was fighting impeachment
by the Florida Senate—that contained Reno's recent seven-part *Special Report*
articles on the 1956 grand jury. The articles Reno wrote contained material critical of Giblin. Asked by Holt's attorney who wrote the articles in the brochure,
Giblin stated: "I think Mr. Heller wrote them [Dan Heller, co-curator of the Dowl-
ing estate], but they appeared under the name of Miss Jane Wood."[2]

Giblin, who had been Al Capone's Miami lawyer in the 1930s, had been one
of the most ardent voices in pressing the grand jury to indict Judge Holt the

previous year. The colorful Giblin once called the judges of the Florida Supreme Court "political pygmies," said he hated half the lawyers in Dade County, and often spoke out against fellow judges.

Reno had become a one-woman Consumer Financial Protection Bureau, as well as an advocate for the handicapped and mentally disturbed, court system reformer, juvenile defender, champion of the Everglades Indians, and all-purpose civics class. Even the winos outside the *Miami Daily News* building knew who she was. Maggy Reno Hurchalla remembered visiting her mother at the newspaper and the winos asking what she was doing there.

"Visiting my mother."

"Who's your mother?"

"Jane Wood."

"Oh, Jane Wood!" they'd cry excitedly.

The *Miami News* was outshining the *Miami Herald* in this era of being all that a community newspaper could be, but that didn't necessarily sell enough newspapers. High-profile crusades and more national and international coverage were what the Miami public seemed to increasingly favor, as well as morning rather than afternoon news. Though Dan Mahoney was the newspaper's publisher and had traditionally been the final authority on hiring and major changes at the paper, the parent company, Cox, decided to assert more direct control over the newspaper's direction.

On July 28, 1957, Cox CEO James M. Cox Jr. announced that Bill Baggs was the new editor of the *Miami Daily News* and that the paper was launching a Washington bureau. He stated that Baggs would "preside over the preparation of all news and features and govern the editorial policy of the newspaper."[3] Editor John McMullan was abandoning ship to go to the *Miami Herald*, and Cox saw the loss as a chance to reinvent the *News* somewhat into a leaner, tighter vessel as it was increasingly struggling to remain competitive. Tolerance of larger-than-life journalist personalities like Jane Reno who kept their own hours and chose their own material was not part of the future plan. Within months, the *News* moved from Freedom Tower into a new building on the Miami River and, two weeks after the move, on November 4, dropped the "Daily" from the name and became simply the *Miami News*.

The first issue of the new paper touted the changes within as an improvement all around, but one of the first things that regular readers noticed in the weeks to come was that Jane Wood's *Special Report* feature had disappeared. Staff writers no longer had "Miami News Staff Writer" bylines but instead were identified as "Reporter for Miami News." Reno's children remembered her not having a particularly good relationship with Bill Baggs, even though they had a shared liberalism, and that as editor he appeared determined to marginalize her role at the paper. It is hard to say how much of the marginalization was a result of the paper's content restructuring and how much was Baggs's personal desire to muzzle her, but her bylines became attached to short city and county reporting articles without any of the depth she'd been allowed to go into before. Reno kept most of her thoughts on her demotion in status to herself and seemed to accept that she wasn't going to regain her past glory under the newspaper's new leadership. She was already looking beyond to greener pastures of salary in different work that would help her afford three children's tuition at expensive private colleges.

"With all the move, and the new editor," she lamented in 1958, "nothing has as yet happened to distinguish the *News* as a newspaper, except that it misses more news coverage all the time."

Nevertheless, writer Howard Van Smith won a Pulitzer Prize for national reporting in 1959 for his articles about the desperate conditions for migrant workers in Immokalee in the winter of early 1958. Reno loved "Howie" Smith, her editor at the paper's Sunday magazine throughout the early part of the decade. She didn't in the least begrudge him being assigned to the articles, but it was a curious snub that Baggs brought Smith away from his old editing job to be a reporter when it was Reno's reporting the year before that had first brought attention to the situation of migrant farmworkers in the area.

Reno's feature article in January 1957, "Someone Has to Pick Those Beans, But . . . ," was a detailed view of the labor conditions at two camps in the Princeton/Redlands area of south Dade. The article began by asking why there was wire around the camps with signs warning that it was electrically charged. A guard said it was because it was a labor camp full of "a lot of damn heathens" but also said that they only turned the current on at night. A camp manager ridiculed the assertion: "That fence never has been charged, isn't charged, can't be charged, and will never be charged as long as I am here. You were being kidded." One of the partners of B & L Farms, C. E. Lounsbury, expressed surprise at learning there was such a fence and guessed it was for the protection of the workers from outsiders coming in to steal. The camp manager echoed the sentiment. Reno went on to write:

"The increasing stream of migrant farm workers flowing here in the winter since the end of the war has been hurting such conscience as Dade County has in periodic twinges. That life behind wire is such a shocking contrast to the tourist season 25 miles away. Average citizens, from winter to winter, rediscover the squalor. They are embarrassed, guilty, angry when they see it, and tend to lash out and try to make villains out of individual farm operators. Actually, as far as farm labor camps go, the B & L Mexican camp is a good one. It is kept quite clean. That our food is being harvested by people who live on the thin edge of nothing is not a local problem. The Mexicans, mostly from Texas, rate the camp good. There is no easy out, no ready-made solution of the great inequity in the life of those harvest hands.

"To keep farm labor camps from being figuratively as well as literally shocking is going to need—not laws, restrictions, regulations—but creative imagination. We can't legislate against the ways we have of growing food with laws tough enough to stop the camps, because that would stop the food growing now. We have to find better ways. This is how it's being done in the Redlands.

"For 10 years a lot of imaginative ingenuity has been going into building big, highly specialized farm machinery to bulldoze, disc, fertilize, and spray thousand acre vegetable patches. Smart scientists and manufacturers have improved and tailored fertilizer mixes to give plants all the major and trace elements they need in proper proportion. Chemistry and industry have cooperated to produce sprays to control bugs and fungus.

"The same sun that nurtures the tourist crop on the beach ripens the tomatoes in February in south Dade. The beautiful green sea of young corn rippling into the Everglades west of Krome today would have been quite impossible before the war. Thousands of acres are producing food today that were once impossible for profitable farming. So far, fine. But nobody has invented a machine that can pick tomatoes, beans, and sweet corn. The thousands of acres of vegetables have to have thousands of human harvesters.

"Once Negroes picked the crops around here. About 1948 a few Puerto Ricans began to trickle in, and that trickle has grown into a stream. A few years after that, the Mexicans wandered down. The migrant Negroes this year come mostly from Mississippi, and most of them will go back there when work ends here for them.

"The cars and the trucks that bring the Mexicans have mostly Texas licenses. A few are from California. The Mexicans are not sad, frightened people like many of the Puerto Ricans become when they migrate. They are more husky. They have a gay, curious, and robust air about them. They aren't intimidated. Some wear sombreros and boots with a verve. Many have an Indian look about their high cheekbones and copper skin.

"The Puerto Ricans are the Okies of the East Coast. They have established a vast, migratory loop. They begin to leave here in mid-March to go by truck and bus to the 'Delmarva' peninsula—that composite of Delaware, Maryland, and Virginia where a spring vegetable empire is growing. From there they go on up to the Great Lakes' borders to pick fall crops of tomatoes and wax beans. Some get as far as Maine and Minnesota, where they work in the potato harvest. They go home to Puerto Rico for a fall visit, return here between September and January to begin the cycle again.

"The ragged army returns, each year a little larger, with new recruits. B & L Farms, with its 6,500 acres owned or leased this year, is much the biggest operation in an area of huge farms. They come penniless and hungry. They borrow company money for food, in $3, $5 driblets. A little more than $20,000 in such small debts are on B & L books now. Thompson pulls a batch of ledger cards to show that though debts may accumulate to $50, to $100, the company doesn't take more than $10 a week out of a man's pay. No interest is charged. The company gives them a roof over their heads, rent free. There seems to be no good reason to have an electrically charged fence around a farm labor camp. The general belief in the Redlands is that it was set up last summer with the idea of keeping migrants who were not working for B & L from sneaking in and sleeping there.

"The necessity of such camps is rather obvious. How else can a horde of penniless wanderers find shelter on the Gold Coast at the peak of the winter season—or any other time? An incredibly bare minimum of shelter it is. In the Mexican camp near Krome Ave, there are almost 400 unpainted, tin-roofed new cabins, each 16 feet square. A plank partition splits each in half. A family lives in one room of that duplex, eight feet wide by sixteen feet long. If the family has six children, all eight live there and do their cooking there. The camp covers about 40 acres. In the 800 box-like homes are stuffed about 2500 people, with their bunks, cots, and worldly goods. A few dark, sagging tents are still pitched there, for the camp began as a tent-town. . . .

"The little, little children growing up so meagerly, toddling around the bare rock in the dust are the poignant notes of the camps. About 300 children, mostly from the Mexican B & L camp, are enrolled in Redlands Elemtary school now, says Jim Rice, attendance officer.

"'Attendance varies with the family,' Rice says. 'Some come just as regularly as any other children. I'd say that the attendance of migrant farm children who enroll is about 85 percent. . . . But we have never made a concentrated drive to force attendance on migrant farm workers. When you try to force those kids in school against their parents' will, the whole family just vanishes. They pick up and leave.'

"And the toddlers playing behind those fences will grow up to fill the next generation's farm labor camps—unless somebody can think of a better way to get our vegetables picked."[4]

The humanitarian crisis in Immokalee and other farm towns that Howard Van Smith and the *Miami News* brought to light at the beginning of 1958 was the result of heavy December rains and a January freeze that brought widespread crop failure throughout the state. Thousands of migrant workers were stranded in hovels in places like "Shacktown" in Immokalee with no work, no food, and no money to leave. Southern Dade County was also hit hard, losing half the $25 million vegetable crop. The stories drew the attention of Governor LeRoy Collins, who vowed to get involved in supplying aid and relocating the stranded workers. A stream of follow-up articles by Smith continued throughout the year to push for a replacement of Shacktown with a migrant labor camp with at least basic sanitary levels and accommodations. Instead, rather than upgrade, most Shacktown landlords just shut down their camps by the end of the year.

The question Reno posed in her 1957 migrant worker article was never really answered: How to change generations of these workers having to live and toil in the same conditions year after year? Closing down the migrant camps was seen as progress in the same way that closing down substandard public housing projects has often been seen as progress. The obvious eyesore was gone, and society could feel better. But where did the people go? They usually dispersed into substandard individual hovels throughout the community.[5]

While her former editor was tackling the migrant worker story, Reno was relatively absent from major reporting once her *Special Report* feature was taken away. She did some work on flood control, a few articles on the doings of the Miccosukees, and was assigned a variety of mundane short city-reporting pieces. In March she was assigned a series for the women's section, "Women You'll Remember," utilizing her extensive knowledge of Miami history to highlight remarkable women's contributions to the city. She had fun with the series, writing about characters outside the usual realm of knowledge like Old Lady Marg Hamochee, a Miccosukee woman who experienced all the Seminole Wars and lived to the age of 121, dying in 1937.

At the same time in March, she started producing some work more reminiscent of her *Special Report* again, starting with a series on a reform school in north Florida, the Marianna Industrial Training School for Boys, and their extensive use of corporal punishment. Boys could volunteer for beatings at the reform school to make up for low grades, but beatings were also administered for a range of offenses. Reno wrote:

"Boys at the state school for juvenile delinquents at Marianna work their way to release by a complicated grade and point system. Some boys 'have their points taken care of' when they volunteer to take a beating. These beatings with a leather strap have been described by Dr. Eugene Byrd, Miami psychologist and former staff member at Marianna, before the US Senate subcommitte on juvenile delinquency. Other former staff members support him in his condemnation of the punishment. Several resigned because of the abuse and brutality they witnessed.

"Under the individual rating system at Marianna, as described in a booklet they print there, a boy might never get released from the training school, except for the fact that state law requires he be turned loose at 21 years of age. However the average length of stays of boys under this system today is just one year. This is because boys 'have their points taken care of' by beatings.

"Graduates explain, 'Well, they don't want you to stay there forever, so if you get a low grade you can go to Mr. Dozier and ask him if you can have your points taken care of.' Some times they will let you take a beating to erase a low grade, say the boys. All boys who ask for a beating are not granted paddlings, says Assistant Superintendent H. B. Mitchell, who comments, 'If I spanked all boys who ask for a spanking, I'd be spanking boys all Saturday.'

"Most who are paddled on Saturdays at the 'White House,' the school's old solitary confinement building, have no choice. A list of their names is read each Saturday morning. They usually receive about 15 blows with a leather strap from Assistant Superintendent R. W. Hatton, while Superintendent Art Dozier or Mr. Mitchell counts. A study of 250 white boys committed at one time to Marianna showed they had at that point been given 691 whippings among them. Eleven year old boys had received 265 or 38 percent of the beatings and 17 year old boys received 21, or but three per cent. The older the boy, the fewer beatings he received, records of the school showed at the time. Mr. Mitchell says the personality of the boy is carefully considered before he is given any spanking. . . . Superintendent Dozier says he abhors these paddlings, but knows of nothing better."[1]

Many boys were at the school for relatively low-grade offenses like running away from home, though there was also a fair share of hard cases. Dozier was well liked in Tallahassee and usually got all the funding he wanted for the school, so Governor Collins expressed alarm when Reno's reporting made him aware of the corporal punishment. The ever-moderate Collins chose to keep his head in the sand, though, proclaiming, "I can't believe that there is any brutality going on there or that Mr. Dozier would be permitting anything wrong," adding that he was "shocked that anyone would have serious fault to find with Mr. Dozier's operation, which I have heard described many times both in and outside the state as an almost model institution of its type."[2]

For a politician whom Reno liked and respected, LeRoy Collins was very good at doing nothing a great deal of the time. The Immokalee Chamber of Commerce had notified his office of the impending farmworker crisis in December 1957, but nothing reached his desk. He had to read about it in the *Miami News*. Because Dr. Byrd's testimony before the Senate subcommittee didn't name the Marianna school, it was left to Jane Reno to put the pieces together and bring the story to the governor's attention. But Collins failed to act on it.

Representative Jack Orr, one of young Janet Reno's political heroes for his lone vote in the Florida State House against a bill in 1956 to circumvent the US Supreme Court ruling on desegregation, also weighed in, singing the praises of Dozier:

"I disapprove of corporal punishment, but Art Dozier is one of the very best public officials we have in this state. I don't know of a public official in whom I have more confidence. I've supported every appropriation he has asked of the legislature. I've been to Marianna. That's a good school. You can feel the terrific amount of respect the boys have for Mr. Dozier, and they do not seem to be afraid of him. I wasn't aware they use corporal punishment, and I never knew of the beatings. I have to side against the use of corporal punishment. I don't approve of it."[3]

Whether Orr ever would have acted on his disapproval became a moot point when he was voted out of his House seat in 1958 for his courageous stance in support of school desegregation. One after another, politicians expressed surprise and dismay but refused to believe that Dozier could really be doing anything wrong. The testimony of former staff psychologist Dr. Byrd before the Senate subcommittee was graphic. He testified that the boys were required to spread out across a cot, grab the headrails, and be whipped savagely with a three-and-a-half-inch leather strap. If they let loose their grip on the headrails or moved on the bed, they were lashed more times.[4] A letter to the editor shortly after Reno's articles came out from a former boy at the school confirmed that everything she had written in her articles was true. A former staff psychologist came to Reno after the article and told her that Dozier's assistants made boys reveal naked bottoms at times for whipping and appeared to take sexual pleasure in the process.

Fifty years later, the school remained open, and the name had been changed to the Dozier School for Boys in honor of its longtime superintendent. Governor Charlie Crist launched an investigation in 2008 when thirty-two unmarked graves were found in the school burial ground. Eventually the number grew to fifty-one. Boys who had attended the school remembered the beatings. They told horror stories of being whipped so hard that underwear had to be surgically removed and of being forced to bite down on a pillow soaked in blood, spit, and mucus.

The victims of the systematic abuse, who became known as the "White

House Boys," filed lawsuits and told of boys who were taken away never to be seen again. A study of the remains by the University of South Florida proved inconclusive, unable to support the charges of foul play or even to provide much identification of the bodies. In 2011 the Dozier School was shuttered for good, a dark stain on the community that no one wished to remember. A reporter for the *Tampa Bay Times* who worked on the story told Maggy Reno Hurchalla that her mother's reporting in 1958 had provided some of their most important source material in investigating the school's history.

Reno followed the Marianna series with a series on the Ocala Girls School, a reform school for girls that suffered from far less controversy about their practices. The main difference between the boys' and girls' schools that Reno brought to light concerned who ended up at the schools. The girls were more uniformly poor and from broken homes, often having suffered sexual abuse. Quite a few of the boys at Marianna were from wealthier families, and their delinquency was more a matter of choice than a result of their environment.

Delving even further into the lives of people society left behind, Reno did a deeply disturbing series on psychotic and other severely damaged children in Dade County, subjects she had touched upon before in *Special Report* in 1956 and 1957. The first article began:

"Danny is a handsome 10-year old boy. Soon he will go to a new home. In this home, children are locked in cages. Danny will enter this home because he jumped out a second story window and because he is an aggressive homosexual at 10. He goes berserk and attacks other children with knives, scissors, fists. He has to be locked up somewhere to keep him from hurting or killing himself or someone else. Danny cannot go to public school. He can't live at home, because he is a menace to his younger brothers. The Hope and the Haven schools for mentally retarded children can't control him. He is too much, even for the Montanari Clinical School for emotionally disturbed children.[5]

In the second article in the series, she wrote:

"More dangerous than so much dynamite are several hundred profoundly disturbed and psychotic children who sit in back rooms of Dade County today. Many will kill or be killed, rape or be raped. Jail or the grave will solve the problem of finding a safe place for them, say Miamians who have for years tried and failed to get the State of Florida to do something for them.

"Lurline, 11 years old, has raving temper tantrums, leaves home, comes back nude in the middle of the night and gets in bed with her younger brother. She cuts her mattress with razor blades, tears up her clothes, refuses to bathe or comb her hair. Her mother has threatened suicide because there is no place for the child.

"A. J. Montanari in his clinical school works with 35 disturbed children who can't go to public school. The Juvenile Court and the family welfare agencies know them. Children who can't afford his charge get financial help to stay there from the Opti-Mrs. Club of Miami Beach. Many, many children are too dangeroous, too volatile, too destructive, for his school."[6]

Reno's daughter Maggy went to work for Montanari, who went by the nickname of "Monty," during the summer before she started college at Swarthmore. She returned to work at his clinic the following summer. It was an eye-opening experience and helped motivate her to major in psychology. She remembered a ten-year-old psychotic named Billy: "What struck me at the tender age of 17 was that they *were* children. Even psychotic children are less bizarre and frighteningly horrible than adults. Monty said of Billy: 'He will be in jail for the rest of his life. We can't cure him. We can leave him with one relatively happy time.'"

After a Florida Bar Association banquet in May 1958, Reno wrote to her son Bob, praising his desire to be a lawyer. She had reached a new appreciation for the law, partly due to the admirable work Morton Silver had been doing for the Miccosukees. Earlier in the decade she had been implacably against the idea of her daughter Janet becoming a lawyer, but her views had changed. Receiving an honorable-mention Press Award for the second year in a row for her contributions to Florida justice, she was disappointed because, more than anything, she wanted the two-hundred-dollar first prize.

One of her favorite memories of the evening was the toastmaster, who drew a great round of laughter with his introduction of the Florida governor: "And now I want to introduce a moderate lawyer, who practiced in a moderate town, before moderate judges, for moderate fees, and who will undoubtedly in the hereafter go to a moderate hell—LeRoy Collins."

Collins was one of the few Florida politicians for whom she had a good deal of respect, even though he was dragging his feet on resolving the Miccosukee claims. He was helping Florida navigate slowly but smoothly through the era of integration, and he would later be tapped by President Johnson to act as peacemaker in ugly confrontations at Selma, Alabama, and to ease racial tensions in other volatile hotspots of the South. In 1968, his efforts caused him to lose a bid for the US Senate. His opponent appealed to the still deep-seated racism of much of central and north Florida by calling him "Liberal LeRoy" and showing pictures of Collins side by side with blacks.

Reno's tablemates at the Florida Bar banquet included former state attorney George Brautigam, whose reputation she had helped salvage the previous year with her reporting on the grand juries, along with the young attorney Dan Heller, who had also been smeared.[7] In response to the *Miami Herald* coverage of the 1956 grand jury, Brautigam brought libel charges against the paper. Columnists at the *Miami News* had been guilty of joining the crusade, too, and reporter Bill Baggs was forced to write a column apologizing to Brautigam. During the libel trial against the *Miami Herald* early in 1958, Reno tracked down a copy of Baggs's apology column after "three hours of frantic legwork" and supplied it to Brautigam's legal team. Paul Louis, who was part of a Brautigam legal team that was headed by a young Melvin Belli, told Reno that it was the display of that column that won the case for his client. Brautigam had scant time to savor his vindication, though, as he died not long after in August.

Conceding Brautigam's courage and his own mistakes in judging him, Baggs wrote a *mea culpa* obituary of Brautigam for the *Miami News*:

"George Brautigam paused before the small circle of gossips in the corridor. His eyes grinned at the fellows there. 'What are you gentlemen talking about?' he asked. 'You,' one of the gossips replied. 'What about me?' asked Brautigam. 'We were discussing how completely you committed political suicide,' someone of the circle explained. A larger grin crawled across George Brautigam's face. He chuckled. It wasn't a laugh. It was a chuckle, with humor in it, and obviously with much thought in it. 'Well, gentlemen,' he said, 'it was rather complete.'

"Mr. Brautigam walked on, and the remark was made that sometimes he seemed to be brilliant and sometimes he seemed not very smart, but he was the most consistent man on guts in Dade County. He had more than his share of courage. This was the summer of 1956. Or perhaps it was early in the fall. In any event, by this time the affairs from April of that year had indicated plainly that Mr. Brautigam had indeed performed suicide of a political nature with thoroughness."

Baggs recounted the story of the events that had transpired, how he and others had thought Brautigam wrong at the time, and how the Florida Supreme Court had vindicated Brautigam, before continuing:

"The court thereby ruled that Mr. Brautigam was right and the mob was wrong. There is a great lesson in this story of George Brautigam and I, for one, am not ashamed to admit that I learned my lesson and made my apology. Someone remarked yesterday that when Mr. Brautigam died on Sunday, he did not leave his wife and children much of an estate. Someone said he left pennies, not dollars. But Mr. Brautigam really left his family something much larger and stronger and richer. He left a heritage of courage."[8]

The night before the Bar banquet, Reno attended the annual newspaper fraternity's Ribs n Roast affair, where journalists from all the area newspapers skewered politicians and public officials of the day. While she enjoyed participating in her own skit and thought the dress rehearsals went more smoothly than the year before, she didn't enjoy all of the affair. A skit depicting the Whiteside case was a sour note for Reno.

Thurmond "Whitie" Whiteside, a prominent local attorney and the husband of her old friend and social worker Ellen Whiteside, was charged with corruptly influencing an FCC commissioner, Richard Mack, to win approval for the purchase of the Channel 10 television station in Miami. The first trial, which occurred a year later in 1959, resulted in a hung jury, and the second trial in 1960 resulted in Whiteside's acquittal. His reputation was ruined, though, and he committed suicide in 1961.[9] Although Reno knew that Miami was rife with corruption and that there were few saints among anyone she knew, she also deeply distrusted some of the witch hunts that were taking place to root corruption out.

The skit was put on by longtime *Miami Herald* columnist Jack Bell, who wrote the "Town Crier" column. Reno loathed Bell, having known him since first going to work for the *Miami Daily News* in 1933, when he was a sports columnist there. The source of her dislike for him was unclear, but it likely had to do with him being a somewhat older paternalistic chauvinist. He was a decorated veteran who lost an arm in World War I, and he spent eighteen grueling months of World War II traveling on the front lines with the troops while reporting for the *Miami Herald*. In the skit, Bell played Whitie and sang a ditty to characters playing Richard Mack and Judge George Holt, called "You May Get Pennies from Heaven (But You Won't Get a Cent from Me)."

"The Mack-Whiteside skit, written by Jack Bell, who played Whitie, was a mean, humorless bitch of a thing," Reno wrote. "Nobody laughed, the disapproval was palpable. It was a tribute to the good taste of the audience, and their knowledge of Whitie and the facts."

As at most roasts, the targets didn't always like the ribbing, but the skit did show a take-no-prisoners defensiveness on the part of *Miami Herald* columnists about the paper's recent excesses. The *Herald*'s backing of the grand jury in the crusade against Judge Holt had already been shown to be overzealous, attempts to impeach Holt had failed in the state Senate, and the paper had just lost a libel lawsuit brought by George Brautigam. With the Whiteside case unproven in court at that point, it was questionable to use comedy to further tarnish Holt and prejudge Whiteside.

While Reno's workload for the *Miami News* had lessened, she considered surviving the week an accomplishment that made her "more of a Mr Jack the Giant Killer than I thought." The rehearsals for the Ribs n Roast had lasted until midnight or one o'clock in the morning each night, and she stayed up after to do public relations work for Hank Meyer Associates, resulting in her getting only two to three hours sleep per night. Money was a constant worry, and to pay for college costs, she did as much side work for Hank Meyer as she could manage.

"It was an interesting experience, for once in a lifetime," she wrote, "but cost me too much time and hence money when I might have been working for Hank. And in the end there are so many feuds going on within the cast that it is painful in spots."

The favor Reno did for George Brautigam ended up coming back to Reno in an odd sort of way, confirming what had led to the scoop on the police-directed robbery ring; going the extra mile in journalism could reap unlikely rewards. Mark Reno had come back from his year in Maine with a handful of fake driver's licenses ready to be made up, replete with the seal of the State of Maine. With fresh licenses proclaiming they were twenty-one, Mark and brother, Bob, set out one night for an unassuming bar in northeast Coral Gables called the Golden Nugget. At six foot four and six foot three, they had little trouble convincing the barmaid, and the licenses were as genuine-looking an article as one could ask for. Bob ordered a Tom Collins, Mark got a drink for himself, and they were enjoying themselves until state agents dropped in for impromptu ID checks. Mark produced his Maine license and the agents gave him their okay. When Bob handed over his wallet, though, his Florida license was still in it as well, revealing him to be only eighteen.

While the charges got dropped by the local police, Bob still had to appear before the Florida State Beverage Department for a hearing. The barmaid had been arrested as well, and the owner of the Golden Nugget faced a possible suspension of his liquor license. Bob felt extremely guilty about the barmaid because she couldn't have been expected to second-guess the validity of a license that the state agents had accepted from Mark. Unfortunately, Bob was back at school at Tulane in 1958 and unable to attend a hearing, so his mother tried to see if she could defer it. She was taking a rewrite story from the State Beverage Department one day when the man she was talking to asked:

"Who is this?"

"Jane Wood."

"Mrs. Reno, did your son get his subpoena?"

"No, when is the hearing?"

He said it was set for the next week and that the subpoena was in the mail. Reno explained that Bob couldn't make it and asked whether the hearing could be postponed so that he could testify on behalf of the barmaid. The man suggested she call the State Beverage Department's legal advisor.

"Who?" she asked

"Paul Louis."

What luck, she thought. Louis had been the lawyer to tell her, "Without you, Brautigam couldn't have won." She called him.

"Why Janie, you own $100,000 worth of me," he said. "I'll just throw that case out when it gets to me. Don't worry about it anymore."

This was the first time Jane discovered herself in a position as a fixer, and she was amused and delighted by the turn of events.

"Cast your bread upon the water," she wrote, "the best investment of all."

On the other hand, she found that the power of the press could work both ways, and word trickled down from Judge Culbreath that he was aware of the "wild stag Wheel parties at the Reno house" and that he was going to send the police to raid the next one. The Wheel Club was a youth version of the Rotary Club that Mark Reno belonged to in high school, which his mother thought had done him good because "he is one of the boys and companionable, and it seems to me a little less of a sot." There had only been one party at the house, so Reno found the judge's warning "a bitchy thing to remark" and had to warn Mark off of having any more parties.

With Janet at Cornell, Bob at Tulane, and Maggy entering Swarthmore, Jane and Henry sold more of the property to finance their children's educations. Jane's skills in the part-time work she had been doing for Hank Meyer Associates were obvious. She had always loved drama, and public relations work was the perfect stage for showing off. The costs of keeping three children in private colleges were beyond the means of a pair of reporters, even ones as frugal as Henry and Jane. With the burden of paying some support to her parents, too, she cut back her own expenses to a bare minimum. Almost all material items became luxuries. Shoes, dresses, cars—she made do with what she had for as long as she could possibly get use out of it. For these reasons and others, the temptation of a better-paying career became great.

Reno's typical wide range of reporting continued into the summer, but most of it was somewhat mundane city and county reporting—news on the county welfare department, flood control, future infrastructure planning, taxes, hospitals. Certainly many of the topics were the same ones she had touched on time and again in her *Special Report* feature, but with all depth removed from her reporting, it was just somewhat tedious short-form news that any cub reporter could do. Seeing a limited future at the *Miami News* and needing a better paycheck, Jane Reno told publicist Hank Meyer that she would go to work for him full-time if the *News* would let her go. Meyer recalled steeling himself and dialing a number one day in the summer of 1958.

"Uncle Dan," he said, "I have a favor to ask. I want to hire one of your people."

Curiously, publisher Dan Mahoney was one of the people at the paper whom Jane adored. They got along well because his chauvinism didn't faze her, and she wasn't like any woman he knew. Ever since Reno had beat up the boys on her block as a child to prove it was okay to be a genius, she kept up a frontal assault on life. Mahoney knew that he had a great journalist in her. When Hank Meyer told him that he wanted to hire Mahoney's star reporter away from him, a less-than-friendly exchange of remarks took place.

"You want her that much?" Mahoney said, after calming down. "She's one of the best we have. It hurts."

"It wasn't easy, but I got her," Meyer remembered. "She is a constant joy and revelation. She lives with nature, close to earth, is unpretentious. Jane doesn't have time for mundane things. A sense of great balance and great beauty is demonstrated in her work and in her life. There is no frustration, no vanity. Her makeup is her soul and spirit.

"She's a nonconformist, never needs editing, can tear down the walls of Madison Avenue. Such spirit. And staying power. In any situation she shows excellent judgment. Doesn't preach. No crusades, but always involved. And she takes her shoes off anywhere.

"Some people don't understand Jane. They are the kind of people who feed their bodies with food, rarely read a book, early to bed. Their closed minds sap their spirit. They have no purpose or goal. Jane is their opposite: she's free. The most beautiful person I know."[10]

The *Miami News* announced Reno's resignation on July 20. With Reno's departure from the Miami journalism scene, the editor of a Sunday supplement over at the *Miami Herald*, Betty Garnet, was looking to see if she might assume the mantle of the city's top woman journalist. A brash blonde with a penchant for cigar smoking, Garnet had no trouble fitting in to what was generally considered a male domain. It didn't hurt that she was something of a bombshell. Henry Reno was quite fond of Garnet and took her under his wing to help her get more experience on hard-news stories. In 1959 Garnet wrote a front-page story about illegal gambling in Islamorada that appeared to have the stamp of Henry Reno all over it in terms of knowledge of the town, the people, and the gambling:

"After the Golden Beach raid near Miami Beach last week in which 25 persons were arrested, everybody is a little nervous and the crowd around the dice table at the Sport Fisherman's Club in Islamorada is thinner than usual. But the right guy still has no trouble finding the opportunity to lose his money. In fact, two teams of Herald reporters found the dice rattling on two successive weekends. At the bar in Islamorada's swank Hafway House, run by Ralph (Whitey) Martin, a bit of small talk with the bartender brings out Bob Pick, who is ready to oblige on a horse bet and who, if asked, will confide that there is a 'little action' out back come nightfall. This in turn brings an introduction to Martin, on whose approval rests admittance to the Sport Fisherman's Club gaming tables."[11]

Pat Murphy, who wrote for the *Herald* in the 1950s, recalled:

"Betty was either adored or disliked—the cigar smoking turned off some people, though I admired her and thought it showed character. She came across as a bit aloof and superior to some people—but there were worse personalities in the newsroom. My guess is there was a little cattiness toward her. She had a great perch at the back of the newsroom up against a wall where she could survey the whole newsroom.

"There was a certain collegiality among everyone off in 'features row' that Betty enjoyed and shared. She had a wonderful laugh—sincere, spontaneous, lusty, endearing. She was very much 'one of the boys.' She was a damned fine editor, took her job seriously, had no compunctions about going back into the sweaty, smelly, dirty composing room to work with the makeup guys on her section to make sure it's done right. She always dressed like she might have to go to a party unexpectedly—not frilly, just immaculate, tasteful, tailored. Shoes always high or medium heels. She had a very female walk that attracted male attention—some might say seductive, I'd say womanly."[12]

Unfortunately, the sea changes that were taking place at Miami newspapers doomed Garnet's future as well. A new corporate environment took hold that spelled the end of old-time newspapering in the city. A lot of new staff was brought in to the *Miami Herald* during the early 1960s, and Garnet's husband, Tony Villanova, was demoted as a photographer at the paper. Garnet resigned from the paper in protest in 1962. She went to work for the *Miami News* for a brief time before following Jane Reno's path to Hank Meyer Associates. Doors were opened for other women to follow, but most in the future were transplants, as were most of the citizens of the rapidly changing Miami. Few had the kind of long history in the town that Reno and Garnet did, and the knowledge that went with it.

Thus began yet another phase of Jane Reno's life, creating instead of covering stories. She had always thought of the newspaper reporting she had done on the Miccosukees as public relations to some degree. At the beginning of 1958, the Miccosukee tribe declared her Princess Apoongo Stahnegee, an honorary Seminole princess.

"When the Miccosukee council decided to make me a princess, one cold January day, I wept," she said over a decade later. "I had made a reputation as a writer in my town, Miami, but when I went among the Indians I knew it didn't mean a thing, that they measured me all over again. Smallpox Tommie pinned this egret headdress around my head, and Howard Osceola said, 'Jane Wood, we do this because we like the way you do things.' And I cried. It was the greatest honor I ever received."

"There aren't any princesses in the Seminoles, the Miccosukees!" Reno laughed. "They just thought it would be fun and I would like it. They decided they'd name me Princess Apoongo Stahnegee."

Morton Silver told her it meant "rumor bearer," knowing the reaction it would get from her. Reno did not realize her leg was being pulled and protested:

"Howard!"

"Morton, don't be ridiculous," Osceola said. "Apoongo Stahnegee is the man, he's a messenger, he goes around to all the villages telling them what arrangements are being made this year for the Green Corn Dance and the Snake Dance. He's a messenger."

Still, everyone derived some amusement out of Silver's translation.

Reno was honored at a large Miccosukee gathering to celebrate their new courthouse, thirty miles west of Miami on the Tamiami Trail. Federal and state Indian Affairs commissioners were at the gathering, and it was a festive time with a great deal of hope in the air. For once, everyone seemed to be on the same page. The state Indian commisioner, Colonel Max Denton, assured the Miccosukees that the State of Florida was going to give two hundred thousand acres of land back to them, as they requested. He said that Governor LeRoy Collins and his cabinet were wholeheartedly behind the return of the land, and he expected legal technicalities to be ironed out within weeks. The only hitch in negotiations, he said, was in the creation of a trust so the land could never be taken away from them.

The federal representative, US Indian Commissioner Glenn Emmons, was fully supportive of the agreement, but, invoking states' rights, he reiterated that the federal government had no part in it. The federal government had authority only over reservation Indians of recognized tribes. It was engaged in negotiating the money claim with the reservation-based, newly formed Seminole Tribe of Florida. After being pressed by Howard Osceola, Emmons did agree to at least recognize the Miccosukees as a state organization. This would help define a legal status for the Miccosukees in their negotiations with the State of Florida. Colonel Denton assured the Miccosukees that the Seminole Tribe lawsuit against the federal government would have no bearing on the Miccosukee state land claims. For his part, Emmons assured the Miccosukees that he would let the Seminole Tribe know that they had no authority over nonreservation Indians.

Denton returned on an unannounced visit in March during a trailer trip of Florida, and his good relations with the Miccosukees dissolved by the end of the meeting. He was pressed on the point of whether the proposed trust could allow the government to take away the land in the future. When Everglades National Park was created, federal officials had taken away land from a reservation group of Seminoles and relocated them to Devil's Garden in Big Cypress, where Jane Reno had her first encounter with them. Denton admitted that the state could take away the land if they chose. The Miccosukees restated their unbreakable position—land in perpetuity or nothing. Angrily, Denton told the Miccosukees they should fire their lawyers, Morton Silver and former governor Millard Caldwell, if that was what they were advising. The Miccosukees held firm, and Denton stormed out.

On September 20, 1958, the Miccosukees released a legal brief that Silver had written, detailing the long history of broken treaties and promises. In Silver's brief, the tribe gave the government an ultimatum: resolve their claim in sixty days or they would take the matter to the International Court of Justice at the Hague. "The Miccosukee nation could fare no worse by presenting its case to those other small nations of the world that are hungrily eyed by the larger ones," wrote Silver, "and to those nations whose memory of their struggle to defend their homeland is fresher in their minds, or even to those larger nations that in their policy and tactics, however distasteful these may be to the United States, at least do not attempt to conceal their actions under the hypocritical mask of a noble ideology ignored in practice."

On September 21, Bob Reno, who was working a summer job at the *Miami Herald* between semesters at Tulane, wrote an article that relayed the Miccosukee demands. Bob's article featured the bold title, "Settle All Our Land Claims Now!" Previous threats by the Miccosukees to take their case to the United Nations had not been acted upon, but along with Silver's brief they prepared a buckskin declaring the sovereignty of the Miccosukee Seminole Nation, which accepted the obligations spelled out in the Charter of the United Nations.

Governor Collins's response to the ultimatum was almost inexplicable, given what he then knew of the Miccosukees. He drafted a group of five venerable white men from the greater community who had almost no knowledge whatsoever of the Miccosukees and their land claim, save for Louis Capron, an author and lifelong friend of the Seminoles, and tasked them to study the "Seminole problem." The other four men were newspaper editors Bill Baggs and John Pennekamp, and circuit court judges Harold Vann and Grady Crawford. They held five meetings with a wide variety of people—but not a single Miccosukee—and delivered a report in February 1959. Their conclusions reflected a profound lack of understanding of the Miccosukees that Collins, even in limited interactions with the Miccosukees, had already progressed well beyond.

The report stated that Seminoles in Florida were defined by the federal government as only those who lived on reservations; that only the federal government, and not the state, could negotiate with tribes; and that, therefore, any claim by Everglades Miccosukees against the state was basically untenable. Furthermore, they asserted that the Everglades Miccosukees didn't even want to live on the lands they were seeking but merely wanted to lease them for profit. Thus they recommended that the Miccosukees be denied the land grant but that some small concessions be made to buy Miccosukee camps along the Tamiami Trail to ensure they could continue living in them.

The General Council of the Miccosukee Seminole Nation wondered in a let-

ter to the governor how these conclusions had been arrived at without committee members ever once meeting with the Miccosukees. They also asked,
reminding Collins that he once had suggested they needed to be protected
from their lawyers, that Millard Caldwell no longer be recognized as part of
their legal team as he was attempting to switch sides to work for the reservation Seminoles. Meanwhile, Buffalo Tiger composed a letter of complaint
against Caldwell from the Miccosukees to the Florida Bar. Tiger wrote: "Our
former lawyer, former Gov. Millard Caldwell is trying to switch sides in a case
we hired him to work on for us, and which is still going on. We also hear he is
saying things we don't want him to say to other people about our case, that
he learned while working for us as our lawyer."[1]

Caldwell disputed the accusation from Tallahassee, stating that he had become "associated" with Morton Silver but also at the same time with a reservation attorney, John O. Jackson, and that he had understood his role to be
merely that of a peacemaker between the Miccosukees and the reservation
Seminoles. When he was unable to bring them together, he said, he withdrew.
This was clearly not the understanding of the Miccosukees when they brought
him on to help represent them, nor was it the memory of Jane Reno. Later in
the year in the court case to determine whether Caldwell could represent the
reservation Seminoles, Caldwell testified that his firm stopped representing
the Miccosukees because he disagreed with Morton Silver. Reno remembered
the meeting where they lost their trust in Caldwell:

"One of the most fascinating things I ever saw: Millard Caldwell was associated with Morton Silver and the Miccosukees in their land claim, obviously
for his potency because he was a former governor of Florida, a long-legged
man, with all that Southern long-legged authority, and he came out there and
gave them a pitch that they should join the Indians of the reservations in their
money claim.

"Those old Indians got up and talked, and talked to him through Buffalo
Tiger, their spokesman. They said no, and they shamed that man, and he
walked—that long-legged, arrogant ex-governor of Florida walked—down the
aisle in shame. Because he had suggested, in effect, that they sell out."

Despite the citizens' committee findings being a step backward in understanding, given all that had already been established in negotiations, the governor's cabinet accepted the committee's report without question. Indian Com-

missioner Max Denton was instructed to come up with a plan to "encourage the Miccosukees to accept white schools, medical care and modern life."[2]

At a meeting at Hialeah City Hall in May, Howard Osceola, Buffalo Tiger, and Morton Silver got a chance to question three of the committee members about their findings. Chairman of the committee Judge Grady Crawford, Judge Harold Vann, and John Pennekamp appeared at the meeting. Crawford argued that they made only suggestions, not recommendations to be acted on. He said the purpose of the committee was to discover how the Seminoles were divided and to whom they looked for leadership.

"We understood it was impossible for the state to give you the lands because of your contract with counsel," Crawford told Tiger and Osceola.

Morton Silver acknowledged his original contract had contained a protective clause that would allow him to place a lien on Miccosukee land if he wasn't paid, but he said that he had formally waived the right to allow the land trust to proceed.

"And the state knows it," Silver said.

Crawford said that the committee never met with the Miccosukees because the tribe refused to meet without their attorney Silver present. An exasperated Buffalo Tiger declared: "Looks like to me somebody is trying to confuse this whole thing. We won't be led around by the hand like those weak-minded Seminoles on the reservations."[3]

On April 28 the Board of Commisioners of State Institutions—which was Governor Collins and six other members of his cabinet—approved a bill to go to the Florida Legislature authorizing 143,000 acres to be put aside for use by all the Seminoles. The legislature approved the authorization in June, and it was passed back to the governor's cabinet to proceed upon. As nothing was yet guaranteed or spelled out, the Miccosukees, tired of being jerked around, accepted an opportunity to embarrass the US government in spectacular fashion. An invitation landed on the Miccosukees' doorstep from Cuban revolutionary leader Fidel Castro, inviting them to take part in the first 26th of July celebration since the Cuban Revolution. The Miccosukees saw this as a good chance to press the issue of their claims to being a sovereign nation and ratchet up the pressure for a settlement. On one of their trips to Washington, Howard Osceola and Buffalo Tiger had met the Tuscarora Iroquois activist Mad Bear, who was keen to join them on the trip. Wallace "Mad Bear" Anderson had served in World War II and the Korean War yet had been denied a loan to buy a home under the GI Bill, launching his career as a sovereignty advocate for native tribes.

Jane Reno recalled how it came about:

"The tail end of our organized Indian effort to embarrass the government of the U.S.A. came when I was called and asked how I would like to go with a group of Seminole Indians to be a guest of Fidel Castro in Cuba. And by that time, we hadn't broken off with Fidel, but I was working for Hank Meyer Associates in public relations, no longer newspapering. I said, 'Oh God, how I envy you.' This was the first anniversary of Castro's revolution. 'Why don't you take my son Bobby Reno, who is working on the *Miami Herald*?' I said.

"So they took Bobby. They had the thirteenth floor of the Hilton Hotel,

Bob Reno with new friends from the 26th of July Movement, Havana, July 1959.

and Bobby said it was the wildest and most beautiful weekend. The crowds and everything, and all the Indians, including me, he said, were on the balcony with Castro and he kissed us with the tears streaming down his cheeks. We all got drunk on champagne on the thirteenth floor of the Hilton, he said, and those Indians can drink up a storm. That was the last gasp, in effect, of the Miccosukee Revolution of 1950, which was a public relations revolution, an attempt to embarrass the U.S. Government into behaving. I always wished I'd been there."[4]

It actually wasn't the first anniversary of Castro's revolution, but the first celebration of the 26th of July, after the rebels had taken power seven months before. The day marked a failed assault on the Moncada barracks in 1953, which had been the first serious attempt at unseating the dictator Batista by force, and the bulk of Castro's revolutionaries belonged to the revolutionary force called the 26th of July Movement. In his article for the *Miami Herald*, Bob Reno wrote:

"The Miccosukees, as colorful in their tribal garb as Fidel's rebels, were 'personal guest of honor' of the revolutionary chief at his 26th of July celebrations here over the weekend. And the Indians got VIP treatment start to finish of their three-day stay.

"When they arrived Saturday they were whisked through the jammed streets in a fleet of six shiny, flag-decked Cadillacs after being greeted by bearded Castro officers at the airport. Everywhere they went, the Indians were escorted by machinegun-toting 26th of July soldiers—even through the throng in front of Castro's speaking stand at the giant rally Sunday to be given a personal welcome by the revolutionary leader himself.

"Castro urged the Indians to extend their visit for another week. The visit of the Indians reached diplomatic proportions when the Miccosukees presented Castro with a declaration written on buckskin praising his 'victory over tyranny and oppression' and giving the revolutionary government formal recognition. In return, Castro formally recognized the 'duly constituted government of the sovereign Miccosukee Seminole nation.'"[5]

If the Miccosukees were looking for reaction, they got it. Though Castro was still independent and seeking relations with the United States, the Eisenhower administration had made no secret about their hostility toward the Cuban revolutionaries. While countries throughout the Third World had

*Left to right*: Morton Silver, Fidel Castro, Wild Bill Osceola, and Mad Bear, Havana, July 26, 1959.

been casting aside colonialism and establishing independence throughout the Eisenhower years, most of these efforts were viewed with suspicion by the virulently anticommunist Dulles brothers, Allen and John Foster, who respectively ran the CIA and the State Department. The communist paranoia of American society in the 1950s kept any progressive voices in check, and great opportunities were missed to encourage fledgling independent democracies in the world. Instead, America saw all independence movements and revolutionary efforts as being guided by the Soviet Union. Some were, and some weren't, but those revolutionaries who had no alliance with either superpower usually ended up being pushed to seek Soviet help in the face of American hostility. In a letter to her aunt Peg a few years before, when the globe-trotting Balfours were based in India, Jane Reno had expressed her thoughts on the Eisenhower administration:

"We are so hoping you will have a chance to get down here before your return to India. Tink's Christmas card, with her girls' picture, made my heart

Miccosukee delegation with Cuban authorities, Havana, July 1959. Wild Bill Osceola is shown in the lower left, holding the buckskin.

turn over—they looked so like Nina and Tinker at that age. Fifteen Odos Deli-yanni came back to me with quite a dreadful rush, because it is so long gone, and breakfasts under the pines on Odos Strofili. I don't write letters very well, anymore, for the same reason ditch diggers don't cultivate a garden in their spare time. So I don't get any, gradually, and feel spasms of remoteness that could simply be cured by some coffee together.

"We enjoy your letters, my children and I. They are especially pleased to know that the elder generation of your branch of the family is staunchly liberal Democratic in politics. All my sisters and brother are Eisenhower devotees, from living with or among Republicans. Daddy and I devoutly dote on Adlai, and Bob Reno does to the extent of sending a campaign contribution of $1 to the Stevenson campaign fund. We chuckled at your last letter, saying that we must not blame Indians for not doing things our way. Hell, I think the American Republican way is often so bad in so many things, including foreign policy, that I find Nehru's path easier to champion, on the whole, than Dulles. Dulles' difficulty lies principally, I feel, in being for so many years the minority and irresponsible party's spokesman in world affairs, that he can never learn the feel of the helm. This is, of course, true of the Republicans in general, I feel."

While Bob Reno had seen the Cuba trip as an innocent lark, he was surprised at how much it angered American officialdom.

"I won't answer any questions until I talk to my counsel," he wrote home jokingly from Tulane. "I have enraged the Governor, the State Department, the Indian Commissioner, and the Florida Bar, all for a story I didn't even get paid for. Since the *Herald* refused to call me a staff writer, the least they could have done was pay me."

The outrage reflected how stacked the odds were against the Miccosukees in the popular view. It was somewhat interesting that the government actually took the Miccosukees seriously and negotiated in reasonably good faith, whereas most news coverage aside from Jane Reno's reporting treated the Indians like some sort of cartoon relic. The *Miami Herald* editorial page blasted the trip by the Miccosukees with arrogant and dismissive paternalism, writing on July 29:

"The silly season seems to be with us again. It blossomed in a bit of grandstanding by a dozen of Florida's Seminole Indians. They junketed to Cuba for the big doings in Havana last weekend. There they swapped documents with Premier Fidel Castro. The little band from Florida 'recognized' Castro's revolutionary government. He, in turn, 'recognized' the 'duly constituted government of the sovereign Miccosukee Seminole Nation.' Most, if not all, of the members of this expedition presumably are members of the United States. As such, they should settle any differences they may have with this nation's government through the orderly processes provided by law. There is no such thing as divided loyalty. The Cuban gambit was the latest in a long series of headline-hunting antics by this ill-advised group, which must embarrass most of the 1000 Seminoles in Florida. We'd blush, too, if we took such foolishness seriously, which we don't."[6]

The editorial was almost certainly the work of associate editor John Pennekamp, who had been best man at Henry Reno's wedding to Jane, but whom, by the late 1950s, Henry Reno regarded as a "vain and possibly corrupt old ass," according to Reno's daughter Maggy. It was further evidence that Pennekamp had no useful insight into the Miccosukees, and even a fair degree of malice toward their cause.

Despite the outrage it provoked, the Cuba trip did not derail efforts to move forward with the claim. On August 12, the Board of Trustees of the Internal Improvement Fund in the state cabinet agreed to create a 143,000-acre land trust. Max Denton continued to argue that the reservation Seminoles should manage the land, but Governor Collins overruled him, stating, "I am afraid we might start a civil war among the Indians if we turned it over to the reservation tribal council."[7] The land was to be used for year-round subsistence hunting and fishing for all Seminoles, and a variety of small commercial enterprises consistent with traditional ways. The Miccosukee Council congratulated Collins in a telegram: "We are happy to hear that you did not agree to help them try to take over these lands. The Miccosukee tribe has always been separate from the Muskogee Seminole tribe on the reservations. We speak different languages. Our religion will not let our Miccosukee tribe die or give up this land."[8]

Even still, Collins told his cabinet that the state was reluctant to give the Miccosukees control of the land because attorney Morton Silver would be able to place a lien on it. Silver reiterated that he had relinquished any lien rights and that this had been put into a signed contract, which the Miccosukee Council confirmed in its telegram. Still, Collins would obstinately keep repeating this falsehood at future meetings. His Indian commissioner, Max Denton, also kept stating falsehoods, claiming that the Everglades Miccosukee Tribe was constituted of "a small minority of 35 adults." Buffalo Tiger responded indignantly to Denton's assertion: "Col. Denton knows nothing about Indians. If he ever visited the Everglades and talked to our people he would know that we represent over 300 Indians who choose to be left alone on this land which we have occupied for over 100 years."[9]

In fact Denton had been a few times, visits that included his attendance at the large Miccosukee tribal gathering at which Jane Reno was crowned an honorary princess. He knew full well the tribe was made up of far more than thirty-five members. But the falsehood was related to a "problem" the authorities kept bemoaning, that the Miccosukees were too divided to know who really spoke for them. As Jane Reno knew from her experiences, no one had ever tried to speak for the Trail Miccosukees except the Miccosukee Council through Buffalo Tiger, and Howard and Homer Osceola. This was quite clear to anyone who had spent time among them. The "other group" that Denton regularly mentioned was the Ingraham Billie and Corey Osceola faction, who stated they wanted only to be left alone, so the council that was fighting for land that would allow them to be left alone could hardly be seen as misrepresenting them. Denton fabricated numbers without basis to claim they were a larger group than that represented by the Miccosukee Council.

If anything, the Cuba trip accelerated negotiations on a federal level, as it was an enormous embarrassment to Secretary of State Dulles and the Eisenhower administration. Commissioner Emmons was dispatched on behalf of the federal government to renew efforts toward a settlement, and he brought all parties to the table at the Everglades Hotel in Miami on November 15, 1959. The Miccosukee General Council was represented along with the Board of Directors of the Seminole Tribe of Florida. Though various reservation members like Mike Osceola kept arguing for reservation control of the new lands, without too much rancor Emmons got the two sides to agree that the Seminole Tribe would exert full control over reservation life and the Miccosukees would exert full control over the 143,620 acres in Flood Control Area Three. A proposal by State Indian Commissioner Max Denton to grant the Seminole Tribe control of the Area Three land was dismissed.

Emmons kept the results of the meeting under wraps until he could present them to Collins and his cabinet two days later. Collins refused to accept the results of the Everglades Hotel meeting and cast doubt on whether it was possible for the state to give the Miccosukees control of the land in a way that would satify them and be acceptable to the state.[10] He claimed there were no protocols for giving the land in irrevocable trust and that they could only offer a "license privilege" sort of lease.

Collins referred the issue back to committee for further study. In February the Miccouskee Council announced they were rejecting the offering of the land under licence privilege, as the government could revoke the privilege at any time. In April 1960, a board of commisioners of the state cabinet voted to approve the 143,620 acres for Miccosukee use. The cabinet would retain administrative control, and it would be available for all Seminoles under the license privilege system the state proposed. The state was done negotiating, and this was their final offer. Max Denton stated: "The land is now there for the Indians to use. If the Indians want to take advantage of it, they may do so. If they don't, it's their business."[11]

Nevertheless, Attorney General Richard Ervin later declared that necessary paperwork had not been filed and the transfer was nonbinding. A few small patches of land were made available for traditional use, but the promised acreage of Area Three was not made available to the Seminoles as promised.

Although Collins was liberal in nature and went on to do important work civil rights work for President John F. Kennedy, as governor he proved to be indecisive on a number of issues and easily swayed by bad advice. Time and again, he became aware of dramatic state problems through newspaper reporting rather than from his own staff. When his point man for the Miccosukee problem, Max Denton, told him the Miccosukees were split apart and manipulated by lawyers, he largely accepted the misinformation. When a panel of "respected white people" who had no useful insight into the Seminoles or the facts of the Miccosukee land claim gave him bad advice, he accepted it.

One of the issues throughout that bothered white authorities the most was the Miccosukees' insistence on their interests being carefully protected by their lawyers. Max Denton had told the Miccosukees to be wary of white men speaking for them and told the Miccosukees to fire their lawyers. Collins voiced the concern about liens repeatedly in meetings well after that was no longer an issue. The citizens' committee Collins appointed chose not to meet with the Miccouskees because the tribe wouldn't meet without attorney Morton Silver present. As Collins himself was a lawyer, and former governor Millard Caldwell had worked on the Miccosukee legal team, the target seemed not to be lawyers in general but, rather, their particular lawyer, Morton Silver.

Jane Reno believed Silver's Jewish heritage had a lot to do with the disdain for him:

"Once upon a time I was out at the Green Corn Dance about three o'clock in the morning with my daughter Janet Reno, a lovely, long-legged girl. At the Green Corn Dance you're not allowed to go to sleep, you're not allowed to eat, but you drink. So I said to Homer Osceola:

"'Homer, some day Morton will die as all men must and you're still gonna have an Indian land claim going on, and my daughter Janny Baby, who's a Harvard Law School student, can take it over.'

"And Homer looked at Janny and he said: 'Janny Baby, you will never make a good Indian lawyer, because you're too beautiful and too young, and you will want to be popular. Morton Silver's a Jew and he doesn't care whether he's popular or not and he makes a great Indian lawyer.' [12]

"When I first met him everybody was saying 'Eeennh! This Jew lawyer, he's trying to get in on those land claims and make all that money.' His family remembers it and the Indians remember it as the time Morton was wasting all his time and not making much money at all on Indian claims. He got really roughed up. He was a crusader. And I thought to a certain extent Homer might have been right, because he was Jewish—which is a minority—and then I realized another thing. Morton had fallen out of a window when he was a boy and had to lay in bed for about a year and was crippled and had to have several operations. He was not only a Jew but he was a crippled Jew, and he was on the side of every Indian in that swamp. He wasted more time and a great deal of money, and Indians knew it. They knew it." [13]

As a new decade began, the Reno children were building their own lives away from home, and the Reno porch became a gathering place for an eclectic mixture of people unrelated to the family. The first Seminole newspaper, the *Seminole Indian News*, was created on the Reno porch in August 1961, bridging the divide between the Trail Miccosukees and the Seminole Tribe, which had been narrowing since the November 1959 agreement. Betty Mae Jumper was the editor bringing news from the Seminole Tribe, and Alice Osceola reported on the doings of the independent Miccosukees. Reno described the process:

"It was the last gasp of the Miccosukees—Kennedy had just been elected— and it was before they dropped their land claim and decided to join the money claim. And so, Betty Mae Jumper was the editor from the reservation. A lot of city people call her the 'lady Indian chief' or something like that, but she's the chairman of the council of the Dania reservation, and of the Seminole Tribe. Alice Osceola was the other editor. The two lady editors met on my porch.

"The editorial board consisted of Alice's five brothers, and the whole editorial board had to bring her a six-pack of beer apiece, and they would tell me what they wanted to say, and I would turn around and put it in my typewriter and read it back to them then and there. So we had a lot of fun. May I say that my great and good friend Morton Silver made it up and laid it out."[14]

The daughter of a Seminole Indian woman named Ada Tiger and a French trapper, Betty Mae Jumper was born in 1923 near Indiantown east of Lake Okeechobee. She was lucky to survive, given the Seminoles' feelings about mixed blood at the time. Corey Osceola, an Indian medicine man and an uncle of Alice Osceola, wanted Jumper to be put to death. He was one of the most militant of the Miccosukees and wary of the white man's influence. The others joked that he was always ready to go off to war, about which his daughter Marie once wryly commented, "if you knew his wife, you'd understand why." Jumper explained to Reno what happened:

"My father was a white man. When I was born the tribe leaders wanted to kill me because I was half white. They wanted to put me out away from the camp under a pine tree and leave me. My grandfather wouldn't let them. He picked up a shotgun and said, 'If anyone does anything to hurt this baby, I'll kill him.' That's why I've always loved my grandmother and grandfather. They were Indian. Later I got along well enough with Corey Osceola. My mother's cousin had a baby by a white man at the same time I was born. And the tribe put it out under a pine tree and stuffed its mouth full of clay and it died."[15]

Reno loved the company of Jumper and Alice Osceola because she had discovered in her dealings with the Miccosukee and Seminole tribes that they had a matriarchal society. Although she found that most outsiders were under the impression that men ran things, she recognized a similar illusion in her southern lineage. Her great-grandmother in the Civil War had run the plantation, and southern men generally delegated the authority to their wives to make decisions and run their lives. With the Miccosukees, Reno found the same was true except in reverse.

"In the Indian tribe it is *delegated* to the old men," Reno said, "you do the deciding about these kind of things, you make these decisions, you do this stuff.

"And with the younger men, this and this is delegated. The mother delegates the authority: husband, you go here and make the decision. The blood flows with the mother. It is the mother's camp. You are your mother's tribe. Buffalo Tiger is a member of the Wind clan, which is his mother's tribe. There were Wind, Panther, Frog, Beaver, and other clans. I remember Janet said to Wild Bill: 'How do you know how to deliver your babies?'

"Wild Bill had just delivered his fifth. He said: 'Janny Baby, my mother taught me how.'

"It's delegated authority. We just run the world. I felt quite at home among Indian women."

Unfortunately, the success in producing the *Seminole Indian News*, which published four issues from August to December 1961, was soon interrupted by tribal infighting. Buffalo Tiger resigned from the Miccosukee General Council early in 1961, stating that it was due to health reasons, and in December he formed a breakaway tribe. According to Morton Silver, Tiger walked over to the other side of the Tamiami Trail and held an election with a dozen people present. Half of them were family members, said Silver, and the other half were Seminole Tribe members from the Dania Reservation. They declared themselves a new Miccosukee tribe, with Buffalo Tiger as their leader. Immediately they began pursuing federal recognition and a financial settlement of Miccosukee claims.

With the state having quit negotiations for good and the federal authorities consistently making clear that reservation Indians were their only purview, Tiger thought it was time for the Miccosukees to adapt to the "realities" they had so forcefully rejected to date. Having spent his adult life living in the white man's world in Hialeah, Tiger did not feel the same unbreakable attachment to the old ways in the Everglades that the Osceola family did. He saw himself as a pragmatist. The Osceolas saw him as a traitor. Reno recalled Howard Osceola telling her: "My daddy told me never to sign away the land I love, Jane Wood. If we get that money, what will it be? Divided up after this and that—$30,000 or $40,000 an Indian. We'll buy cars, drive 'em in the canal, get drunk and get cheated by white men, and it'll all be gone. All be gone."[16]

Despite Tiger himself admitting the elections of the new tribe were voted on by no more than 20 percent of the Miccosukees, the tribe quickly attained credibility with the US government. The Miccosukee General Council warned anyone they could against dealing with Tiger, but their pleas fell on deaf ears. For a few reasons, the small splinter group was able to wrest control of the Miccosukee tribe away from the council. One was that Tiger was an articulate spokesman. As Jane Reno noted in 1955, she knew no other Seminole who spoke English as well as he did. The qualities that had made the Miccosukees elect him to be their interpreter in pursuit of the land claim were exactly the qualities that Tiger now used to work against the council. Without Buffalo to relay their views eloquently translated into English, it was very difficult to be heard. The second reason was that the federal government was ready and willing to recognize and deal with any tribe that only wanted a financial claim and a reservation, almost no matter how fractional the group was. The third was that the Miccosukees had been portrayed in media reports since 1957 as being in a greater state of disunity than they actually were, ever since Ingraham Billie had retreated with a small faction to ally with Corey Osceola.

The Miccosukee Tribe of Indians of Florida was born, and the government granted reservation lands to it on either side of the Tamiami Trail. Twenty years later, the tribe finally gained a lease on 189,000 acres in Flood Control Area Three. Spurning the reservation tribe for the most part, the Osceola siblings chose to continue living their lives independently as the Everglades Miccosukee Tribe of Seminole Indians, never having surrendered a claim to their native lands. To them Buffalo Tiger was not a Miccosukee leader but a paid agent of the Bureau of Indian Affairs. They lived by the words of their proud Osceola ancestor, who had stuck a knife in a table and declared, "We need no agent, the land is ours."

For his part, Tiger casually dismissed the bitterness of the Osceolas. Unfortunately he echoed what white men had suggested for Miccosukees a quarter century before. After hearing criticism of him from Homer Osceola, he said in 1983: "Just because their last name is Osceola, they still think they're great leaders like Chief Osceola, but they're wrong. The man died long, long ago. These people better wake up and be like everybody else."[17]

Jane Reno maintained her friendships with all of those to whom she had become close among the Miccosukees and Seminoles in the coming years, though her strongest affection was for the Osceolas. She shared their deep attachment to the Everglades and their way of doing things. Reno wished her reservation friends the best of success and loved strong Seminole women like Betty Mae Jumper, but her heart was in the Miccosukee camps on the Tamiami Trail. Her son Mark formed his own relationships in the 1960s, trading and spending time with the Trail Indians. Still, Mark Reno noted, almost all his relationships with them for the rest of his life were with those in his mother's generation. Among the Seminoles there was not the expectation common in white society that children would become friends with the children of their parents' friends. New relationships with one's own generation had to be forged separately, based on hard-won trust over a long period.

# 19 | Publicity!

Henry Reno had a heart attack in 1960, and the thoughts of mortality that had been sweeping over Jane—because of her aging parents and the death of Henry's father—were compounded yet further. To her surprise, though, the event helped their relationship. Henry was fairly set in his ways, almost sixty years old, and some of his crime-beat friends and drinking buddies weren't necessarily people whom Jane cared for. Both of them had been drinking quite a lot, which made them more likely to be disagreeable with each other. The chronic shortage of money didn't help, as they tried to support their children in college. Over the previous few years, with her combative journalist life at its peak and her alcohol consumption on the rise, she had become more and more likely to explode at people. She was aware of the fact and was surprised and pleased with herself one evening when a policeman stopped her on her way home from a party, and "we had a pleasant and courteous chat and he let me go. No incident, no rudeness on either side."

When Henry had his heart attack, though, he was forced to stop drinking. He adjusted surprisingly well, and both Jane and Henry's doctor agreed that he was an excellent example of a recovered coronary patient.

"He sticks to a resting regime," Jane wrote, and "his only excess is inordinate cups of coffee, and he is very benign about getting all his little drunken friends and colleagues out of jail and other troubles, and did not go off into the horrid self-righteous attitude of the dried-up drunk. So he is serene and pleasant and a source of strength to me."

Hurricanes continued to invade the Reno existence, making Jane marvel anew at their staggering power. After a decade that had been free of any serious storms, Hurricane Donna came roaring into south Florida with a vengeance. It hit the Florida Keys as a Category 4, with winds of 145 miles per hour, and meandered across the Everglades to hit Naples with 120 mile-per-hour winds. Miami itself was not hit that hard. Donna crossed out into the Gulf of Mexico, back across the state into the Atlantic and regained strength,

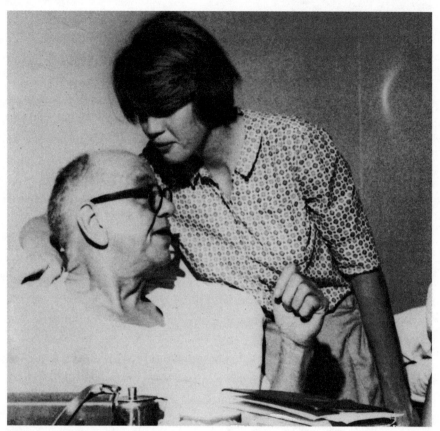

Janet Reno with her father, Henry, in the hospital, 1960.

roared north, and even battered daughter Janet with some wind and rain in Boston.

"Here the maximum winds, in gusts, were 97 [mph]," Jane wrote of the storm, "and I would say the sustained wind was no more than about 85. Not as bad as '45, '47, or '50. The trees didn't take that permanent set that we saw in '45. Nothing went over or broke off here much, though Dai lost her mango and avocado. The worst was right about dawn Saturday. (We stayed up all night.) The rain sheeted past. We had about a foot of water in the drive at one time, and a sheet in the yard, but after a fair day today it is almost gone everywhere."

One of the great humorists of the era, John Keasler, worked on the *Miami News* with Reno in the 1950s, and his family stayed with the Renos during the hurricane.

"The house would have been very peaceful," Reno wrote, "minus the Keasler children to leave doors open when the wind turned to the south. But they are really a most wonderful family, and Henry and I were glad Henry thought to ask them over when Key Biscayne was asked to evacuate and all the hotels were full. John Senior dropped a bottle on his foot just before they left the house, and had to have eight stitches taken in his foot at Kendall Hospital."

Keasler wrote a column twenty years later remembering the storm and the prank he never confessed to the Renos:

"We had been finishing up our columns fast, to drop off at The News, before heading out to the Renos. We did four daily columns between us, then. My wife did a daily column under her maiden name, Margery Dougherty, and an advice column under the name Jane Dare. I did the column I do now, and a satirical advice column named Dear George. Margery did most of all four of them that day as I nailed up.

"We counted noses; were ready to take off in our two cars, an old Buick and the even older Pontiac station wagon. I ran back in to get the new bottle of Irish whiskey for the hurricane party. Coming back out the front door, my elbow hit the jamb. The bottle fell, did a freak bounce, came down and cut my instep wide jagged open. I tied my foot up tight with a ripped sheet and tried not to think about it.

"Cats mewling, dogs whimpering, babies yowling, and me cussing, we took off, dropped off our literary gems and, rocking in wind gusts, sped toward the home of our host and hostess. Jane was home, Henry was still on duty at The Herald, but expected. We had a drink or two. It was late afternoon when the power went off.

"My wife and Jane sat out in the sedans listening to the car radio bulletins. The rain got harder and began to go sideways. They came back in. Jane took a look at my foot; insisted I get to an emergency room of a hospital a couple of miles away. I tried to start the Buick. They had run the battery down listening to the radio. I started toward the hospital in my station wagon. I ran out of gas a quarter mile away and slopped through a field on foot. It was blowing pretty good now.

"The lone intern seemed glad to see me. 'How'd you do it?' he asked. 'I was hit in the foot with a bottle of John Jameson,' I told him. He shrugged and kept leaving to fix the hospital generator, after cleaning my wound, and pouring antiseptic into it. I sat for what seemed like forever, waiting for him to bandage me. The emergency room phone started ringing. I kept trying to outlast it. But I can't handle a ringing phone.

"My mood was not good. A drink or two had worn off. As a columnist, I wasn't really working the hurricane story—my assignment was to 'gather color.' Not working the main story can make you restless. Finally, I snarled at the phone and hopped across the room a bit bloodily and snapped, 'Yeah?'

"And a voice said crisply, 'This is the Miami Herald, running a check. Any hurricane casualties?'

"'Uh, what?' I said to the competing newspaper, trying to gather my wits.

"'This is the Herald,' the voice said imperiously. 'Are there any hurricane casualties?'

"Hm. 'No,' I said. 'The only casualties we have are from the train wreck.'

"Then I hung up, immediately took the phone back off the hook, lay it on the desk and left it there. So much for the competition.

"My foot finally bandaged, I wangled a ride back to the Renos. Henry eventually got there (and drove his car into a deep water hole) and we all rode out the wild and windy night that was Donna. 'What are you laughing at?' he asked me a couple of times, but I didn't dare tell him. Certain rules of etiquette apply when your hurricane host is on the opposition paper. To get thrown out into the hurricane. . . ."[1]

Jane Reno found Margery's extraordinary composure throughout the storm somewhat off-putting, until it was explained that both Margery and one of her boys suffered from epileptic fits. Since having her first ones a year or two before, Margery had been taking a phenobarbitol prescription, which explained her unruffled and mildly sedated state. John Keasler and Henry Reno left the house not long after dawn in 65-mile-per-hour winds as the storm wound down, with Henry facing a twelve-hour work shift ahead. Despite the strain, Henry had learned to relax after his heart attack, and Jane was impressed at how easily he dealt with events. At home, the only structural damage was two screen doors wrenched off and some shingles along the edge of the porch beaten off the roof by the gumbo limbo tree near the air conditioner. In the aftermath of the storm, Mark Reno stopped by to inspect, and wondering at the damage inflicted by the Keasler family, pronounced: "Looks like the hurricane hit you inside more than outside."

One of Jane's friends from the neighborhood, Joan Cronin, stopped by the following night to take a bath. Electricity was back on at the Reno house, but Cronin's family was still without. Joan had put all her children in their overflowing swimming pool with a bar of ivory soap, but she couldn't bear to face the cold water herself.

The Upper Keys, which had born the brunt of the devastating 1935 hurricane, were not so fortunate as Miami. Once again the area received a direct hit, with the most devastating winds experienced in Florida since the 1935 storm. In the following week, Jane Reno drove down to observe the damage and check on Phil and Daisy Winslow's house near Tavernier. The Winslows' house had come through intact, but Reno was shocked to see what had happened to a group of well-built concrete block homes on Lower Matecumbe Key. Great holes had appeared beneath their foundations where the sand and earth had been scooped out, and the houses had fallen in on themselves and split in two.

"As a measure of the storm in the Key Largo area," Reno wrote, "Buttonwood Sound, a shallow bay connecting with the Gulf west of Tavernier, had the water blown the hell entirely out of it, and was bare, when the water was over the highway.

"They have done a good job of road mending, bridge repairing, restoring utilities, and beginning to clean up. But there are places about Islamorada that you feel, better scrape it all with a bulldozer and start again. The funny thing is the way landmarks are lost, and you can't remember what they were.

"The one happy source of amazement to us, and delight, was five beautiful flamingoes wading in the mud and water at Whale Harbour, right beside the road. We stopped and walked out within twenty feet of them, and watched them for a long time. They don't fly off, and are undisturbed by the traffic, and scrounge for edibles after making puddling motions with their feet in the mud. They may well turn out to come from some rare bird place nearby, but it gave me a tremendous heart lift to see them. I would have bet heavily against the possibility of my ever seeing flamingoes strolling near the highway on the Keys.

"But so many of the people's faces looked deeply grooved and remote in expression. I gather the Red Cross is being as muddled as ever. To a lady in a soaking wet dress, chilled, who walked up from Tavernier after the storm to a Red Cross station, a Red Cross worker with a pile of clothes said, 'We are sorting these today, we won't distribute them until tomorrow.' To the same lady who stood in line to get coffee. 'The coffee is for working men only.'

"If I had put my life in the Keys at the Matecumbes, I would just turn my back on it all and walk away. In too many places it smells of death—dead fish, I suppose. You could cry looking at it, but you are too shocked."

While Janet attended a huge Kennedy rally in Cambridge as the 1960 election approached and was, according to her mother, "transmogrified with enthusiasm," Jane was still reserving judgment on the Democratic candidate.

"I have an idea Kennedy will win, and heavily," she wrote. "But you can't tell about the Catholic thing. It is the ghost. He is far smarter than Nixon, and has more guts, and will I am quite sure be better for the country. But as yet he is still so unfamiliar, and I feel unpredictable, that I do not have a trust, a feeling of any safety with him. Just a hope. Now and then I have a real surge, listening to him, that he might be a young Roosevelt, but not derivative. I think he knows what a president of the U.S. should be. Whether he can be it is another thing."

Though Reno had been wary about her husband becoming aggravatingly censorious after drying out, as happened with so many reformed alcoholics, the opposite was true. She became able to relax herself and reflect on some of the problems that had been contributing to her increased volatility. Her new awareness came too late for her to correct some of the harm she had done, drunkenly insulting friends and relatives to such a degree that some never forgave her for it. In the first half of the 1950s, the inner anger had been primarily the result of Henry withdrawing into himself. The latter half of the decade had brought a number of other factors to bear that sharpened her tongue more than ever:

"Not only is he himself again, more than he has been in years," she wrote of her husband to her son Bob, "but the terrible angst that has been haunting me seems to have lifted and gone away. I can tell because when I drink I do not get cross or sad, and when I have a hangover I just have a headache, and not terrible shame about memories of things I said. I think it is many things, probably including hormones, but basically I think it is two major ones.

"#1. For some years I have had a feeling that my personal universe was expanding and that my children were going away from me with the speed of light. For some reason since Christmas I no longer feel this at all, but feel instead that we are all in parallel orbits and always will be, and that actually if I should ever need any of you to reach out and hold my hand, I could have you there very quickly. Finally I feel that the world is my neighborhood—that we will rendezvous in Milan at *La Scala* some week-end, and will take another week off together in New Zealand some year. Or meet in the Marquesas.

"#2. Since Far's death [Henry Reno's father], I have had a most terrible fear of old, plaintive, querulous age—that I was being pulled toward and into it, and that everything was headed downhill toward gloom. And I think Dai-Dai's example has cured me of that. I realize more and more keenly how much my mother has contributed to me, in peacefulness and sanity, in the last few years. She has an air of having dropped all reins, and that she will go henceforth where life wills her to go, and trust what it brings to her to be happy and loving and kind. And she has not been proved wrong. This makes you feel it is worth living to be 76, and it is a great help."

In her new career, Jane Wood Reno was at a stage where being a show-off was more fun than ever. In public relations she was allowed to let herself go wild and be as fanciful as she wished. One of her first coups was convincing Buckminster Fuller, the notorious inventor and philosopher who made his name with geodesic domes, to come down to the Miami Seaquarium for a ceremony dedicating the new "Golden Aquadome."

"He looks like Pnin," she wrote to daughter Maggy, "on the cover of that Nabokov book of short stories.

"Sixty-three, a little deaf, thick lens glasses, very Boston accent. Five minutes after he lands at the airport he tells me, 'Miss Wood, I didn't know I was to speak until I received the invitation. You know, I get $1,000 a speech.' So, I laid myself out to be charming to this man, so he would speak, for nothing, and say nice things. We needed fair weather for our ceremony, which we didn't get. But we had the thing in the snack bar. Fuller advised the young people present to look to the porpoise for inspiration. (He employs life's gifts so fully, generates 1,000 horsepower of energy in seconds when he leaps 15 feet from the water for a fish.) Fuller is a darling man. And Johnny and Susie dePoo, your Daddy, Janny, Bobby, John Keasler, Burton Clark and I entertained each other at various meals at the Pup and Jamaica Inn.[2] Fuller, who got kicked out of Harvard for helling around, stopped drinking in 1940, but he is still a convivial man at heart, and he adored Johnny and Susie, who are truly adorable.

"We learned about Fuller's most recent corporation. He is, in addition to being president of Synergetics, Inc., Plydomes, Inc., and Geodesics, Inc., also president of the newly formed Obnoxico. It makes obnoxious things people don't need. Such as, a telephone with a lamp on it in the form of a naked woman with a French lampshade on her hair. Also: a baby's diaper, sprayed with pink plastic and curled up on the ends, to plant ivy in. He is going to make Johnny dePoo executive vice president, and me press agent of Obnoxico."

The two biggest accounts Reno had while working for Hank Meyer were the Miami Seaquarium and National Airlines, and she often planned promotional events involving both of them. After the Miami Seaquarium received a plea from the small town of Cesenatico in Italy, Reno dreamed up a public relations coup. The town had a lonely female bottlenose dolphin named Lalla living in a canal, pining away for a mate. The Seaquarium, under Reno's encouragement, offered a male dolphin, and National Airlines came through with an offer of transportation for the groom to Italy. John Keasler became escort and best man, and was aided by humorist Art Buchwald. Surrounded by a great hoopla, Palooza, the male porpoise, flew to his bride in Cesenatico. In August 1961, Reno received a charmingly garbled letter from Dante Matassoni, president of the Cesenatico Tourist Board:

"Palooza, the American porpoise living in the Aquarium of Cesenatico, thanks to the intensive cure of vitamins to which has been submitted for a very long time, is now as regenerate. He is so brisk that he is flirting with Ciumba, the best friend of his wife Lalla. Palooza seems to follow the vogue of Italian boys: he swims and turns as a perfect Italian—dandy.

"To call more attention to his love evolutions, Palooza jumps very often: this is very strange, because till now, Palooza, always so sluggish, seemed to fail the well known tradition of American marines, who fascinate Italian girls, too. Unfortunately this passing rapidly from Ciumba to Lalla, did not give the 'fruit of the sin': of course, that's natural! For a regular procreation is necessary an honest and faithful union, and Palooza. . . . well, he doesn't know it at all.

"We do hope in 1962.

"What will happen till then? Divorce or not divorce between Lalla and Palooza?

"Ciumba, Palooza's passionate lover, has all the physical requisites and Palooza seems to like her very much. All this has been observed particularly during this summer time: sun, blue sky, moon, are the fittest ingredients to favour the most ungovernable loves.

"We have to acknowledge that Palooza has become a really latin lover and has lost that kind of appreciable ingenuity of American boys with their hairs cut very short. Therefore we have to conclude it is the Italian climate that transforms a whatever temper, as we have mentioned above. Consequently we advise all the American young people to come to Cesenatico, where, well . . . perhaps they can all become like Palooza."

Mark Reno was the only child still at home at this time, and one of his hunting expeditions led to another of Jane's publicity ideas. An irony of the "sharp lookout for game wardens" in this story was that Mark went on to become one himself. Jane wrote:

"Marky and Steve shot a deer, and then they went back with Chisholm and found a very young fawn down in the brush, because Chisholm had noted the lower pair of eyes just before the boys shot. Mark brought it home, and I crawled in the dog house to give it a bottle. That fawn came to me, licked my cheek, and blew into my ear in the sexiest manner of any animal I ever met.

"Doe Winslow came along, while I was trying to think of an appropriate name for the deer, and named him Bucky. Henry, who cut up carrots, beans, and bits of bread to his whim every evening, took up the name.

"The fawn lived in Mark's bedroom for three weeks, sleeping on the foot of his bed, while Mark was building a big deer corral. Its elegant, affectionate trust of anybody who came along was enough to restore the guiltiest mortal to decent self-esteem.

"At one point, before the fawn lost its spots, Mark trained it to lead him on a leash; he would slip a dog harness on the deer, and Bucky would cavort across the yard with Marky running fast behind him.

"We had the Lincoln Road account at that time, and I decided to get a photo of a beautiful young blond model in Easter clothes being led by Bucky down Lincoln Road. The Easter Parade was my idea. What came out was Adrienne Boudreau taking one buck shopping on Lincoln Road.

"Steve brought the deer over for the photos, keeping a sharp lookout for game wardens. The model, Adrienne, was charming. Bucky got nervous, I fed him Coke, he spilled the Coke on Adrienne's dress, but she was really gracious. In this cavorting, we gathered a small crowd around us.

"'Tell me,' said a nice elderly Jewish lady, 'is it a dog?'

"'No lady,' I said, 'it's a goat we got fixed up to look like a deer. It's for publicity.'

"'Oh,' she said. 'Publicity!' And her tone made my heart surge with delight that I am in this business, and no other."

Reno eagerly anticipated becoming a grandmother and was overjoyed at the birth of her first grandchild, Maggy's son Jimmy, in the summer of 1961. When she heard the news over the phone, she whooped with delight. The operator asked her to stop shouting. Reno's response to the operator was so rude that her phone was cut off for an hour. Maggy Reno had married Jim Hurchalla the year before, while she was only a junior at Swarthmore College, and she took her baby to lectures with her when she was a senior. Her college yearbook contained these dubious words of wisdom: "I'm working twice as hard but having three times as much fun. Every college girl should have a baby."

Taking a cue from her mother, she had four children in a little over five years so that she could get on with other things herself. Although Henry Reno was unable to attend Maggy's graduation in 1962, he wrote a letter congratulating her:

"Not coming to your graduation has been a deeper disappointment than I have let anybody know, but I shall think of you, Jimmy, James, and Janny Baby every moment of the time. My motto has become 'don't look back.' So a man challenged me the other day and said, 'but you are looking back when you read Stonewall Jackson.' My answer was that all people worth writing about are in fact immortal.

"One critic said that if I did peep back I would indeed recall many a day and night on a bar stool. I thought for awhile and conceded the fact, but allowing that sifting the sordid from the good, one could even find bits of immortality on a bar stool."

After graduating from Tulane, Bob Reno returned to the *Miami Herald* and did what his mother had wanted to do at his age. He moved to Key West. Leading an idyllic life, he worked as the *Herald* bureau chief in what his mother called a "distinguished, elegant little town, where you meet Tallulah Bankhead at splendid parties in walled gardens."

"The politics are hilarious and vigorous," wrote Jane Reno. "The proximity to

Cuba makes it explosive. He is buying a Pontiac, smoking big cigars, and dating Little Audrey, the most beautiful girl in Key West. It is a sort of peak of life that few men are fortunate enough to have happen. He may also someday become a fine writer—he has gifts."

One of the gifts Bob Reno had displayed in his final semester at Tulane was the inherited art of enjoying himself to the hilt on very little money. In one letter home, he described how it was possible to spend a fine night on the town in New Orleans for the princely sum of a quarter. He had dated Sally Godchaux, from a well-known New Orleans family, and had met her grandmother and two great-aunts one night, "who are all over 80, sisters-in-law who outlived their wealthy husbands and just sit around and sign checks." Godchaux's grandmother regaled them with memories of a 1928 picnic with J. P. Morgan's daughter, the comment of President Taft when Sally's father was born—"a fine boy"—the time the chauffeur ran over Governor Parker, and the bra that she designed, patented, and sold for the Belgian Relief Fund in World War I. The next time Reno encountered them was by random chance in the midst of an extraordinary day.

"I went to a wedding in the morning," he wrote, "and met there a charming, beautiful girl from Beaumont, Texas.

"We proceeded to paint the town together after the reception with a bankroll of exactly 25 cents.

"We started by lifting a bottle of champagne from the bridal suite at the hotel. In the lobby while throwing rice we met Sally Godchaux's Aunt Edna, age 85. (She's a professional wedding crasher.) We invited her to help drink the champagne and she took us to Mrs. Jules Godchaux's penthouse in the hotel, where the butler served the champagne followed by more of their own. Thereafter Aunt Edna took us to Mrs. Albert Godchaux's apartment for more drinks and more stories about how the chauffeur ran over Governor Parker. From there we left Aunt Edna, and the girl and I took the streetcar (20 cents) to Iona's and Walter's. We listened to a folk singer Pete-Seeger-style over more drinks. Walter told him his singing stank and an argument ensued. Walter took us all to the Bourbon House and the Good Friends bar to cool off hostilities. At the Good Friends I tended bar when the barmaid left for an hour. We lost Walter and went to Pat O'Brien's (with 5 cents now) where the girl (Susan) met Rev. and Mrs. Plumley and Mr. and Mrs. So and So. Susan and the Plumleys' daughter were former roommates. Becoming a subtle but unabashed moocher by now, I snowed Mrs. Plumley and they invited us to their table for drinks and to watch the floor show. Afterwards they took us to the Blue Room of the Roosevelt Hotel, New Orleans' most elegant and expensive night club. They left us there and we stayed dancing and enjoying the show at their table for two hours. At 4 o'clock a.m. I used the last 5 cents to call a friend at an all night poker game who came and took us home."

Mark Reno spent a somewhat aimless year after dropping out of Tulane, working at odd jobs like scuba diving for the Wildlife Commission. Then he joined the Army. He wanted to apply for Officer Candidate School but was concerned about his background of juvenile arrests. They had been for underage drinking, or for the time he and his friend Eddie Kay broke into a church so they could turn off the offensive neon light in the steeple. Henry Reno began looking into the arrests to see if Mark's record could be cleaned up, and he received a note from a colleague in the Naples bureau: "Mark Wood Reno, 18, was arrested 7-25-59 by Sgt. Ed Helenek, Naples police, at 10:06 p.m., and charged with possession of alcoholic beverages by a minor. Incidentally, Helenek was dropped last year after he went psycho and shot the chief and another sergeant who was his father-in-law. He has now been decommitted but is not on the force. Hope it'll help."

After a year in the Army, Mark still was the only one of the children whose future was a mystery to his mother. He was a formidable outdoorsman and waterman who could live equally off the bounty of the ocean or hunting in the woods. Of the children, he had formed the closest relationship with the Miccosukees, and he spent a great deal of time trading with them out in the Everglades. Unlike his siblings, however, he had no set idea of what he wanted to do with his life. He entered Officer Candidate School at Fort Benning in early 1962, and by the summer he was a second lieutenant paratrooper in the 101st Airborne Division. His mother described him as "profoundly bored by everything in the army except jumping out of airplanes." As Mark remembers, that wasn't true, because he derived no special thrill from even that. Jumping didn't do much for him one way or another, and his days as a paratrooper were the last times he ever strapped on a parachute. In response to her mother's expressed concern, Janet offered an eloquent defense of her brother:

Mark Reno wrestling a gator at a Miccosukee camp on the Tamiami Trail, early 1960s.

"I mean not to sound preachy, but tread an easy line with your youngest son and let him feel free, and let him feel beloved, and let him feel approved of, and don't lecture him, and don't show your worry, and don't treat him as a little boy anymore. You know even more than I do that he is great and wonderful, that he is out of Conrad and Isak Dinesen, that he has said more truthfully than most of us—*I know not where I go*—but they say to me 'seek and ye shall find' and so *I propose 'to sail beyond the sunset and the baths of the western stars.'* This is far better than doing as most of his contemporaries have, sitting in classrooms in their senior year at the University of Florida, drinking up a storm, learning nothing, going blindly on to law school. No, your youngest son is great, his course is beautiful."

Janet breezed along happily through Harvard Law School, spending her weekends hiking through the countryside. Her greatest quandaries revolved around whether it was a worse cultural loss for Christmas carols to be banished from public schools by civil libertarians, or whether the constitutional lawyer in her should stand with people offended by such secular traditions. During her first summer home from school Janet got a job at the small law firm of Ed Brigham. He was the younger brother of Jane Reno's old friend Peg Brigham, whose family friendship with the Renos dated back to the Depression.

Very few lawyers were willing to encourage a woman's desire to practice law at the time, and Ed Brigham's support gave Janet Reno's legal dreams a huge boost. In a letter home from Harvard, Janet reflected on why she had decided on law, and the initial and unlikely violent opposition of her own mother to the idea. Since at one point Jane Reno had praised her son Bob's desire to be a lawyer, her stance was somewhat inexplicable.

"When I was nine I can remember thinking that despite ranches, etc.," wrote Janet, "what I really wanted to do was be a lawyer like my grandfather and Thomas Jefferson. Then came ranches, nuclear physics, foreign service, and generals. In my last year of high school I distinctly remember commenting to Ma that what I really wanted to do and should do was to be a lawyer and Mummy firmly saying that was the only thing she would ever forbid me to be. Such unexpected dogmatism from that corner squelched me for a long time and I never thought much about it again till my junior year, and then Howard Hughes. Then without really deciding I took the Law Aptitude Test—thinking nothing great was at stake—and then I did well and I can remember Christmastime my senior year at Cornell asking Ma what she thought about me applying to Harvard, etc. All she said was 'might as well.' And I still hadn't decided to go to law school. And then came Harvard and then Ed Brigham. Maggy explains it all by saying I do exactly what Mummy doesn't want me to do."

Jane Reno could hardly complain. Her daughters were a perfect model of her independent nature. The more that law led Janet toward an ideal of justice for all peoples, the more strongly she felt about the civil rights movement. Shortly after the riots at the University of Mississippi in 1962, when James Meredith was admitted as the first black student and the governor tried to block his enrollment, Janet questioned the Kennedys' commitment to the cause.[1]

"Mississippi—" Janet wrote, "my reaction is thank God it's over. The law gives no express mandate, but to me the implied mandate to the executive to enforce the laws in this fashion comes through loud and clear. I wonder if Jack might not have paid more attention to Oxford than he in fact did to the America's Cup races. This last minute appeal Sunday night seemed unnecessary, too late, and irrelevant. Some words might have been appropriate earlier? Perhaps as early as January 1961? But then the South might have raised up and snorted. Bessie[2] has the answer—when the stink gets too strong in God's nose he's going to do something about it."

Jane Reno's father, George Washington Wood II, died in 1962. She had seen it coming for a while and was steadfastly impressed at how her mother handled it and carried herself despite a lifetime of frail health. The day that George Wood died, Reno found her mother out in the yard sobbing.

"Jane," she said, "I was always afraid until I met your father. And when I met your father, I was never afraid again."

In describing her mother in recent years to her aunt Peg, Reno mirrored some of what she had written about Grandmother Lil a quarter century before. It concerned the indefatigable strength of southern women:

"My mother is a wonderful model of excellence to me in how to be very old, and very ill. You know, she built up a reputation about herself about not being brave, but all her life she had all the courage a crisis required. And she has been so splendid in her strong and kind care of Daddy in the last few years—a faithful and gracious standing up under a heavy load that would have been beyond the strength of spirit of many much younger people. And she has done it all with such elegance, and without any self-pity, or heroics, or plaintiveness.

And so she had come already to seem a true hero to me, one of the few people I ever saw grow marvelously in stature at such an age. So she has robbed old age of some of the terrors that had gathered around it for me—the terror of becoming dull and querulous and a burden."

When National Airlines began their Miami-Baltimore service, Reno suggested to the mayor of Miami Beach that it might be a great gesture of goodwill to send the mayor of Baltimore an alligator for the Baltimore Zoo. Reno even offered to supply the alligator. She went out to her Miccosukee friends in the Everglades to get a small gator from them, quickly taped up its jaws, and brought it home.

While the alligator took its rest on the Reno porch in the hours before the trip to the airport, the tape came loose. She quickly grabbed another roll of tape and prepared to secure its mouth again, but the alligator was quicker. Her son Bob said at the time: "It was the kind of thing I always knew would happen. I come home, there is a sign on the door saying, 'Mean alligator on the loose in the kitchen, watch out.' There is blood all over the porch, and there is nobody there but the mean alligator in the fireplace."

Jane Reno later recalled: "I wasn't fast enough, I hesitated—I forgot what I used to preach about being quick and smooth. I stopped for just an instant when I had my fingers under his jaws and was coming around to clamp the top of his snout. He jerked his head sideways and chomped off the end of my finger."

Blood poured out of the finger. Reno's daughter-in-law Vera helped her pen the alligator away in the fireplace behind a makeshift fence, and they rushed for the emergency room.

"There wasn't really that much blood," Reno recalled, "about three dozen drops the size of a quarter, and Vera and I were giggling, and Henry was asleep. It didn't hurt so much when he bit because I was anaesthetized by beer and he didn't really bite the tip end of my finger off, just gave it a compound fracture with stitches."

The family doctor, John Dix, long used to the bizarre injuries of the perennially active Renos, sighed and said to the emergency room nurses, "You probably won't treat many grandmothers with alligator bites."

To Reno he observed, "You keep the practice of medicine from becoming boring, Jane."

With her finger stitched up, Reno went home, started taping up the alligator's jaws all over again, and finally got the creature safely off to Baltimore.

The event made her more cautious in her alligator handling, and her demonstrations to her friends on how to hypnotize an alligator involved progressively smaller creatures. On one trip out to the Osceola camp, she caught the tail of a small alligator, pulled him out, and showed how to put it to sleep. A four-year-old Indian boy ran up to her, and she thought for a moment that she was getting to be something of a legend.

"Jane Wood," he said accusingly, "you caught the littlest."

The *Miami Herald* moved into a new building on Biscayne Bay on March 23, 1963, and Reno's ever-mischievous husband, Henry, stopped by in April to check out the newspaper's new home. Columnist Jack Bell wrote that the new receptionist called up to the City Desk and told Art Himbert that "Mr. Greeley is here to see you. Mr. H. Greeley."

"Horace Greeley?" asked a suspicious Himbert, referencing the legendary nineteenth-century New York newspaperman.

The receptionist paused. "Yes, Horace Greeley," she confirmed.

"Don't send him in, I'll come out," Himbert replied, wondering who was pulling his leg, only to be greeted by a smiling Henry Reno.

When Himbert got rid of him and went out a half hour later, he told the receptionist, "If Arthur Brisbane calls, I'll be back soon."

The receptionist, unfamiliar with newspaperman humor, dutifully replied, "I'll watch out for him."[3]

The love of spring-hopping remained a steady passion, and weekend trips to the Suwannee country of north Florida became a ritual. Gathering up family and friends, she would lead a caravan upstate, navigating from one spring to the next with the help of a worm-ridden and pencil-marked Florida Geological Survey book. From the surface far, far above, they snorkeled and gazed at the wondrous, subterranean world, and collected fossilized alligator droppings millenniums old. Afternoons lazed by with cool melons and beer, and blue crabs netted in the grasses just off the Gulf. Reno traded stories with the boat-shack man and set camp near the boil that marked the origins of the Ichetucknee River. Around the campfire, they told and retold stories until they could no longer stay awake.

In a letter from her youngest and favorite cousin, Peter Hunter, he joked

Tubing at Ichetucknee Springs, mid-1950s.

about the spring-hopping life while stationed as an Air Force pilot in France. Like Reno, Hunter was a lover of the classics and possessed a similar intellectual combination of romanticism and realism. He also was a devoted fan of the *Pogo* comic strip, which was a key to understanding a great deal of the Reno family. The quirky blend of sophistication and irreverence in a group of swamp critters was as much a part of the Renos as it was of Howland Owl, Churchy LaFemme, Albert the Alligator, and the other *Pogo* characters. Hunter wrote:

"The mind reels (as Howland Owl would say) at the possibilities for self-realization as a Down-streamer, and all the refinements which could be developed, awaiting the user of the Floating Chaise! The height of the ridiculous would be to lash together a group of Floating Chaises, with a table and a life-raft filled with provender, including an ice-chest, and float in magnificent convoy! But this is only one suggestion . . . maybe a 20-man Air Force life raft (the round style), to serve as a base of operations, with as many Floating Chaises, kickboards, inner tubes, etc., as necessary to insure naval superiority, would be better long-range military planning."

Reno and Hunter shared a love of poetry that ran deep, and their letters back and forth traded verse of their favorite poets and discussions of poetry. In 1964, Reno wrote to Hunter in regard to the poem "Tetelestai" by Conrad Aiken:

"I would disagree, however, that *Tetelestai* is like Whitman—it's much more musical, not really in a Whitman mood . . . and there's very little of Whitman that ever moved me much. It (*Tetelestai*) is a beautiful evocation of a mood, colored light blue. I am reminded by it of how happy it makes one to phrase a melancholy mood nicely, it is indeed the perfect prescription for a cure of the blues. One time when my chillun went off to college, I was going sailing with Barbara Wyatt, and I had been very low in spirits, until, on the dock, I announced: 'The long legged ghosts are walking, through my house and through my heart.' With that, I felt perfectly delightful."

After Henry Reno's heart attack, he didn't try to keep up with his wife's bound-less energy and sense of adventure. He had his own separate network of friends after four decades at the *Miami Herald* and still enjoyed his newspaper work as much as ever. Visiting with his son Mark and daughter-in-law Vera in Montserrat in 1964, he was so charmed by the island that he decided he want to retire there.

"Henry came back gayer and happier than since he went deaf in one ear in 1948," wrote Jane. "He has his eye on a lot, where a neighboring lady walks a pig on a leash."

Henry continued to be an important part of her life. He retired from the *Herald* in 1965, where he had become an institution. Among rewrite men, Henry's reporting was legendary, both for the enormous amount of information he compacted into his telephone calls and for the eloquence and gentleness of his storytelling. His reports were often gruesome, yet he told them without unnecessary embellishments—almost like fairy tales, his wife remembered. When former *Herald* reporter and editor Gene Miller was a young rewrite man, Reno would call up, tell him everything he had for a story, and then say to Miller, "But really, don't use me as a source."

"Henry Reno liked cops better than reporters," Miller observed.[1]

Most historical familiarity with Miami crime reporting doesn't predate the celebrated crime novelist Edna Buchanan, but it sometimes extends to Gene Miller, who showed her the ropes at the *Miami Herald* when she began there in 1973. Calvin Trillin wrote a story about Buchanan for the *New Yorker* in 1986, the year she won a Pulitzer Prize:

"All connoisseurs would agree, I think, that the classic Edna lead would have to include one staple of crime reporting—the simple, matter-of-fact statement that registers with a jolt. The question is where the jolt should be. There's a lot to be said for starting right out with it. I'm rather partial to the Edna lead on a story last year about a woman about to go on trial for a murder conspiracy: 'Bad things happen to the husbands of Widow Elkin.' On the other hand, I can understand the preference that others have for the device of beginning a crime story with a more or less conventional sentence or two, then snapping the reader back in his chair with an abbreviated sentence that is used like a blunt instrument.

"One student of the form at the Herald refers to that device as the Miller Chop. The reference is to Gene Miller, now a Herald editor, who, in a remarkable reporting career that concentrated on the felonious, won the Pulitzer Prize twice for stories that resulted in the release of people in prison for murder. Miller likes short sentences in general—it is sometimes said at the Herald that he writes as if he were paid by the period—and he particularly likes to use a short sentence after a couple of rather long ones."[2]

The so-called Miller Chop and the terseness of style that influenced Buchanan was, in fact, a style perfected by Henry Reno over forty years at the *Herald*, and a style that Miller largely learned from working with Reno. While the acclaim and recognition of a Pulitzer was afforded to Gene Miller and Edna Buchanan individually for their crime reporting, Reno effectively had been the co-winner of one himself in 1951. Pulitzers for public service were awarded to the newspaper, however, not the individual. Although the *Herald* did not shy away from crediting the reporting of Henry Reno and Red McGee for the award, over time their names disappeared from history in association with it.

In Reno's position as a crime reporter, he received volumes of information on the dark secrets of countless Miami citizens. His children found that occasionally he would confirm something if it could not harm anyone, but he virtually never betrayed a trust and never gossiped. There were occasionally exceptions, if something was a fairly common rumor. Though Jane Reno thought State Attorney Richard Gerstein was getting a bum rap during the 1957-era grand jury investigations of the state attorney's office, she admitted it was only because they were accusing him of the wrong things. Henry Reno had told his family that the word among the bookies on Miami Beach was that Gerstein was shaking them down for payoffs.

The year Henry retired, Jane chose to undertake one of her most ambitious adventures. Life in Miami was not as quiet as it had once been, and she wanted to forget about civilization for a while. The result of this idea was to set off on a beach walk by herself up the coast of Florida. The story of her walk was published in the *Miami Herald* on September 26, 1965:

"For six days I walked 104 miles up the beaches of the Florida east coast, from Jupiter Light to Patrick Air Force Base. Two nights I slept on the beach, walking on between naps. In a bag slung on one shoulder I carried cheese, raisins, and bell peppers, water in a plastic one-pint detergent bottle, a bug-bomb, a very light water-repellent jacket with hood, a plastic bag to keep my legs warm, plenty of matches, cigarettes, comb, Kleenex, a map, lipstick and enough money.

"After noting on the first day that I could skinny-dip in complete privacy almost anywhere along that beach, I left my bathing suit behind to lighten the load and had no cause to regret it until the last day, when I reached a populated beach.

"The idea that walking up the beach would be a good vacation came to me after the phone had rung incessantly all one day and into the evening. After studying the map, I picked that stretch because it seemed the least populated on Florida's east coast. Unpopulated it proved to be, for many, many miles.

"I knew that Jonathan Dickinson, his wife, baby, and others had been ship-wrecked along there in the eighteenth century and found it so desolate that a number of their party died before they finished their walk to St. Augustine. But they walked hungry, naked, in the winter, and were prisoners of hostile Indians.

"I picked the first week in May, and on the nights I did not sleep on the beach, I called my daughter-in-law, Vera, who lives in Stuart. She came and picked me up, fed me a good dinner, and I slept comfortably in her house.

"The thing I learned was faith.

"Have faith that walking is a means of getting somewhere, and the blue headlands before you will fade into the blue distance behind you. If, upon walking on the second day, you totter along the sand with new muscles in your legs and feet complaining, put one foot in front of the other for three minutes and the kinks and pains will go, and you can step out happily. The same thing holds true with a cramp in the calf of the leg in mid-afternoon.

"Have faith that you can walk twenty miles on a pint of water, and you will find you can, especially if the water tastes slightly of detergent. This will deter you from wanting too much water. The same dense, beautiful, and inpenetrable green that was so forbidding to Jonathan Dickinson mantles the rolling dune behind the beach today for many miles. Sea grapes, palmettos, and coco plum

Jane Reno resting at Blowing Rocks in Jupiter during her 104-mile, six-day solo beach walk in 1965.

are woven together into a wall. Only the shore birds that were laying pink eggs, raccoons, and a little animal that left tiny tracks and wedge-shaped holes in the sand seemed to find the underbrush hospitable.

"The little tracks proved to be those of armadillos; they like to stick their noses in the sand now and then. There were no signs of the small bears that used to come down to Jupiter Beach to eat turtle eggs when Captain Bill Gray and his brother Herman camped out there in 1909.

"That coast is fringed by long, narrow islands, and it was on the beaches of those islands I walked. There is no bridge across the St. Lucie Inlet at the northern tip of Jupiter Island, the first stretch of my journey. I should have had to backtrack eight miles or so had a fisherman not ferried me across that inlet to the southern tip of Hutchinson Island.

"To me the Stuart House of Refuge, about two miles north of St. Lucie Inlet, was just that. Built in the 1880s to afford succor to shipwrecked sailors who might otherwise have perished from hunger and thirst on that desolate coast, it is today maintained as a fascinating little museum by the local historical society, and I rested there luxuriously. Just off shore treasure hunters were working.

"A road is being built the length of Hutchinson Island, but it is not yet completed, and access to the beach for many miles north of Jensen Beach is only possible by foot or by beach buggy. That shimmering, firm, level strand was populated mostly by birds. There is no bridge across Ft. Pierce Inlet, at the northern tip of this island, and I went back to the mainland there across the Ft. Pierce causeway.

"The third island, which I was told is also called Hutchinson Island, is about thirty miles long. My map showed no road north of Wabasso Beach, and no bridge over Sebastian Inlet. Just at dawn I rounded the northern tip of that island, and there was the most beautiful new bridge arching over Sebastian Inlet. Later I found it was opened in February. That was when I really pondered on the message: Have faith.

"For six days I walked when I wanted to walk, ate when I wanted to eat, and slept when and where I wanted to sleep. In the nights when I got sleepy, I combed the eroding sandy bluff to a casuarina tree, scraped up some needles and small dead twigs and branches, and started a little fire.

"After my feet were warm, I put out the fire and raked the hot sand out to make a bed. My bag was my pillow, and I wiggled out curves in the sand to fit. Never did I have a sounder, sweeter sleep—even though I usually waked chilly in two or three hours. The chill went away when I walked. The nights were most magical after the moon had set, for the stars were higher and so lavish in their brightness that I could see the white crests of all the curling waves.

"At the end, I backtracked, and my walk ended in a little white board building overlooking a splendid beach opposite Melbourne Beach trailer village. The sign says simply, 'The Bar.' For six days I had talked to almost no strangers. I plodded in and over my beer visited with the bartenders, Janie and Jamie.

"I told them what I had been doing. Jamie came from behind the bar and put soothing drops in my eyes and rubbed my ankles. Bob Jacobs, a customer, sent across the street to the trailer village for an electric vibrating machine, unplugged the juke box, and massaged my legs. Nobody would let me buy a beer.

"So . . . it might be that some day I shall be drowned by the sea, or die of pneumonia from sleeping out at night, or be robbed and strangled by strangers. These things happen. Even so, I shall be ahead because of trusting the beach, the night, and strangers."[3]

Though she enjoyed her career in public relations, work alone could never begin to satisfy Reno. Although publicity was a chance to have a lot of fun, it was less mentally challenging than journalism had been. Reaching the heart of middle age, her intellectual curiosity wasn't dimming, and her body had no desire to slow down either. She became more contemplative, questioning things constantly to avoid falling into a rut.

About discussing life with her friend and neighbor Joan Cronin, Reno wrote: "I told Joan about what the stars said to me when I was somewhat distressed a couple of months ago and went down and got stuck in the mud near Cape Sable. Stars talk to me down there, there being little but stars, mosquitoes, and mangroves. They said, 'Don't let 'em get you down.' Also, that was what the night and ocean said to me last year when I was walking."

She wrote to daughter Maggy around this time:

"I got to thinking last night what I would really most like to do when I am about 55, because at best most business is to a degree a con game, and newspapers and trade writing worse. Of course, what I, and anybody else would like, if they could afford it, would be to be good and kind to people. How? I thought and thought. I thought of teaching crazy children, and I thought of nursing, and I thought of teaching normal children. Nothing clicked. Then I thought of being a masseur. Yeah, I know all about the classified ads in the *Herald*, category 89, and I have nothing immoral in mind. If this should happen, you needn't tell people your mother is a masseuse, say she has retired. I will be in a very moral solarium."

The separate lifestyles and desires of Jane and Henry caused them to spend less and less time together. For the past few years, she had often abandoned him but for a couple of meals together on the weekends.

"He would have a right to be sulky," she wrote, "and has been in early years over much less."

Instead, she thought him to be angelic, both in his treatment of her mother and his serenity. He was retired, restful, and content with his friends and memories. When he retired, he did go through with his plan to live in Montserrat for a while.

Janet Reno wrote to him at his residence at the Coconut Hill Hotel, updating him on the news at home. She had moved back into the house with her family after completing Harvard Law School and was getting an inkling of what living with her mother for the next few decades was going to be like: "Guess what we did? We almost traded the red car in on a 1965 dark blue Mustang for you. Someone offered $1950 on a trade in. See what happens or almost happens when you leave us by ourselves? Mummy's foot is mending whereas Mummy is going to hell in a handbasket."

Jane Reno's drinking had become fairly pronounced. She had taken to bar-hopping more frequently, whereas most of her drinking in the past had been social. She was in the midst of a particularly unpleasant point in relations with her siblings, and the equanimity she had discovered only a few years before was rapidly fading. Her sisters and brother offered a great deal of criticism about how she was caring for their mother, though Reno was the only one of them willing to take care of Daisy Wood. For Reno's part, she was furious with her siblings not only for their carping but for their unwillingness to part with money for their mother's care.

Doe Winslow, daughter of Reno's sister Daisy, was witness to an enlightening day when she was ten years old. Reno's siblings had decided Jane was out of control, and they were going to do an intervention. The whole notion of an intervention went against every grain of Reno's being: it was the ultimate act of censoriousness. Never in the family history had such group judgment been exhibited, and Reno did not respond well.

"When I think of Jane now," recalls Winslow, "I think of her as being like my view on Dorothy Parker: too bright, too fond of drink, too contemptuous of less colorful mortals.

"And when I was 10-ish, I thought she was the coolest person in the world.

Then one day, she picked me up at Dai-Dai's to go for a ride or run errands or something. To make a long story short, we were gone all day and into the evening. She was drunk and full of hard feelings for her sisters and my father and Uncle George and she told me plenty of dirt intended to, I don't know . . . win me over to her way of thinking? But it was all news to me. What did I know? I thought the whole Wood family was funny and smart and I loved being around them and I thought they all felt the same about each other.

"I remember exactly what I felt the moment we finally got back to 5500 S.W. 74th St: I couldn't get away from her fast enough. I remember a whole bunch of adult family milling around inside the house, anxious and angry. And I remember an explosion of accusations and name-calling among them all as soon as Jane came into sight. Talk about a sibling rivalry."

For years her sisters had been tolerating Reno's barbs, which could be particularly vicious if she had been drinking. The Dorothy Parker tongue never got any less sharp. Though she loved her siblings, she felt a compulsive need to wound them in different ways. None of Jane Reno's children can explain where the anger came from. Part of the answer may be in her early rejection of her mother's southern gentility, and frustration that her siblings inherited it. Reno believed in living larger than life, and her siblings bore the brunt of her contempt for "less colorful mortals." With Dolly, who was most resistant, the digs were subtle. In the case of Daisy, Jane had always resented her charm and flirtatiousness, and found it easy to hurt her. Winifred had always been the closest to Jane, but that didn't stop Jane from mocking Winifred's conventionality. One night during one of Winifred's visits, both of them were drunk and arguing when Winifred exasperatedly burst out, "Goddamn it, Jane, you have no humility!"

"Of course I don't!" Reno roared back proudly.

Unable or unwilling to match her antagonism, Reno's siblings found that criticizing her care of their mother was a way to get back at her. Bitter words flew often, and Jane's volatility only grew more pronounced.

Janet, who was working as a young lawyer and living at home with her mother, was a match for her in terms of will. Furthermore, she was unfazed by any of her mother's behavior. When it got excessive, Janet would simply yell, "Goddammit, Mummy, straighten up!"

Janet's first taste of politics came when she helped her friend and soon-to-be law partner, Gerald Lewis, win a seat in the state legislature in 1966. The Lewis campaign had been warned off campaigning in Matheson Hammock, so Janet improvised an idea of how to get around the ban on campaigning in the popular county park. She took her mother and a whole cast of family and friends out on her boat and anchored it just offshore. They all blew up campaign balloons and cast them on the waters, letting them float to shore. Following that, Janet waded through the shallows, carrying more balloons in to distribute to mothers of clamoring children. Lewis went on to win, giving Reno the idea that she wanted to pursue a seat in the state legislature herself. She estimated the campaign would cost no more than $4,500, which would be enough to buy all the balloons they needed to ensure victory.

Out on the west edge of the Everglades, near Immokalee in the Big Cypress Swamp, Henry Reno owned a small cabin. Upon returning from Montserrat, he spent more time there enjoying the quiet peace of one of the emptiest regions in the state. His wife's drinking and explosiveness were proving too difficult to live with for someone seeking rest, and one of the things he and Jane shared most strongly—their love of solitude and wild, remote places—helped keep their lives separate. In 1967 he moved out to the cabin full-time but came in every two weeks to visit and pick up his heart medicine. Family and friends had a party for Jane and Henry's thirtieth anniversary that he came home for, and he was delighted. Someone asked him what it had been like.

"Has it been thirty years?" he said, marveling at the thought. "Thirty years with such a woman! Well, to tell the truth, I wouldn't have missed a minute, not for a million."[4]

Only a few weeks after their thirtieth anniversary, Henry Olaf Reno, who had covered crime in Miami from the wild boom days of the 1920s to the reign of Meyer Lansky, died of an aneurysm at his cabin. He was sixty-six years old. He had seen the worst Miami could offer in that time, as well as the comic side of crime—he took a particular delight in stories like the one of a police bloodhound that was picked up by a dogcatcher while it was in pursuit of a criminal. The trademark of his journalism was the same characteristic that carried him through his marriage to Jane: he was never judgemental, never censorious.

"Henry watched life as a parade," recalled Jane. "He could have written many, many books, but instead he chose to enjoy all the things he knew in his own way."

A few nights after her husband died, Reno wrote to her cousin Peter:

"In the middle of the night we have been playing Beethoven's Seventh, especially the second movement. But tonight with your sweet gift revealed by a letter from a nice man at the University of Miami, I have been playing *La Traviata*, and I cried and cried. He loved those dying sopranos so: Camille, Mimi, Aida, et al.

"A week after we were married, I was crying with him over the death of Mimi. And I am sure you, as we do, associate Aida's death with Maggy's marriage. My feeling has always been that the message was: Go to Heaven, thy native land, and so with my friend Henry. Thank you for going along this path with me."

By the time Jane did turn fifty-five, she wasn't in a "very moral solarium," but she was relatively unconcerned with riots in Paris, riots in America, the war in Vietnam, and much of the world turmoil that was taking place. The death of her husband had settled her to some degree, and she had decided that grandchildren were reason enough alone for one's existence.

"I have, of course, plenty of balm for any soreness of heart I may have," she wrote.

"Though I tell my long-legged children, 'You're nice to have around even though you passed the prime of life a long time ago,' they *do* have children. If I could be sure of keeping enough of them around me under age six I should possibly be willing to live forever.

"Bobby Hurchalla and I were sleeping together in the same sleeping bag one night and he awaked with some night fears as the morning star came up. After I had assuaged them, he said: 'Grandmud, I wish there were no rattlesnakes, and no hurricanes, and no trees fell on you, and no heart attacks, and nobody died till the end of their life.'

"It makes, I think, a good prayer."

Her drinking slowed very little, and she continued an alarmingly casual habit of driving drunk. One time she was driving home on a dark and drizzly night, feeling no pain after a business evening involving many cocktails, when two blocks from her house she saw a man stumping along briskly. He was headed west, and there was nothing beyond her house but the black night and eventually the Everglades. Because it was drizzling and he seemed old, she stopped. She recalled that she would have even if she had been sober, but when she was drunk she made a point of always stopping for people.

"Where are you going, sir, can I give you a ride?" she asked.

"Thank you," he said. "Is this the way to Chicago?"

"Hop in!"

She took him home and gave him a dry shirt. Her son Mark helped him change, and they made a little fire and dried his shoes and socks. They also gave him a cup of tea, because he didn't drink. He told them his name was William Schneider and that he was ninety-one years old and born in Estonia.

"Schneider?" Reno asked. "Are you Jewish or German?"

"I am Jewish!" Schneider replied, with robust pride.

Mark Reno and his wife, Donna, along with Jane, took the man home to his niece, who fussed at him in such a way that they understood why he was walking to Chicago. He offered Jane five dollars, which she refused, though she could tell that he was moderately well-to-do. She was also impressed by his fitness. Between 7:30 a.m.—when he had left his house—and 8:00 p.m., he had walked fifteen miles and had still been going strong. The following Friday a brief letter from William Schneider arrived that began "Dear Friends"; included with it was a ten-dollar gift certificate for the Jordan Marsh department store: "Thank you again. You were so very kind. Please accept this expression of my gratitude. It is good to know that Christianity is not dead!"

Jane Reno was touched and amused. She hated to tell him that they were atheists. The incident was hardly the most unusual one of the winter, however. With the family gathered at Christmas—Janet, Maggy's family, and Bob Reno and his Turkish wife, Challa—they were all sitting around the fire on a Friday night. The fire had been going for only about five minutes, when there was a great fluttering sound. Sparks leapt all around the fire.

"A peacock has fallen down the chimney!" proclaimed Challa Reno.

"Don't be ridiculous, Challa," replied Janet, accustomed already to her sister-in-law's drunken exuberances.

"Tsk-tsk, Challa," said Jane Reno quietly to herself.

More flapping and sparks occurred, and Challa insisted with increasing certainty: "It *is* a peacock that has fallen down the chimney."

Jane Reno got down on her hands and knees, and craned her neck to peer up the chimney. Indeed, there was a dying peacock's head and one wing, flapping feebly. The fire was doused, but too late to save the peacock. Eventually, after everyone else but the Hurchalla family had gone to a party, Jane Reno wrestled the dead peacock out of the chimney and disposed of it. Reno wondered about her daughter-in-law's perceptiveness:

"Challa, you couldn't see anything, how did you know it was a peacock?"

"He sounded like I would feel," she replied, "if I was a peacock and fell down the chimney."

Reno kept up a vigorous workload for herself, writing in her spare time for a Viennese photographer who did small color books on places like Eleuthera and other islands in the Bahamas. The writing part for each book only took her two days, and she was paid two hundred dollars per book. Still, it could hold her attention for only so long because it was too much like her regular work. She found herself rising from the typewriter one afternoon, roaring, "Screw you, Eleuthera!" and sitting down to read the Maurice Sendak–illustrated book *The Beeman of Orn.*

After working on the Eleuthera book for three hours one morning, Reno noticed that she had a cut and a big goose egg on her forehead.

"How did I get that?" she asked Mark's ex-wife Vera, who was staying with her.

"I don't know," Vera replied.

Reno remembered that she had been at the beach by the Sand-Bar Lounge the day before with Joan Cronin and her daughter Stephanie and that they had walked down the beach and slept. On the way back, Reno had been carrying Stephanie and fell across a breakwater; Stephanie was unhurt. While her memory was cloudy, Reno's alcoholic humor remained unaffected.

"My amnesia," wrote Reno, "seems to be due to the two six-packs of Busch and two vodka martinis I had comforted and warmed, rather than the blow on the head."

Words never ceased to be a source of joy for Reno, whether written or spoken. Riding up in the elevator at Hank Meyer Associates in 1969, she pondered over a new theory of hers that it was rarely excusable to invent or to use words of more than two syllables.

"Like Churchill, I like the small, old words," she wrote to her cousin Peter.

"I think I could also invent, given a little more time, a racist theory to the effect that nations that invent a lot of polysyllabic words are stupid, trivial nations that should properly be condemned to having to spell and pronounce them. (i.e., the Germans and the French).

"My proof for my theory are the lines of English poetry which I at present consider the finest and the most useful for the purpose of making me feel good by saying them to myself when I ride around in my car depressed by the foolishness of much of the world's work. They are from *The Tempest*:

> Our revels now are ended. These our actors,
> As I foretold you, were all spirits and
> Are melted into air, into thin air:
> And, like the baseless fabric of this vision,
> The cloud-capp'd towers, the gorgeous palaces,
> The solemn temples, the great globe itself,
> Yea, all which it inherit, shall dissolve,
> And, like this insubstantial pageant faded,
> Leave not a rack behind. We are such stuff
> As dreams are made on, and our little life
> Is rounded with a sleep!

"The beauty of this particular line of thought is that I consider words of more than two syllables insubstantial words, so its use in that place by Shakespeare is supremely fitting and shows a very rare something."

With the birth of her sixth grandchild, Douglas, in 1970, Reno had an assortment of little ones to expose to the same parts of wild Florida that she had shared with her children. Maggy Reno Hurchalla had four children—James Alan, Robert Hunter, Jane Elizabeth, and George—and Mark Reno had Karin Hunter and Douglas. To her grandchildren she was known as Grandmud. The "Grand" part wasn't important to her, and any abbreviation to "Gran" drew a stern rebuke. She told them, "Just call me Mud."

Her adventures with her family continued to take unusual twists. A canoe trip down the Wacissa and Aucilla Rivers of north Florida in 1971 taught her grandchildren things they didn't know were possible.

The spring-fed and crystal-clear Wacissa River connects to the Aucilla, a dark tannic river, in two different ways. The way the Reno trip was aiming for was the connection via the Slave Canal, a three-mile shallow channel built by slaves around 1850 to help cotton plantations get their product downriver more quickly. The brutal work of picking through rock never managed to excavate the canal to more than a half foot deep in places, and the canal was never suitable for navigation. Over time it became one of the finest canoe trails in the state, with one caveat—"if you could find it." The entrance to the Slave Canal from the Wacissa River has always been a notoriously elusive creature, overgrown by thick vegetation and hidden from view.

Not surprisingly, they missed it. They chose the path less traveled, one of many threads of the river through a region where the Wacissa River aimlessly dead-ends in a giant swamp. By sheer chance, they managed to navigate through this section across to the Aucilla River, at a place called Half Mile Rise. Unfortunately, at the end of the half mile the Aucilla disappeared underground. A large hole dropped into some Tolkien-esque dimension of Middle Earth, and they were not so ambitious as to see where that would take them. The river simply ended in the middle of the forest.

The idea that a river could abruptly go down a hole was somewhat perplexing to the grandchildren, but they knew already they were part of a family that seemed doomed to discover all such things. Half Mile Rise is one of the longest sections of above-ground river in the Aucilla Sinks, an area of a few miles where the Aucilla River randomly disappears and reappears. This disconnect was what prevented planters from shipping their cotton down the Aucilla River and the reason the Slave Canal was built. Although the family knew they were on the Aucilla, they didn't know where they were or why they were stranded.

Jane Reno, Janet Reno, Maggy Hurchalla, and her husband, Jim, contemplated what to do. As adults, they seemed stoic about the situation, suggesting they had seen all this before. Jim Hurchalla and Janet Reno were elected to go off for help because they were the only ones on the trip who had shoes. The remainder of them slept in a briar patch, using soggy towels for blankets to ward off the mosquitoes. In the morning, Jim and Janet eventually returned with a ranger from Fish and Game. There turned out to be a dirt road not too far away, where they were able to bring the van and load the canoes.

Janet had started up a law practice in 1967 with her friend Gerald Lewis after helping him win a seat in the Florida Senate, but they dissolved the practice by 1970 when it became apparent that Lewis didn't have the time for it. In March 1971, a few months before the Slave Canal adventure, Janet took a job in Tallahassee as a staff director for the House Judiciary Committee headed by legislator Talbot "Sandy" D'Alemberte. Her primary work was on divorce reform, to streamline the process and make no-fault divorces possible.

She was still thoroughly her mother's daughter, as a *Miami News* article entitled "Drafting Laws a Snap for Lady Legal Eagle" showed:

"If the Florida House of Representatives Judiciary Committee can't find its new staff directors some weekend, she's probably guiding a boat down the Caloosahatchie River. Better yet, she might be skimming along the St Johns River in a big rubber innertube.

"'I love both politics and law so I couldn't be more pleased,' said Janet. 'Also, anybody who knows me, knows how I feel about Florida. I love to explore the little known spots, go down the dirt roads, get a 20-horsepower aluminum boat and take it down the wild rivers, study the odd trees, do some diving, roam around the swamp country.'"

Later in the article she admitted a love for her sister Maggy's life, as well as the family she had been brought up in: "I'd like to get married and have four children. I wouldn't mind at all trading a political career for that."

In November 1971, the legislature approved the reform as Article V of the State Constitution, and the following March it was approved by the voters of Florida. Janet received a standing ovation before the legislature for the work she had done. The rise of liberal politicians like Florida House Speaker Dick Pettigrew, the new Florida governor Reubin Askew, and Georgia governor Jimmy

Carter had her more optimistic than ever. She enjoyed Tallahassee greatly and wrote to her mother of her impressions of the political stage.

"This is a lovely town. I do not believe I've ever seen a more beautiful spring in any place I've ever lived—the azaleas and dogwood border on being a miracle. I had not realized it but Tallahassee is a border between the rolling hills of the Piedmont Plateau and the sandy pine barrens sloping to the Gulf. A mile south of Tallahassee the red clay turns to sand and the oaks and great pines give way to the slash pine, occasional tall cabbage palms, bays, and magnolias—you almost feel you're coming around a bend to Maggy's. Within the first week I was here, two reporters came up to say 'Your daddy was more responsible for breaking me in as a reporter than anyone else. He was wonderful to me.'

"The grim-faced, hatchet-voiced cracker woman, and the Sheriff Crews have given way to long-haired FSU youth. The old and the new have blended so beautifully and I say to the rest of the country beware! The South is rising in a beautiful, liberal, elegant way that bespeaks its heritage. That fact was forecast and it's happening! Jimmy Carter, Dick Pettigrew, 'Reubin the Pure'—race is not an issue. The meanness that hung like a heavy pall across this land is going. You no longer have the feeling as you drive through the oak woods that there is some intangible sinister doom in the air. The disappearance of the racists, and prosperity are responsible. You drive down a little dirt road and you come across the same heartbreakingly squalid shack. But a teenage black boy rides by on a new bike and gives you a thumbs up sign and a big smile. Even the shacks are giving way to trailers. Mr. Jefferson is breathing a great sigh of relief I'm sure as he looks down on this land he put his stamp on. You suppose he might be saying 'we have overcome!'"

Her admiration for Governor Askew was reciprocated, as he was deeply impressed at her dogged tenacity in seeing the judicial reform process through. "Reubin the Pure" was a lifelong nonsmoker and teetotaler and very formal for the most part, so his display of affection for Reno after the judicial reform raised a few eyebrows in Tallahassee. A UPI story reported:

"Gov. Reubin Askew, a politician given more to dignified handshakes than kissing, exclaimed 'Janet, Dear!' and gave Janet Reno a big kiss after the judicial reform Askew had pulled strings for and Miss Reno had sweated over cleared the legislature. . . . Askew, jubilant and smiling, rushed from his second floor office on the far side of the Capitol to the door of the House Chamber and shook hands with House members as they left. The Governor entered the chamber and kissed Miss Reno, the staff director of the House Judiciary Committee who sat through the tedious series of joint committee meetings in the closing days of the 11-day special session."[1]

Filled with enthusiasm for the political process, Janet ran for the House District 113 seat of the Florida Legislature in 1972. She took care to run for an open seat so as not to alienate any of the many Democratic Party connections she'd already made in Tallahassee, and she easily won the primary. She reminded her mother that at the age of ten, Jane had told her that "politics is the great frontier today, that there aren't any jungles to conquer anymore." As Dade was a heavily Democratic county, it was expected that the primary had decided the general election. To the shock of her supporters and her own great dismay, she narrowly lost to a Republican novice named John Malloy. It was a big Republican year with Nixon crushing McGovern for the presidency, and being a bold, physically imposing woman probably didn't help. "She was outspoken, and everybody she told she was voting for McGovern probably voted against him and her," recalled Richard Pettigrew years later, one of her former state legislator idols and later a member of the Carter administration.[2] From what she had been told by polls and supporters, she also took it slightly for granted her own race was in the bag and devoted much of her time to campaigning for other Democrats. It was a hard lesson for a political rookie, and she never let herself become complacent again.

Janet dealt with the setback by reading a biography of Abraham Lincoln and contemplating the advice of the local mayor, Jack Orr. The mayor had been a longtime hero of hers for being the only Florida House legislator to vote in favor of school desegregation in the late 1950s, at the cost of his political career for the next decade. Only recently had he been judged to have been on the right side of history and elected to political office again.

"Be absolutely honest," he told her. "Don't pull any punches. If you do that, you'll wake up in the morning feeling wonderful. If not, you'll wake up feeling awful. But if you're honest, and the voters turn you away, then it's their problem, not yours."

The porch parties continued unabated, drawing the usual wide range of Miami characters from different walks of life. A potter's wheel was installed on the breezeway to encourage anyone feeling artistic. As the parties grew into affairs that sometimes consumed an entire weekend, a social column in the *Miami News* noted one request from Reno about an upcoming one: "The invitations are the sort only Jane Reno would send out; her parties have always lasted far longer than she intended them to, so this time she's taking that into account. Jane's giving a party that starts tomorrow, ends officially Sunday night, and her only plaintive note is she hopes all the guests will go home by 7 a.m. Monday so she can go back to work."[3]

The family did the first reroofing of the house in 1973, and in typical Reno fashion invited all their friends to bring their own hammers, nails, and drinks to help out. It was just another porch party but with work involved. As family friend and *Miami Herald* staff writer Margaria Fichtner pointed out, so many unusual things happened at the Renos and so many great stories were told that few could refuse the invitation.

"So you went," Fichtner wrote. "You took your hammer and your nails and your liquor, and even though you knew you'd come home with two smashed thumbs and a sunburned neck, you drove out to that house in the woods off North Kendall Drive and pitched in to help these people with their damn fool roof because they'd asked you to."

One of Jane Reno's oldest friends, the social worker Ellen Whiteside, offered: "You can't be a part of the Reno circle without a lot of sparklers going up. There is warmth and love and life lived at a high intensity. The Renos have always had the capacity to take people just as they come—regardless of age, brains, or previous condition of servitude—and go from there. They don't require that you change to suit them."

The flip side of that, Fichtner noted, was that they didn't change to suit you either. She quoted one family friend: "They exist in a real climate of ideas that's as much a part of them as the air they breathe. When they turn their hands to something, they put their mind to it, too, and their minds have had great exercise since they came into this world. Ideas are not something the Renos strive for. They are part of the currency of their lives."[4]

In 1972 Jane Reno began acting on the realization of the past decade that the world was her neighborhood. She visited the Galapagos Islands with grandchildren Jane and Bobby Hurchalla, and Mark Reno's wife, Donna. Jane Hurchalla, who was seven at the time, remembers fragments:

"I saw little penguins, and Bobby got to go scuba diving with some of the crew.

"I used to go up to the empty bar every afternoon by myself and have a 7-Up and chat with the bartender. There were large tortoises crawling around sandy islands. Just saying blue footed boobies made me laugh. I remember wandering around Guayaquil and buying a painted wooden dove and a silver spoon."

In the summer of 1973, with daughter Maggy and grandchildren Jimmy and George in tow, Reno set out on an ambitious adventure to Turkey, Greece, and Iran.

They traveled to Tehran, and on to Isfahan, where the six-year-old George wandered off on his own in a bazaar without his family realizing it. Fascinated by the sights and smells of the vast labyrinth, George only came to discover that his solo perambulations were causing deep concern when a group of laughing, young Iranian boys a few years his senior tracked him down and shepherded him back to his mother and grandmother.

In Isfahan, a guide smuggled them up into the minarets of a mosque, an act of sacrilege that even under the pro-Western government of the Shah Reza Pahlevi was still dangerous. Posters of the Shah and his family graced nearly every shopfront, to be replaced five years later by ones of Ayatollah Khomeini. During siesta, the children were exposed to the howl of air-raid sirens for the first time, which were tested with some regularity in the city. Leaving the children in the hotel to sleep, Jane Reno and her daughter let themselves be herded down a back street by a guide, who had a camel he wanted to show them.

"The camel was walking in slow circles around a grinding wheel," recalled Maggy Reno Hurchalla, "and there was a huge sycamore tree, which may have dated back to the heyday of Isfahan in the 1400's. Our guide released the camel from its harness, beat it on the nose to make it fold down on the ground, and bid me to mount it. Just before I did it erupted upward. The guide rapped it on the nose some more, said foul things to it, and once again it sat down. That time I managed to get on and he led me on a leisurely amble around the courtyard."

In Shiraz, they visited the tomb of the fourteenth-century poet Hafiz, which Reno had been wanting to do ever since she had become entranced with his poetry as a teenager in Greece. In a cemetery near the gardens of Bagh i Dilgushi and the tomb of the other great poet of Shiraz, Sa'di, was a marble sarcophagus with two of Hafiz's poems chiseled in relief on the marble. Reno remembered one set of lines well and quoted them often for the rest of her life:

When you hear the words of the high in heart
Don't say that they are wrong
It is you who do not understand the words, my friend . . .

From Iran, Reno flew with her family to Turkey, spending time in Istanbul and Trebizon. More than forty years had passed since Reno had seen the old city of Constantinople. She relived some of her youth by taking the Hurchallas on a boat across the Bosphorus. In a taxi ride from their hotel out to a castle in the country, another memory came back to Reno. The ways of Turkish taxi men were apparently a constant, whether their mode of transport was a modern car or a rowboat four decades before plying the Sweet Waters of Europe. After quoting a small fare for the trip, the taxi driver casually informed Reno midway along that the fare would be dramatically increased. She let forth a torrent of abuse and cursing the likes of which the Hurchalla boys had scarcely heard before, which lasted almost all the way to the castle. Little did the driver know that he was not dealing with a typical foreign woman and her family, but with someone who had bargained in Istanbul bazaars like a veteran in the time of Ataturk.

Last on the agenda was Greece, which remained close to the heart of Jane Reno. The family wandered the Parthenon, and something about the lines of the columns that had once reminded Reno of a cocktail shaker seemed to make an impact on young George Hurchalla. He took the elevator every day to the roof of their hotel to stare up at the ruins. They traveled out to Mycenae, to the home of Agamemnon, and went swimming in the Mediterranean. At a wine festival, it was time for grandson Jimmy to get lost, when an inebriated Reno couldn't find him on the tour bus.

"I was sitting on the bus squashed between a pair of drunk Canadians," recalls Hurchalla, "so that it was impossible to see me. They were singing 'Roll Out the Barrel' so loudly that I couldn't get myself heard."

A confusion with their flights forced them back to Athens early, and they got split up when there was only room for Maggy and her son Jimmy on the original flight. Jane Reno stayed behind with grandson George, waiting eight hours for the next flight. To Reno's surprise, when she finally landed in Miami with George, she discovered that the others had not yet arrived. While Jimmy had been looking out the window of his flight soon after takeoff on the second leg from London, he noticed with a small measure of alarm that the Pratt & Whitney engine was on fire. As his father designed engines for Pratt & Whitney Aircraft, this could have been a bad moment for Jimmy's faith in his father's engineering skills, but since Maggy's husband designed engines only for military aircraft, he was off the hook. A number of other passengers had an even better view of the fire, and there was a stir of mild panic. The pilot droned something calmly about "problems with the left wing" and told the passengers that they were returning to London Heathrow.

The Hurchallas had been put up the night before by friends Colin and Silvia Smith, whom they had to ring up again and ask if they could impose for another night. Colin Smith worked for the *London Observer* and had met Jane Reno eight months before, when his editors sent him to Florida to do a story. Because National Airlines had recently opened the first nonstop flights from London to Miami, and Reno handled the publicity for National, she was the person who arranged a whirlwind tour of the state for him. The Florida story was a convenient way for his editors to get Smith out of London, where he was understood to be an IRA target as a result of some unflattering articles he had written on their bombing campaign in London that year. Fearing for his family as well, he returned to London and brought them back to Florida for a three-week vacation in January 1973, part of which was spent at the Reno household in Miami and part at the Hurchalla house in Stuart. While his family was in Stuart, Smith showed how deep his paranoia ran. Maggy Reno Hurchalla recalls, "We took him along to a birthday party for our friend Joan Jefferson, and he was worried our friends might be with the IRA, because of Joan's red hair and the fact that Charlie Porter appeared at the party dressed up in drag as her sister Charlene."

While Maggy and her son had been somewhat bemused by their engine catching fire, the Londoners on the flight to Miami had reason for their panic. Terrorism was an immediate and real part of everyday life in London at the time. The passengers were hustled through a back way after deplaning and were not allowed to speak to anyone at the airport. It was only later that Maggy Hurchalla realized what innocents they were as Americans traveling the world.

A letter from Colin Smith to Jane Reno four months later, on January 8, 1974, brought this reality home:

"Your letter arrived exactly a year to the day we set out for Florida and a holiday none of us are ever liable to forget. So much has happened since: Watergate, the Yom Kippur War, the collapse of the British economy, more Watergate. On Saturday we had our first warnings of a military takeover when the army surrounded London airport with tanks, ostensibly against an Arab terrorist threat. Later they admitted that it was to accustom us to the sight of police and troops working together—just like Ireland. The miners are sticking to their overtime ban (and I don't blame them) and if Heath does call and win an election the confrontation between the Conservatives and the workers is going to be even harder. Meanwhile, the IRA keep letting off bombs in town—the last place was Madame Tussaud's—and we'd be short of milk bottles if the energy crisis didn't mean that the cows' production level had dropped in cold cow sheds. I tell you all this to set the stage, no, the backcloth: We're very happy.

"In a moment I am going up to town to see an insurance broker about a policy to cover my new mortgage. We have found an Edwardian semi in the suburb of Dulwich which is not so far from where we are now, though slightly nearer to the city center, and famous for its school which P. G. Wodehouse attended. We were disappointed you didn't turn up after Maggy; Athens seems so close. Now I must go and arrange my next 25 years of heavy debt—barring the reprieve of a civil war. Perhaps Orwell got one thing wrong: it should have been 1974, but then one shouldn't over react to a few silly tanks around an airport. Really nothing much changes: as usual I'm just about to go to Vietnam. Last year I covered the Middle East war from the Israeli side.

"A Happy New Year and much love, not to speak of Peace and Groovy, to you all and please postpone the bean picking until after your London visit."

Reno was on the verge of retirement and had suggested to Smith that she might go off to work as a dishwasher in Colorado or pick beans to keep herself busy. She did retire from Hank Meyer Associates in 1974 and instead directed her energies toward improving her property on Kendall Drive, an oasis among the encroaching townhouse developments. Everywhere on the wooded part of the property, Brazilian pepper trees—also known as Florida holly—had begun to shade out the native vegetation. Day after day she started up the chainsaw, and swinging it about with her sinewy, gnarled arms, went to battle the pepper trees. Simply cutting them down didn't work because they always grew back. Using herbicides on their stumps to eradicate them, she eventually won the battle, resulting in a lush native habitat that was a far cry from the barren, rocky property of scattered pines and palmettos that she had built her house on in 1950.

Reno also continued one of her passive full-time pursuits, which was to exasperate her daughter Janet, usually with drinking involved. After leaving her daughter Maggy's house in Stuart one day with her friend Margery Keasler, Jane and Margery made it as far as Fort Lauderdale before the car broke down. Finding a bar nearby, they wandered into it and started drinking. Eventually they met a truck driver. Janet was woken in the middle of the night by the roar of a semi truck in the driveway and greeted by a truck driver yelling, "Hey lady, I got a delivery for you!" About to give him a piece of her mind, she then heard familiar cackles emanating from the cab.

In the winter of 1975, the next of her international trips with her grand-children led Jane Reno to Australia and New Zealand. This time she took her son-in-law Jim Hurchalla and his children Bobby and George. They drove the Queensland coast of Australia from Brisbane up to Cairns, hiked through rain-forests, and snorkeled on the Great Barrier Reef. In New Zealand they explored the hot springs of Rotorua, gave the children their first sight of snow on Mount Cook, and flew them across the fjords between Te Anau and Milford Sound. Reno fell in a tearoom near Rotorua and broke her leg but was fixed up free of charge courtesy of New Zealand's national health care.

A longtime dream came to fruition in the summer of 1976, when an ex-tended family group and friends gathered near Folkston in south Georgia to paddle the Okefenokee Swamp. Aside from being the headquarters of the Su-wannee River that Reno cherished so much, the Okefenokee was the home of the mythological characters that Walt Kelly had brought to life since the early 1950s in his comic strip *Pogo*. The complex number of levels of humor and satire that *Pogo* encapsulated was a mirror to Reno and her family. Virtually every member of the gathered canoeists for the Okefenokee expedition was a die-hard *Pogo* fan. Walt Kelly had died in 1973, and the trip seemed a fitting tribute to the man who had made the swamp famous. Janet Reno had recently left her job working for Dade County State Attorney Richard Gerstein to go into private practice with the prestigious Miami law firm of Steel, Hector & Davis. The firm had turned her down when she graduated from Harvard Law School a decade before because she was a woman. The day before the Okefenokee trip started she won her first court case with them.

Minnette Cummings, a family friend who was assistant senate majority leader in the state senate of Maine at the time, described meeting up with the Renos: "Janet Reno met us and drove us toward Folkston, Georgia. First attempt brought us right back to airport! No matter. Picked up oodles of beer, some booze, a few set ups, and proceeded to Howard Johnson in Folkston. Jane—braless bosom adroop, brown alligator skin with deepest wrinkles I've ever seen (many of them from smiling), widely separated teeth with brown sides—arrived with ubiquitous beer can in hand, slightly mulled."

Jane Reno traveled with Cummings and her friend Marcia Chapman to the Okefenokee Wildlife Refuge entrance to confirm the reservations Reno had made the previous summer. The equipment they had reserved added up to ten canoes, twenty-one paddles, seven sleeping bags, air mattresses, two porta-potties, nine lifejackets, and seven tents. The ranger warned them that the first night was going to be on a small platform ("Rather small, you'll get to know each other quite well") and the second in a house on an island ("Lots of rattle-snakes on that island, so be careful"). Reno was somewhat impatient with the ranger's paternalism, and Cummings observed: "Jane, having had three more beers, was slightly obstreperous but still manageable."

The attempt to eat dinner that night, before launching the canoes in the morning, was typical of a Reno-organized adventure. They settled for a truck stop after finding everywhere else closed and waited and waited for their orders while nothing but coffee and ice cream arrived. Finally a woman burst out of the kitchen proclaiming, "He's got it all over his chest and arms!"

Whatever "it" was, no one paid it much attention and they continued to wait patiently for their orders. Finally Marcia Chapman got up to inquire what the delay was. She found out that the stove had exploded and the cook was on his way to the hospital. The pudgy waitress said there was nothing really to offer them and that it was her first day on the job. As they left, she burst into tears.

At five o'clock in the morning the group awoke, and Jane Reno opened her first beer of the day. Her minimum intake on any given day was a six-pack, and sometimes, if she got an early start, she would finish off two six-packs. There was no law she had greater contempt for than the one that prevented her from buying beer before one in the afternoon on a Sunday. The group got assembled with the canoes and spent the next three days enjoying the quiet solitude of the vast Okefenokee. Minnette Cummings recalled one section of the trip:

"We floated along, hearing what could have been frogs with laryngitis, but turned out to be alligators. We heard them everywhere. Then we entered a land of fantastic beauty. A beautifully polished deep brown marble floor of constantly changing dimensions. The ceiling formed by interlacing branches, draped with gray chiffon scarves of moss. High constant twitterings and singing of birds, accompanied by the kettle drum voices of alligators. Huge cypress, like supporting columns, standing in awesome, quiet dignity with no symmetry yet a seeming artistic placing which gave each one a necessary place in the overall scene. No tongue can truly tell the beauty, feelings of expansion— and—strangely enough, love that entered the marrow of my soul for the next few precious miles."

When the Reno family took their friends into swamps, this was how they expected them to feel. The love of solitude in these primordial expanses had been established in the Everglades and was carried everywhere they traveled.

# 23 | Go Gator, and Muddy the Waters

In the autumn of 1977, Richard Gerstein decided to resign after twenty-one years as state attorney of Dade County. Rather than leave the office up for grabs by carrying out his term, he wanted to find a successor who could get elected. Though Janet Reno was still working for Steel, Hector & Davis, Gerstein suggested to Governor Reubin Askew that he appoint either her or one of his chief assistants, Ed Carhart. Tradition would have suggested that an assistant state attorney like Carhart be tapped for the job, and Carhart made it clear that he wanted the position. Instead, the governor chose Janet Reno. Most insiders saw the choice as a foregone conclusion, given the opportunity to put a woman of Reno's caliber in the job.

Janet Reno had been with Gerstein's office from 1972 to 1976, one of his top assistants in charge of administration and creating a new Juvenile division. Gerstein didn't know her when he hired her but was told that she was someone he needed on his team. At the time, she was dumbstruck when offered the job through an intermediary, replying: "I've always been a critic of Richard Gerstein's. Why should he want me?"[1]

He didn't even know precisely himself. But her reputation for detail and hard work preceded her, and as minor scandals always hung over his office—"my father always thought you were a crook," she bluntly told him—he wanted new assistants whose integrity was unimpeachable. After four years with Gerstein, she had moved on to join the powerhouse firm of Steel, Hector & Davis to get an opportunity to practice law again. There she got the chance to work again with her old friend Sandy D'Alemberte, whom she had worked with in Tallahassee when he was a state legislator. Other partners included Wilson Smith, whose family land consisting of thousands of acres in the springs wilderness southwest of Ocala was one of the Reno family's favorite getaway spots.

The only nagging question for Governor Askew about appointing Janet Reno as state attorney was her electability. She had lost her only political campaign, one that she had been expected to win. Gerstein had always won elections effortlessly and had run unopposed in his last election. Although Askew had a great fondness for Janet Reno and knew her capabilities, he still wanted to be sure she was ready for prime time and would get reelected.

"It's Dade—let's face it," said Paul Schnitt, Askew's press secretary at the time. "That's the major league. That's where they play hard ball. The state attorney's office there is the largest law firm in the state. You can imagine the responsibilities."[2]

Explaining his choice at a press conference attended by many of Reno's relatives and friends, Askew described the lengthy selection process that had led to his selection of Reno. "Reubin the Pure" was as prudish and serious a liberal as ever, known for serving nothing stronger than orange juice in the governor's mansion. He pontificated about how the choice had nothing to do with Reno being a woman—as some were suggesting—but that after reviewing the credentials of all the possible candidates for the position, he found "Janet Reno stacks up better."

The audience roared with laughter, and the governor turned red. He stumbled the way through the rest of his speech, slowly regaining his composure. Afterward, he was approached on the stage by a harmless-looking older woman, who seemed safe enough to talk to. It was Jane Reno.

"Governor," she queried him, "do you know what 'stacks' means?"

He turned red all over again.

The family made up T-shirts that read "Janet Reno stacks up better" and proudly wore them in her first campaign. To Jane Reno, it was the perfect tribute to her daughter. The concerns about Janet's electability proved unfounded. In September 1978 she faced a weak Democratic opponent, a little-known taxes and securities lawyer who had led an unsuccessful taxpayers' campaign against financing the Metrorail. She dispatched him handily by a three-to-one margin and faced no opposition in the general election.

Though a popular prosecutor, Janet did not have long in office before the honeymoon was over. Soon she faced some of the strongest personal and professional tests of her life. In early 1979, she had a heated exchange with the Drug Enforcement Administration (DEA) over a botched joint operation with the feds where DEA and Customs Service memos critical of her office were leaked to the press. The DEA threatened to arrest her men, calling her "hysterical," and she stared them down, threatening to arrest DEA agents if they tried to. Later in the year, police raided and beat black suspects in what turned out to be the wrong house, and her office didn't seek convictions against them for a "mistake." In 1980, Fidel Castro emptied the Cuban prisons during the Mariel boatlift, and thousands of violent criminals made a new home in Miami. The murder rate skyrocketed. The same year, a black motorcyclist named Arthur MacDuffie was beaten to death by four white policeman after a high-speed chase, and the state attorney's office had the responsibility of prosecuting the officers. Once again they failed, this time when an all-white jury found the officers innocent. At the same time Janet Reno successfully prosecuted black Dade County Schools Superintendent Johnny Jones for embezzling school funds to pay for gold plumbing for his private home. Although Reno personally didn't have a racist bone in her body, the actions and inactions of her office suggested blatantly otherwise.

Outraged, the Miami black communities of Liberty City and Overtown erupted in bloody riots, and Janet Reno was faced with a barrage of death threats and calls for her resignation. Local activists compared her to Hitler, and Jesse Jackson came to Miami and said "she has become a symbol of oppression to all of us."[3] Her greatest concession to keeping a lower profile throughout the tumultuous time was to let her brother Mark remove the family name from the mailbox until things settled down. Otherwise, the Reno phone number remained listed as it had always been and always would be. The accusations of racism stung sharply, but her mother had taught her never to quit. Janet met with black community leaders and attended meetings endlessly to hear community concerns, and many were surprised that she had the courage to do so. Despite the lowest approval she ever would have in the black community, no one opposed her in the 1980 election. Given the shitstorm that her office faced, it was fairly clear that no one else wanted the job, no matter how poorly they thought she was performing.

Though she loved her children unconditionally, Jane often expressed mock disapproval of her daughters' political careers. A vacation to England, Scotland, and Wales in 1978 had to be postponed because Janet was seeking reelection as state attorney in Dade County. Jane scornfully referred to the campaign as Janet "getting bogged down in her foolery."

The same year, Maggy was seeking her second term on the county commission up in Martin County, and Jane rebelled against the demands public life made on her daughters: "Politics! The hell with politics! It eats up all their time. They're public servants all right, all the time, nights and weekends."

"Mother," Janet responded, "it was you who told me that politics now has the great frontiers, the great battles of ideas to be fought, the challenge of changing things for the better. I believed you, and I believe that's right. You helped lead me into this."

Jane gave up on Janet for a minute to focus her ire on Maggy: "Why in hell would anyone want to run for the county commission?"

"Wouldn't you like to help shape the county your children are growing up in?" Maggy replied with equanimity. It was a rhetorical question. She knew her mother already had done this with her journalism. In fact, her mother had written a lot about the importance of the county commission in planning the future of Dade County after the Metro "home rule" charter was passed by voters in 1957.

"I wish they'd both been disco dancers," sighed Jane. "I do, I do."[4]

During Janet's lowest moments in 1980, this sentiment was considerably reinforced. However, it was merely another one of Reno's playful jabs at her children. Looking back at the work her mother was doing as a journalist during the height of her *Special Report* features, daughter Maggy noted that it was similar to the issues she dealt with as a county commissioner. In the same way that Jane flummoxed her detractors with her ability to grasp complex issues and bring them to public light, Maggy became a thorn in developers' sides and a champion of wetland conservation and slow growth planning in Florida. She had also emulated her mother by having four children and going on to a career once she was finished raising them through their formative years.

With repeated outreach in the coming years, Janet regained much of lost her support in the black community in Miami. Some of her most vocal detractors came to express an admiration for her resolve and were glad she had not listened to their calls for her resignation. In 1982, Janet's college roommate Bettina Dudley received a letter from her that voiced a sentiment that Reno was to echo over a decade later after the Waco disaster: "Simply for telling the truth, I am something of a folk hero and everyone is congratulating me. . . . I will never understand the public."[5]

For periods of time Mark Reno worked as a caretaker on the Smith family's expanse of springs wilderness southwest of Ocala that the Reno family regularly visited. In the early years Jane Reno would drive the grandchildren in through miles of sandy rutted roads in her little Datsun, trying not to high center the car on the way to the rustic house on the main spring. During the day, everyone swam in the springs, canoed the spring run, adventured through the woods, and went on great armadillo "hunts" in the evening. The latter consisted of Mark driving an old pickup truck full of people through the pastures until someone spied an armadillo and a great roar of "Armadillo!" filled the air. The family members then formed a large ring encircling the armadillo and waited for it to try to dash through their ranks. Invariably the children dove for cover if the armadillo came anywhere near them, so few were ever brought home for dinner. At night, copious amounts of drinking took place followed by rousing off-key renditions of "The Wild Colonial Boy" and well-memorized poetry like "The Cremation of Sam McGee" and "The Wreck of the Julie Plante."

Back at the house on Kendall Drive, peacocks continued strutting through the yard, fanning their gorgeous feathers during mating season and erupting in their ear-splitting cacophony each time a visitor arrived. When people called on the phone and wondered what was causing the racket in the background, Jane Reno replied confidingly and with a touch of sadness, "Oh, that's Horace. He's mental, you know."

Thus all the peacocks came to be called Horace. Jane was invariably an early riser, getting up with the sun and playing games of solitaire at the porch table, or sipping a beer and enjoying the quiet breeze before going out to work in the yard. Until the early 1980s, she kept up a steady regimen of at least one six-pack of beer and a pack of cigarettes a day. Her quick wits saved her more than once from arrests on drunk-driving charges. Once a state trooper pulled her over and asked her what was in the brown bag on the floor. Inside were a couple of six-packs, but without hesitating she replied sweetly, "Why, dirty diapers, officer, would you like to see them?"

Eventually the odds caught up with her, and a major fender-bender brought an end to her drinking career. She managed to have the accident in Monroe County, outside the jurisdiction of either of her politician daughters. Janet got her out of jail but insisted that Maggy take her to the trial so there would be no suggestion that the Dade County state attorney was trying to influence the case. Jane not only faced charges for DUI and causing an accident, but she was also charged with resisting arrest and calling the officer "a baby-faced pipsqueak."

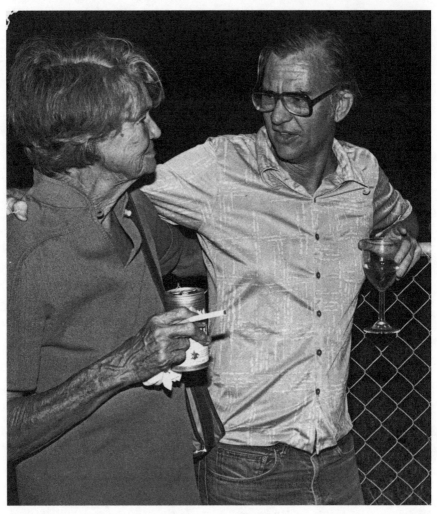

Two legends of Miami journalism arm in arm at a party in the 1970s: Pulitzer Prize–winning reporter (who would later become a *Miami Herald* editor) Gene Miller and Jane Wood Reno. Gene wrote on the back of the photo "last drink I ever had."

She also gave up smoking, though for years after she kept an unlighted cigarette in her hand "just as something to wave around." There were fewer strange animals around now that Jane's children were grown, but possums and raccoons still roamed nocturnally, and a group of skunks showed up at one point and took up residence in the house. Her sense of mischief coupled with her attitude toward authority never abated. After patiently trapping each skunk, she kept taking them over to a nearby police station in the middle of the night and setting them loose.

The elder of Reno's sons, Bob, established himself as a nationally syndicated journalist in New York with *Newsday*. Originally he wrote an economics column, but it evolved into something called "Reno at Large." Blessed with the sharpest writing wit of any of the children and a deep knowledge of history, he skewered Reaganomics and many other sacred cows of conservatism for the next two decades with a remarkable flair and humor.

Mark Reno lived his mother's love of the outdoors. His various careers as paratrooper, game warden, diver, sailor, carpenter, tree nurse, ranch caretaker, electrician, and tugboat captain kept him out of the confines of an office and confirmed what sister Janet told her mother of him—"that he is out of Conrad and Isak Dinesen." Whether freediving to sixty feet in the Bahamas to shoot grouper with a Hawaiian sling, hunting wild hogs armed only with his dogs and a knife, building the Indian *chickee* in his mother's backyard that he lived in, or welcoming guests with the manners of a southern gentleman and the mischievousness of a four-year-old, Mark ensured that another part of his mother's complexity thrived in the family.

One of Jane's favorite companions, her niece Nora Denslow, recalled that Jane "always loved a good protest." Denslow combined the wit of her mother, Dolly, the outrageousness of Jane, and a strong left-wing political conscience. She found any number of causes during the 1980s to protest over, bringing Jane along with her. Reno was disgusted with the Reagan era and the "Fifties Values" she had so abhorred when she lived through them. If there was any chance to show her opposition, she was glad to do so, and if her public antics embarrassed her daughter Janet . . . well, that just made it all the more fun.

In one of the more famous of Denslow's solo protesting endeavors, Nora walked innocently into a crowd of anti-abortion protestors on US 1 in Miami, holding up a pair of signs that read "Masturbation Is Murder" and "Every Sperm Is Sacred." The protestors, unsure of her commitment to their cause and clearly not Monty Python fans, moved away a little bit. She moved with them, yelling her slogans at passing motorists. Looking even more doubtful, the entire crowd of protestors moved to the other side of the street. Denslow moved with them, playing her part deadpan.

Having achieved her goals of spoiling her grandchildren and making the world her neighborhood, Reno relaxed as she entered her seventies and let herself be spoiled. Her eyesight started failing and her hearing got worse, but if asked how she was, she would reply, "I'm blind and I'm deaf, but otherwise I'm perfect!"

She never tired of collecting new stories. Her house retained its open air of welcome, and visitors came from all over the world. Years after Reno's 1975 visit to Australia, a woman named Dianne Brown called the house. She said she had finally made it to Florida and asked Reno if her invitation still stood. Reno had no idea who she was but invited her anyway. The stranger turned out to be a waitress from a coffee shop in Cairns who had taken Reno up on an invitation to visit her should she ever make it to America.

When Reno was diagnosed with lung cancer, her family was determined to make the final years of their matriarch's life as enjoyable as possible. Janet, Robert, Maggy, and Maggy's son Bob took her to Costa Rica, and they visited the rainforest laboratory where her niece Julie Denslow worked. Janet took her to California to visit her sister Winifred. With grandson Doug Reno and niece Sally Winslow, she and Janet crossed the entire length of Canada by train, and Janet also took her on a Caribbean cruise.

"She couldn't get around that well," said Janet, "but she loved exploring and she wanted to GO."

In the final eight months of her life, her children took her on a houseboat down the St. Johns River, and Maggy and Janet traveled with her in a motor home to visit her brother George and his family in Maine. While she was in Miami, she kept up a weekly ritual of going out for lunch with her granddaughter Karin Hunter Reno. The pair turned heads for different reasons. As a successful model who had graced the covers of *Vogue* and numerous other fashion magazines throughout the late 1980s, the tall and beautiful Hunter Reno commanded attention. Jane Reno brought another sort of striking physical presence to bear, Hunter remembers: "We would go to Joe's Stone Crab, and people looked on in horror as this gnarled old woman in a wheelchair slurped down two dozen oysters."

Though Reno thrived on adventure, her family remained her greatest treasure throughout her life. Just before her seventy-ninth birthday, she welcomed with delight a new addition to the family, great-granddaughter Kymberly Hunter Hurchalla, daughter of Jim and Gretchen Hurchalla. Her shouts of joy

Jane and Janet sharing a moment in front of the house that Jane built, mid-1980s.

were not quite as loud as they had been when Jim was born in 1961, but they were still enthusiastic.

On August 24, 1992, she experienced for one last time the power and fury that had made her fall in love with Florida sixty-six years earlier. Hurricane Andrew, one of the most compact and powerful storms to hit south Florida in the twentieth century, cut a swath through South Miami and Kendall on its way down across southern Dade County. The northern edge of the eye passed only a few miles south of the Reno house. During the worst of the storm, Jane and Janet sat comfortably in one of the rooms of the house that Jane had built with her own hands. After listening to the eerie sounds of 160-mile-per-hour gusts of wind whistling through the porch, they moved out to it themselves to watch the tail end of the storm. The roof, which had been reshingled painstakingly by family members in 1990, lost only one shingle, and the only other damage was to a few screens. Not far away, homes in new developments were completely flattened. Janet turned to her when all the chaos subsided and said, "Old woman, you built one hell of a house."

Reno enjoyed her peacocks, her porch, and her life right up to the end. On December 20, 1992, she went into a coma. On the following day, she died peacefully with several of her children holding her hand.

"She did it so perfectly," Janet said of her mother's death.

"She knew she was dying although she would forget the fact when convenient. She did not fear death. But she loved life to the end. Even in these past weeks as I walked with her across her porch, she looked out across the yard, feeling the warm sun and seeing the sparkling blue of the sky against the tapestry of green, and she would say, 'I love this world.'

"She was life itself to me. Whenever I asked myself what life was for or what the meaning of life was, I needed only look over at her, or call her if I was away from her, or in the last days reach over and hold her old and gnarled hand, to know the answer."

A *Miami Herald* editorial attested: "There can be no finer epitaph than this: She did it all."

At the funeral, Janet said to great laughter: "Jane Wood Reno was no saint. One comfort that I have this afternoon is that she will not insult or embarrass anyone. She was responsible for the most excruciating moments of my life. But as I look back over all the years almost all of her outrageous foolishness was directed at puncturing the pomp and arrogance of this world."

Her final wishes were to be cremated and to have her ashes spread over Biscayne Bay while loved ones read poetry—lines from Swinburne and Spender, Shakespeare's *The Tempest*, and a poem of her own:

Dying and fire, being two mysteries
Let me adore them now while I may.
Someday I shall be breathless and fireless
My hands will look living, but I shall be gone;
Because of that day, this day is so lustrous
Death will still be here when I am God.

The family eventually carried out her wishes, sailing out on to Biscayne Bay on Mark Reno's old thirty-four-foot Morgan sailboat the *Karin Reno*. Jane would have been tickled at the voyage honoring her, as it contained one final thumb in the eye of conventionality. Granddaughter Karin Hunter Reno brought her tennis-legend girlfriend Martina Navratilova along with her. Amid the reading of poetry, raised voices debated a family friend at the funeral who had brought up an affair Jane was alleged to have had with one of her Miccosukee friends. Each side claimed they knew what they knew, while the rest of the family members not privy to Jane's deepest secrets had no idea what they knew. Jane Wood Reno wouldn't have had it any other way. She was still causing trouble.

# Notes

## INTRODUCTION: GENIUS

1. On May 20, 1775, Mecklenburg County—which contains the city of Charlotte—formally declared independence from Britain, supposedly becoming the first government in America to do so. Historians are dubious about the authenticity of the declaration, though, which was only discovered in the nineteenth century and may have been created thirty years or more after the fact.

## CHAPTER 1. MIAMI'S ROARING TWENTIES

1. Although identified with liberal causes throughout his career, Bryan was a well-known evangelist and had drafted legislation to banish Darwinist teachings from Florida schools. Having profited heavily from the Florida land boom after moving to Miami in 1921, he was a millionaire. This was the final year of Bryan's life, and that summer he would be humiliated by Clarence Darrow in one of the most famous cross-examinations in legal history, during the "Scopes Trial." Bryan still won the case, in which a Tennessee teacher was sued for teaching Darwinism, but he died a week later.

2. "The Storm Miami Can't Forget," *Miami Herald*, September 18, 1966.

3. "Four Miami U. Co-Eds Elope; Police Looking for Runaways," *Palm Beach Post*, January 30, 1929, 1.

4. "Miami University Students Are Back Home after Tiring of Unchaperoned Tour," *Palm Beach Post*, January 31, 1929, 11.

5. "Miami Pilot Crashes in Field," *Miami Daily News*, April 15, 1930, 3.

## CHAPTER 3. SUMMER 1931

1. The Calvert Home Instruction System was the brainchild of the first headmaster of the private Calvert School in Baltimore, a Harvard graduate named Virgil Hillyer. He introduced the system in 1905 and remained headmaster until 1931, personally editing and collecting materials from his teachers to mail out to students worldwide every week. It was commonly used by Americans on overseas postings seeking the best education for their children, and by 1920 more than three thousand students were using it.

2. The twenty-two-year-old playwright and director that Jane Wood knew as Charles Koon was Charles Koun, or Karolos Koun, who went on to become of the most important theater directors and teachers in twentieth-century Greek life. Born in 1908 as an Ottoman citizen to a Greek mother and a Polish Jewish father, he was educated at an American high school in Istanbul, Robert College, before going on to study at the Sorbonne in France. Due to financial hardship, he had to cut short his studies and take up teaching in Athens, which was where Jane met him in 1930. He was politically active throughout his life and founded the Art Theater group in 1942 to stage lively and subversive plays during the German occupation, along with a drama school that went on to train the golden generation of Greek movie actors. The year he died, 1987, he released a book, We Make Theatre for Our Soul. The Greek Art Theater Karolos Koun and accompanying drama school exist to this day. Though Jane Wood did ask a relative traveling to Greece years later to ask about a Charles Koon or Coon in the drama world, nothing came of it, and tragically resulted in her abandoning further attempts to find what had become of him by the time she took her grandchildren to visit Greece in 1973.

## CHAPTER 4. THE DEPRESSION

1. "South Florida's Crimes of the Century Riveted the Nation," *Miami Herald*, September 15, 2002.

2. Jack Bell, *Miami Daily News*, April 15, 1934, 30.

## CHAPTER 5. THE BEST WE COULD

1. Nicola Sacco and Bartolomeo Vanzetti were Italian anarchists who were convicted of the murder of two employees of a Massachusetts shoe factory during a robbery in 1920. Many viewed their conviction as unjust and based on anti-immigrant fervor. Anarchists retaliated worldwide with a wave of bombings in their support, including the horrific "Wall Street Bombing" two days after their indictment that killed 38 and wounded 134. As appeals went on throughout the 1920s, their case became famous throughout the world, and protests in support of them were held in nearly every major city from Tokyo to Johannesburg. All appeals failed, and they were executed in 1927.

2. "Woman Swims Ashore to Save Companion," *Palm Beach Post*, July 20, 1935, 6.

## CHAPTER 6. BACK TO SCHOOL

1. "The Day of Black Doom," *Miami Daily News*, August 21, 1955.

2. Henry Reno, "Storm's Toll in Keys Set at 25 to 100," *Miami Herald*, September 4, 1935, 1A.

3. Henry Cavendish, "Hundreds of Bodies Are Found in Wreckage on Florida Keys," *Miami Herald*, September 5, 1935, 8A.

4. She was right on the latter count but far ahead of her time in predicting it. Flights over the Arctic were intermittent during the Cold War due to the strict Soviet restrictions on their airspace. A Korean Air Lines flight from Paris to Seoul via Anchorage was shot down by Soviet fighters in 1978 after gross navigational errors by the crew put them far off course. Luckily only two of the 109 aboard were killed. The aircraft managed to make a safe landing on a frozen lake near the Finnish border. Regular transpolar passenger routes over the North Pole wouldn't begin until 1998.

5. "Noted Woman Flier 'Drops In' on Miami," *Miami Herald*, May 24, 1937, 2.

6. Susan Butler, *East to the Dawn* (New York: Da Capo, 1997).

7. Andy Taylor, "Calamity Jane," *Miami Herald*, *Tropic* magazine, March 11, 1979, 45.

## CHAPTER 7. BAREFOOT AND PREGNANT

1. "Attorney Is Called Out and Attacked," *Miami Herald*, September 26, 1937, 1.

## CHAPTER 8. WORLD WAR II

1. Winifred Wood, *We Were WASPs* (Coral Gables, FL: Glade House, 1945).

## CHAPTER 9. THE WASP NEST

1. Janet Reno's speech to WASP fiftieth anniversary gathering in Sweetwater Texas, home of the WASP Museum, 1993.

2. Anne Cooper, *How High She Flies*, with Dorothy Swain Lewis (Chicago: Aviatrix, 1999).

3. Dorothy Jurney, interview by Anne Kasper, National Press Club Foundation.

4. Jurney, interview.

5. Jane Wood, "Do We Need Bears in Everglades Park?," *Miami Daily News*, January 16, 1955, 19.

## CHAPTER 10. GAMBLING AND THE EVERGLADES

1. Henry Reno, "Huttoe Is Down Again in New Political Move," *Miami Herald*, May 28, 1939, 8.

## CHAPTER 11. THE TRAILBLAZER

1. Pulitzer saved up his drama for later in life, when his bizarre and messy divorce trial became the talk of Palm Beach in 1982. His wife, Roxanne, was accused of drug

use—the one charge to which she admitted—as well as sleeping with a trumpet player, a Grand Prix driver, a local French baker, a real estate salesman, and a suspected drug dealer. She, in turn, accused her husband of committing incest with his daughter and using his seventy-three-foot yacht for marijuana smuggling.

2. Madame Mary Lenander was a Danish opera singer and soprano who first gained some notice performing as a student in 1921–22 in the United States. She then primarily lived in Europe, sometimes in New York, and toured with the Andreas Dippel opera company over the next two decades, before coming to Miami as a guest faculty member of the Miami Conservatory of Music in 1940. She thought that Miami could become a great musical center. It is likely that Henry and Jane Reno had social contact with her while she was living in Miami due to her shared nationality with Henry Reno, along with his love of opera.

3. Bob Reno, "Last of the 'Super' Minds Dies in Miami," *Miami Herald*, July 19, 1959, 4F.

4. "4 Bedrooms, 2 Baths, 1 Huge Political Asset," *St. Petersburg Times*, July 21, 2002.

5. Janet Reno, "14 Year Old Miamian Writes Own Story of 9 Months in Europe," *Miami Herald*, July 13, 1952, 3E.

## CHAPTER 12. THE MICCOSUKEES

1. Interview by Marcia Kanner, Samuel Proctor Oral History Program, University of Florida, October 21, 1971.

2. Peter Matthiessen, *Indian Country* (New York: Penguin, 1984).

3. Joshua Giddings, *The Exiles of Florida: The Crimes Committed by Our Government against the Maroons, Who Fled from South Carolina and Other Slave States, Seeking Protection under Spanish Laws* (Columbus, OH: Follett, Foster, 1858).

4. Jane Wood, "Seminoles on War Path for Adviser's Scalp," *Miami Sunday News*, November 25, 1956.

## CHAPTER 13. OSCEOLAS AND TIGERS

1. Jane Wood Reno, interview by Marcia Kanner, Samuel Proctor Oral History Program, University of Florida, October 21, 1971.

2. Jane Wood Reno, interview by Kanner.

3. Reno's memory was faulty. The number discussed in the final years of negotiations was 143,000 acres

4. Jane Wood Reno, interview by Kanner.

5. Jane Wood, "Seminoles Fail to Pin Collins," *Miami Daily News*, July 14, 1957, 15A.

6. Wood, "Seminoles Fail to Pin Collins."

7. Wood, "Seminoles Fail to Pin Collins."

## CHAPTER 14. ADVENTURE

1. Jane Wood, "Navy Removes 260 Mines," *Miami Daily News*, January 14, 1955.

2. Jane Wood, "Fisher's Feat in Ocean Told by Log Book," *Miami Daily News*, July 24, 1954, 11.

3. Jane Wood, "I Went Undersea Sledding in the Gulf Stream," *Florida Living* Sunday magazine, *Miami Daily News*, Aug. 12, 1956, 4.

## CHAPTER 15. BRENDA STARR

1. "Her Beat Ranges from the 'Glades to 20 Feet under the Sea,'" *Miami Daily News*, September 21, 1956, 1A.

2. "George A. Brautigam, State Attorney vs Interim Report of Grand Jury," Case No. 28161, Supreme Court of Florida, February 27, 1957.

3. Hank Meyer Associates was the number-one public relations firm in the city, and Jane had started doing part-time work for them to help pay for college for Janet and Bob.

## CHAPTER 16. A TEST OF WILLS

1. Lewis painted the official portrait of Janet Reno that was hung at the Justice Department in 2001.

2. "Giblin Pressed Grand Jury," *Miami Daily News*, May 16, 1957, 4A.

3. "Announcement," *Miami Daily News*, July 28, 1957, 1A.

4. Jane Wood, Jane, "Someone Has to Pick Those Beans, But . . . ," *Miami Daily News*, January 27, 1957, 1C

5. Real change didn't finally start to come to Immokalee for another forty-five years. In 1993 the migrant workers themselves organized into the Coalition of Immokalee Workers and employed the kind of creative imagination Reno said it would take to change things. They began bargaining directly with fast-food restaurants and large grocery chains, the largest buyers of tomatoes. Even then it took another decade for their first major win, after a national boycott of Taco Bell secured an agreement in 2005. They eventually got commitments from a number of fast-food and grocery corporations to pay a few extra cents per pound for Immokalee tomatoes, with the money going directly to the workers. That provided the first dramatic improvement in the working and living conditions of Immokalee migrant farmworkers in their history.

## CHAPTER 17. A CAREER TURN

1. Jane Wood, "Boys Volunteer for Beatings to Work Way out of Marianna School," *Miami News*, March 6, 1958, 19A.

2. Jane Wood, "Beatings Shock Collins," *Miami News*, March 5, 1958, 1D.

3. Wood, "Beatings Shock Collins."

4. "Miamian Airs Boy Beatings," *Miami News*, March 4, 1958, 1A.

5. Jane Wood, "Kids Are Put in Cages in Danny's New Home," *Miami News*, April 20, 1958, 10A.

6. Jane Wood, "Potential Killers Go Unaided Here," *Miami News*, April 21, 1958, 8A.

7. Brautigam's reputation among leftist circles was never salvaged as he was known during his tenure as state attorney as the "little McCarthy of Miami."

8. Bill Baggs, "George Brautigam Left Heritage of Courage," *Miami News*, August 19, 1958.

9. Ellen Whiteside—who came to have the School of Social Work at Barry University named after her—had pointed Reno to her Depression-era job with FERA, and Whiteside's daughter Kay was a close high school friend of Reno's daughter Maggy, who was also at the roast.

10. *Village Post* (Miami), July 1969.

11. Betty Garnet, "Dice Roll, Wheels Spin in Keys Hideaway," *Miami Herald*, January 13, 1959, 1A.

12. Pat Murphy, interview by the author.

## CHAPTER 18. THE LAST GASP

1. Steve Trumbull, "Seminoles Seek Scalp of Caldwell," *Miami Herald*, February 18, 1959, 1B.

2. *Tampa Tribune*, March 5, 1959.

3. Rick Tuttle, "Indians Challenge Fact Finding Unit," *Miami Herald*, May 17, 1959, 2A.

4. Jane Wood Reno, interview by Marcia Kanner, Samuel Proctor Oral History Program, October 21, 1971.

5. Bob Reno, "Seminoles Win Cuban Approval," *Miami Herald*, July 28, 1959.

6. "Just Short of a Blush," *Miami Herald*, July 29, 1959.

7. John L. Boyles, "Cabinet Gives Indians Huge Tract in Trust," *Miami Herald*, August 12, 1959, 1B.

8. Bob Reno, "Tribe Lays Sole Claim to Tract," *Miami Herald*, August 13, 1959, 14A.

9. John L. Boyles, "Cabinet Gives Indians Huge Tract in Trust," *Miami Herald*, August 12, 1959, 1B.

10. Typed version, tape transcription of meeting held November 17, 1959, Collins Correspondence.

11. "Indian Hassle Ended," *Miami Herald*, April 6, 1960, 10A.

12. Homer Osceola misread young Janet in that regard, as it became a hallmark of her legal career that she never wasted a moment on caring about what would be the popular thing to do.

13. Jane Wood Reno, interview by Kanner.

14. Jane Wood Reno, interview by Kanner.

15. Jane Wood Reno, interview by Kanner.

16. Jane Wood Reno, interview by Kanner.

17. *Miami Herald*, January 9, 1983.

## CHAPTER 19. PUBLICITY!

1. John Keasler, "We Remember Donna—When the World Was Younger and Hurricanes Were Fun," *Miami News*, August 30, 1979, 15.

2. Johnny and Susie dePoo were friends from Key West whom Reno had discovered on the same forays down there that found her drinking with Tennessee Williams. Susie was a talented young artist who became one of the more celebrated artists of the Keys. Burton Clark was head of the Miami Seaquarium.

## CHAPTER 20. AN UNUSUAL GRANDMOTHER

1. President Kennedy federalized the Mississippi National Guard in anticipation of the governor not allowing their use, but he did not use the Guard to ensure Meredith's safety. Instead he relied on a relatively small force of federal marshals, Border Patrol agents, and federal prison guards, who were instructed not to shoot when under attack but only to use tear gas. A mob of more than two thousand people overwhelmed them, and in the fighting two students were killed, thirty-five federal agents shot, and hundreds more injured. The next day, September 30, Kennedy made an address to the nation calling for cooler heads to prevail, and he sent in sixteen thousand troops to keep order. Many civil rights leaders were bitter that he had waited until after violence broke out, compared to the decisive action Eisenhower had taken in integrating Little Rock, Arkansas. When the Arkansas governor had planned to use the Arkansas National Guard to prevent the nine black children from entering school, Eisenhower had federalized the Guard and sent in one thousand paratroopers from the 101st Airborne Division. The tragedy in Oxford, Mississippi, could likely have been prevented by a similar show of force.

2. Bessie was the longtime maid of Daisy Wood, Jane Reno's mother.

3. Jack Bell, "Town Crier," *Miami Herald*, April 12, 1963, 1B.

## CHAPTER 21. LIFE AFTER HENRY

1. "Thirty Years of FOIA: The Challenges Ahead," Deborah Howell presiding at 1996 ASNE convention, March 21, 1997, www.asne.org.

2. Calvin Trillin, "Covering the Cops," *New Yorker*, February 17, 1986.

3. Jane Reno, "The Beachcomber," *Miami Herald*, September 26, 1965, 17E.

4. Andy Taylor, "Calamity Jane," *Miami Herald*, *Tropic* magazine, March 11, 1979, 48.

CHAPTER 22. JUST CALL ME MUD

1. "Askew Kiss Seals Win," *Tallahassee Democrat*, December 10, 1971.

2. "Centerpiece," *Floridian* magazine, *Tampa Bay Times*, January 14, 1979.

3. *Miami News*, February 19, 1972, 20.

4. Margaria Fichtner, "This Is Reno Country . . . It's Wild and Wonderful," *Miami Herald*, January 7, 1973, 1–2BW.

CHAPTER 23. GO GATOR, AND MUDDY THE WATERS

1. "Centerpiece," *Tampa Bay Times, Floridian* magazine, January 14, 1979, 6.

2. "Centerpiece," 6.

3. "Centerpiece," 6.

4. Andy Taylor, "Calamity Jane," *Miami Herald*, *Tropic* magazine, March 11, 1979, 48.

5. Heather C. Sarni, "Janet Reno: The Early Years and Career of a Pioneering Woman Lawyer," paper written for Barbara Babcock's course in women's legal history, Stanford Law School, Autumn 1997.

# Sources

The most important source that this work was founded upon was a collection of Jane Wood Reno's journalism that my mother, Maggy Reno Hurchalla, undertook in the early 1990s to share with family members. In 1994, I expanded upon that and turned it into *The Hell with Politics: The Life and Writings of Jane Wood Reno* (Peachtree). That book contained dozens of her stories for the *Miami Daily News* and *Miami Herald*, as well as some unpublished remembrances of her time as a social worker, and interviews with her by Marcia Kanner about the Miccosukee and Seminole Indians for the University of Florida's Samuel Proctor Oral History Program.

For Wood, Hunter, and Reno early family history, I drew from interviews with family, especially with Maggy Hurchalla; Jane Wood Reno's youngest sister, Winifred Wood; and Lisa Reno, niece of Jane Wood Reno's husband, Henry Reno. In addition, letters from the 1930s between Jane Wood Reno and her aunt, Peg Hunter Balfour, provided detailed information about her early memories of the Wood family house in Sunnyside, Georgia.

The time that Reno spent in Greece as a teenager was a blank spot in family history and muddled in the timeline along with her on/off university education in the late 1920s and 1930s, until my discovery in the early 2000s of a treasure trove of letters in the attic of her house, a decade after her death. These described her life in Greece at the time in exquisite detail. A wealth of information about her life back in Miami during the Depression was found in the letters she wrote to her aunt Peg that the family had collected. Reno's memories of Miami life from the 1920s through the 1950s, which comprised a chapter in *The Hell with Politics*, provided a launching point to research in greater detail many of the episodes she described. Digital archives of the *Miami Daily News* and *Miami Herald* provided details of newsworthy incidents involving Reno throughout the Depression.

As she began to raise children in 1938 and the war commenced in 1941, her personal letters again provided much of the detail of the era, many of them back-and-forths with her aunt Peg. By the time the children were old enough to have their first memories, various conversations I had with her children Mark, Robert, Janet, and Maggy also filled in details of their childhoods. The letters to her from a British RAF bombardier, William Parsons, who had fallen in love with her sister Daisy while he was training with American troops in Miami in 1941, provided an extraordinary insight into the war. *How High She Flies* (Aviatrix, 1999)—the biography of Dot Swain Lewis, a family friend and Women's Airforce Service Pilot (WASP)—was a help with the history of the WASPs, as was a personal interview with WASP Kaddy Landry, and Winifred Wood's book that was published originally at the end of World War II, *We Were WASPs* (Glade House, 1945).

Material on Sippi Morris came from a wealth of Reno family stories about Sippi over the years and the article "Sippi" that Reno wrote for the *Miami Daily News* in 1949 under the alias of Richard Wallace.

Much of the detail of family life in the 1950s came from the letters of Jane Wood Reno to her sister Winifred, as well as her children's memories. The article a fourteen-year-old Janet wrote about her trip to Germany was published in the *Miami Herald* on July 13, 1952. The material on the Miccosukees mainly came from the interview conducted by longtime family friend Marcia Kanner, "Interview with Jane Wood Reno, by Marcia Kanner," Samuel Proctor Oral History Program, October 21, 1971. Some other material came from *Indian Country* by Peter Matthiessen (Penguin, 1992). Jane Wood Reno's articles for the *Miami Daily News* on the Miccosukee efforts were a key source, as no other journalist was continually reporting on the tribal meetings and efforts with an insider's view of the tribe's workings.

Letters to her sister Winifred informed some of the details of her work at the *Miami News*. An extensive researching of the *Miami Daily News* digital archives enabled me to discover all of Reno's published work for the *News* under the name of Jane Wood from 1952 to 1958. The hundreds of articles gave a true sense of the breadth of her work for the first time and her evolution in status as a journalist at the newspaper. The knowledge that she also wrote under male pseudonyms led to the discovery that she wrote exclusively under male names while producing freelance Sunday features for the *News* from 1946 to 1951—Richard Wallace and Don Reynolds, primarily.

For Reno's increasing clashes with new editor Bill Baggs in 1958, Maggy

Reno Hurchalla was a source, along with letters to sister Winifred. The details on *Herald* columnist Betty Garnet were from an interview I did with former *Miami Herald* columnist Pat Murphy.

The final battles Reno undertook on behalf of the nonreservation Miccosukees were once again informed by Marcia Kanner's October 21, 1971, interview of Reno for the Samuel Proctor Oral History Program. Joshua Giddings's fiery tome *The Exiles of Florida: The Crimes Committed by Our Government against the Maroons, Who Fled from South Carolina and Other Slave States, Seeking Protection under Spanish Laws* (Follett, Foster, and Company, 1858) was an invaluable historical source on the Seminole Wars. After Jane Reno quit journalism to go into publicity, I depended on *Miami Herald* coverage of the Miccosukee land claim battle in 1958 and 1959, including articles by her son Bob Reno.

Family letters were responsible for most of the documentation of life during the 1960s as she worked in publicity, with Jane Wood Reno often writing to her children in college—Janet at Cornell and then Harvard Law School, Bob at Tulane, and Maggy at Swarthmore. John Keasler's wonderful memory of his hurricane evacuation to the Reno house, "We Remember Donna—When the World Was Younger and Hurricanes Were Fun," *Miami Daily News,* August 30, 1979, helped round out Jane Wood Reno's own memories of the event.

"Beach Walk," *Miami Herald,* September 26, 1965, captured her six-day journey up the east coast of Florida. An interview I did with family member Doe Winslow gave insight into the heated clashes Reno had with her family over her alcoholism and her care for her mother.

The adventures of the Reno family in the 1970s begin to involve my own personal memories, as well as those of my mother and other family members. Letters to Jane Wood Reno from her daughter Janet, who was living and working in Tallahassee, describe Janet's first experience with legislative politics. The 1973 article for the *Miami Herald* "Reno Country," by longtime *Herald* book editor and family friend Margaria Fichtner, and "Calamity Jane" by *Herald* writer Andy Taylor in 1979, were important early pathways I used into family history before many other documents were available. Various *Miami Herald* articles on Janet Reno throughout the 1970s were also utilized. Memories of family members are the sources for the rest of the years until Jane Reno's death in 1992.

# Index

BORN IN WEST PALM BEACH, FLORIDA, George Hurchalla enjoyed the company of his grandmother, Jane Wood Reno, and by the age of ten, he had traveled with her to Greece, Turkey, Iran, New Zealand, and Australia. He inherited Reno's love of writing and adventure, and after graduating from college with a mechanical engineering degree in 1988, he roamed the planet, from experiencing revolution in Nicaragua to working a Steinbeck-ian life as a fruit picker in Australia. Among Hurchalla's published articles and book are a collection of Jane Wood Reno's newspaper writings, *The Hell With Politics*, *Exploring Florida's Atlantic Coast Beaches*, and *Exploring Florida's Gulf Coast Beaches*. He currently resides in Texas.